Torah Song

The Theological Role of Torah Poetry

GEULA TWERSKY

KODESH PRESS

TORAH SONG: The Theological Role of Torah Poetry
Geula Twersky

© Kodesh Press 2022

Hardcover ISBN: 978-1-947857-73-5
Paperback ISBN: 978-1-947857-74-2

Kodesh Press LLC
New York, NY
www.kodeshpress.com
kodeshpress@gmail.com
sales@kodeshpress.com

Author Photo Credit: "Aliyah" by Geula Twersky
Set in Arno Pro by Raphaël Freeman MISTD, Renana Typesetting
Printed in the United States of America

To YITZCHAK
my beloved husband and teacher
who has taught me *Amittah Shel Torah*

כל השומע יצחק לי

Acknowledgements

I would like to express my heartfelt gratitude to Rabbi Alec Goldstein at Kodesh Press for believing in this project, and for his careful editing of my manuscript. His tireless efforts enhanced the articulate presentation, and the aesthetically pleasing appearance of the present volume. Heartfelt thanks to Rabbi Jeffrey Saks who encouraged me along the way and who played a key role in making sure that this book would become a reality. A special thank you to Dr. Gail Bendheim, Reb Norman Meskin, and Dr. Mark Smilowitz who contributed generously to my book publishing campaign. Thank you to my many dear friends and neighbors from Neve Daniel with whom I am privileged to share Torah, and who contributed to my book fund. My deepest gratitude to my husband Yitzchak, who has not only taught me from his wellspring of Torah knowledge, but has taught me how to learn, and most importantly, to believe in myself.

Contents

Foreword

Torah Song seeks to access the mechanism of biblical poetry and to understand the theological function that it plays in the Torah (i.e., the Pentateuch). An examination of the term *shira*, "song," and its theological implications points to poetry's vital role in the dissemination of Torah theology.

Mining the poetry of the Torah for its theological gems necessitates that we acknowledge the fundamentally distinctive roles of poetry and prose. Poetry, unlike prose, precludes the possibility of pinning it down in an absolute sense. Its allure derives from a certain indefinable harmony between articulation and intimation, best expressed in the language of the fine arts as biblical 'impressionism.' This shift from 'realism' to 'impressionism' calls for an interpretive methodology that relinquishes the insistence upon restrained exactitude, allowing for analytical spontaneity. *Torah Song* articulates a groundbreaking interpretive methodology specific to the unique needs of biblical poetry.

Torah Song's comprehensive evaluation of the three core poems of the Torah, the Song of the Sea, the Song of the Well and the Song of Moshe, is followed by an evaluation of the Torah's three extended blessing units: the Blessings of Yaakov, Bilam, and Moshe. *Torah Song* demonstrates that the poetry of the Torah functions as a loosely connected, broad meditation on קבלת עול מלכות שמים, the recognition of God's manifestation on Earth, and Israel's role as a ממלכת כהנים וגוי קדוש, a kingdom of priests and holy nation, caretakers of the Divine covenant.

Preface

My decision to study Torah poetry came after years of reckless speeding through its obscure language and enigmatic verses as they intermittently cropped up in the landscape. I credit my development as a fine artist with opening my eyes to poetry's evocative power, profoundly altering the way in which I approach Torah study. Art plays a vital role in our lives, affording us the possibility of momentary pause from the whirlwind of daily events, enabling us to survey our inner world. In like fashion, Torah poetry present us with the opportunity to contemplate what we have studied, allowing for clarity of thought and purpose.

Poetry possesses the capacity to surmount the inexorable constraints of spoken language. Unlike prose, it does not allow for a casual reading. Poetry is a fundamentally interactive art form that necessitates a highly attuned ear and full engagement with the text. Immersion in the sea of biblical poetics transforms the passive reader into an active participant. Interaction between the reader and the text imbues biblical poetry with a dynamic vitality, enabling it to surpass the natural limitations of the written word.

In the early stages of my artistic path, I set my sights on mastering realism. Realism shares much in common with the linear approach to Bible study. Both disciplines focus heavily on literal interpretation. My experiences in these two seemingly unrelated fields has led me towards a more seasoned appreciation for biblical poetry's impressionistic qualities. The spontaneity of impressionism's vivid colors, broad strokes, and evasion of precision often surpass the limitations of realism's restrained exactitude. Impressionism in both art and Torah traverses the boundaries of the concrete, offering the possibility of transcendence.

Appreciation of any work of art begins with being able to identify its genre. Using the same interpretive criteria to analyze a Rembrandt portrait and the Monet waterlilies would lead to absurd conclusions. The prevailing practice in much of the current biblical scholarship tends to hold prose and poetry to the same standard of interpretation. Approaching prose and poetry identically reminds me of the events that led to the emergence of the impressionist movement. It was an art critic who disparagingly reviewed Claude Monet's work, referring to it as a mere "impression," who unwittingly placed the new movement on the map, providing it with a fitting name.[1]

When we navigate our way through the text of the Torah, it becomes vitally necessary to take careful note of the shift in terrain from prose to poetics and adjust our interpretive strategies accordingly. Poetry, unlike prose, precludes the possibility of pinning it down in an absolute sense. Its allure derives from a certain indefinable harmony between articulation and intimation. It is with this in mind that I will lay out a methodology for reading biblical poetry that takes into account its unique interpretive needs.

Whereas much of the Torah is written in prose, its text is punctuated by moments of poetic abstraction. The poems of the Torah, like the line spacing method in which they are often recorded, leave far more implied than what is clearly articulated. The elegance of these digressions from the straightforward retelling of events and transmission of the law transcends the shackles of spoken language, pointing the reader in the direction of the Torah's core message, its ineffable soul. In its desire that we seek out its inner message, the Torah speaks in the language of poetics, beckoning us in.

The poetic intervals which dot the landscape of the Torah usher the reader into the innermost chamber of meaning. Understanding the purpose of the poetry recorded in the Torah is critical for accessing its

---

1. Mike Evans, *Defining Moments in Art: Over a Century of the Greatest Artists, Exhibitions, People, Artworks, and Events that Rocked the Art World* (London: Cassell Illustrated, 2008), 17.

very essence. This book attempts to glimpse at the Torah's core message by bridging the gap between realism and impressionism, between prose and poetry.

"Now write down this song and teach it to the Israelites and have them sing it…" (Deut. 31:19).

Introduction

What is Biblical Poetry?

In considering what makes a poem a poem, the words "rhyme," "meter," and "alliteration" immediately come to mind. Poetry, however, is bound by none of these literary devices. Robert Frost, America's renowned poet laureate, is noted for having quipped that poetry is "that which is lost in translation."[1] T.S. Eliot offered the tautological observation that "the only absolute to be drawn is that poetry is written in verse and prose is written in prose."[2] Biblical poetry is even more elusive, for as a general rule it employs neither rhyme nor rhythm. While it would appear self-evident that the Bible contains poetic interludes, the mechanism of biblical poetry remains the subject of ongoing debate. The difficulties involved in articulating a precise definition for biblical poetry bring to mind an oft quoted story involving former U.S. Supreme Court Justice Potter Stewart. When hard-pressed to come up with the decisive parameters of obscenity, Stewart is famous for having remarked, "I know it when I see it."[3] Similarly, whereas identifying poetry remains in many respects intuitive, a systematic guide to the mechanics of biblical poetry remains vexingly elusive. What makes biblical poetic verse any more lyrical than biblical prose, whose nuanced and often ambiguous style has often been interpreted through the rubric of poetics? Indeed, Rashbam classified

---

1. David Connolly, "Poetry translation," *Routledge Encyclopedia of Translation Studies* (ed. Mona Baker and Kirsten Malmkjaer; Abingdon: Psychology Press, 2001), 170–176, esp. 170.
2. T.S. Elliot, "The Borderline of Prose," *New Statesman* 9 (1917), 158.
3. Peter Lattman (September 27, 2007), "The Origins of Justice Stewart's 'I Know It When I See It'," *The Wall Street Journal*.

the entire book of Deuteronomy as poetry (on Deut. 31:19). The Netziv went even further in his characterization of all five books of the Torah as poetry.[4] The Netziv explains that the primary characteristic of poetry is its multivalence. Similarly, the Torah needs to be interpreted on a multiplicity of levels. Whereas the primary message of Torah passages is often implicit as opposed to explicit, a clear approach to Torah poetry remains a desideratum.

Robert Lowth was the first scholar of the modern era to draw attention to the lacunas in our understanding of the fundamental characteristics of biblical poetry. Lowth's insistence upon analyzing biblical poetry through the same lens as classical poetry, however, led him to the dubious conclusion that meter must also be at the crux of biblical poetry. The fact that this assumption is not borne out by the natural rhythm of the text was presumed by him to be due to the mispronunciation of the ancient text. Lowth argued rather circularly that the poetic meter, which he assumed to be implicit in the text, could be inferred from its parallelism.[5] This approach was rejected by Robert Alter, who recognized that biblical poetry has its own special rhythms and need not conform to modern notions of meter. While Alter also embraced parallelism as the single most defining characteristic of biblical poetry, he acknowledged that whereas parallelism is often found in biblical prose, its presence in poetic verse is notable for being richer in images and metaphors and featuring a climax.[6] The unique language which characterizes biblical poetry has also been acknowledged as one of biblical poetry's critical and distinguishing features.[7]

Parallelism's ubiquitous presence in the Bible, and the impossibility of confining it solely to the genre of poetics, led James Kugel to throw the baby out with the bathwater, rejecting the idea of an absolute distinction between biblical poetics and prose altogether.[8] Kugel favors viewing

---

4.   Natali Zvi Yehudah Berlin, *Haamek Davar*, introduction, section C.

5.   Robert Lowth, *Lectures on the Sacred Poetry of the Hebrews* (trans. G. Gregory; London: Elibron Classics, 2005).

6.   Robert Alter, *The Art of Biblical Poetry* (New York: Basic Books, 1985), 3–26, 28.

7.   M.H. Segal, *Introduction to the Bible* (Jerusalem: Kiryat Sefer, 1967), I: 35–39.

8.   J. Kugel, *The Idea of Biblical Poetry: Parallelism and its History* (New Haven, London: John Hopkins Univ. Press, 1981), ch. 6.

poetry and prose in the Bible as operating on a continuum, in which poetic parallelism is a mark of "elevated style."[9] By blurring the parameters between poetics and prose, and rejecting the distinctive character of biblical poetry, Kugel rendered the very idea of biblical poetry an artificial designation.[10] Whereas most would agree that parallelism is not the *sine qua non* of biblical poetry, that is a far cry from Kugel's assertion that the Bible is not offset by clearly defined poetic units. Adele Berlin makes a strong case for the presence of distinct poetic units in the Bible. She understands "compact terseness" to be the essential substance of biblical poetry. "The lines, by virtue of their contiguity, are perceived as connected, while the exact relationship between them is left unspecified."[11] In a similar vein, J.P. Fokkelman refers to "linguistic density," or multiple layers of meaning, to be biblical poetry's most fundamental characteristic.[12]

The ambiguity inherent in the terms "compact terseness" and "linguistic density" brings us back to our original question. What criteria may be used to determine which poetic units of the Torah harbor these specific qualities? In contemplating why Torah prose is punctuated with poetic digressions, we must first be in a position to identify the Torah's poetic units.

We have seen a variety of suggestions for what defines biblical poetry. These have ranged from elevated style, unique meter or rhythm, the presence of parallelism, layers of meaning, and linguistic compactness. On closer examination, however, it was observed that these very

---

9. Ibid., 70; Longman also speaks of prose and poetry as opposite poles on a continuum. Cf. T. Longman, *Literary Approaches to Biblical Interpretation* (Michigan: Zondervan, 1987), 121–134. This idea is very similar to Matthew Arnolds idea of poetry's "sustained tone, numerous allusions, and grand style." Cf. Warren Anderson, "Matthew Arnold and the Grounds of Comparatism," *Comparative Literature Studies* 8.4 (1971), 287–302.

10. Kugel, *The Idea of Biblical Poetry*, 94. Gillingham agrees that "there are in fact no clear-cut distinctions between prose and poetry in Hebrew." S.E. Gillingham, *The Poems and Psalms of the Hebrew Bible* (Oxford: Oxford Univ. Press, 1994), 19.

11. Adele Berlin, *The Dynamics of Biblical Parallelism* (Bloomington and Indianapolis: Indiana Univ. Press, 1985), 4–17, esp. 6.

12. See J.P. Fokkelman, *Reading Biblical poetry: An Introductory Guide* (Louisville: Westminster John Knocks Press, 2001), 15.

same features also characterize the Torah in general. This leaves us to wonder if it is possible to pin down Torah poetry's elusive identifying features.

Identifying the Poetic Units of the Torah

The Torah itself labels three of its poetic units as poetry, שירה, in its introductory verses leading into the Song of the Sea (Ex. 15:1–18), the Song of the Well (Num. 21:17–20), and the Song of Moshe (Deut. 32). Through its invocation of the term for poetry at these specific intervals, the Bible would seem to have excluded other poetic texts, most notably, the Blessings of Yaakov, Bilam, and Moshe. When the Sages mandated the graphic rules for writing biblical poetry, they made it clear that they viewed specific units of the Torah to be poetic, although they neglected to clearly identify these poems (BT *Megillah* 16b). Elsewhere in the Rabbinic literature where the songs of the Bible are listed, the Song of the Sea, the Song of the Well, and the Song of Moshe are included in the list, to the exclusion of other poetic units of the Torah.[13]

The ability to determine the poetic units of the Bible is critical for getting at the purpose for their inclusion in the text.[14] Ascertaining the

---

13. Cf. Mechilta, *Beshalah, Mesechta DeShira* 1; *Midrash Pitron Torah, Haazinu,* ed. Ohrbach, 321; *Midrash Zuta, Shir Hashirim,* Buber ed., 4a. Interestingly, the Sages mandated that a different format be used for writing the Song of Moshe from Deuteronomy 32 than that used for other biblical poems. Cf. JT *Megillah* 3:7; Tractate *Sofrim* 1:11.

14. Alter notes the difficulty in determining the poetic units of the Bible. See Alter, *Biblical Poetry,* 5; Kaufmann lists Yaakov's Blessings (Gen. 49: 1–26), the Song of the Sea, (Ex. 15:1–21), the Song of the Well, (Num. 21:14–20), Bilam's Blessings, (Num. 23–24), and the Blessings of Moshe, (Deut. 33). See Y. Kaufmann, *Toldot ha-Emunah ha-Yisraelit,* B (Tel Aviv: Bialik Institute/Devir, 1960), 150, (Heb.); Segal adds the song of Lamech (Gen. 4:23–24), the curse of Canaan (Gen. 9:25–27), the blessing of Rebecca (Gen. 24:60), the blessings of Rebecca's children (Gen. 25:23), Yitzchak's blessings (Gen. 27:27–29), the song of the Ark (Num. 10:35–36), and the song of *Haazinu* (Deut. 32:1–43). Meir adds to this list the song at the end of the war with Amalek (Ex. 17:16) and the song of the Moshelim in (Num. 21:27–30). See Amira Meir, "On the Study of Pentateuchal Poetry'" pages 96–113 in *God's Word for Our World Vol. 1* (ed. Debrah Ellens, Harold Ellens, et al.; A&C Black, 2004),

primary objectives of biblical poetry will help lead the way to identifying the poetic units of the Torah.

The Purpose of Biblical Poetry

The punctuation of prose narrative with sudden poetic interludes didn't tend to disturb the equanimity of the traditional interpreters of the text, who were more inclined towards queries of a narrower scope such as the interpretation of enigmatic words and phrases and the resolution of textual anomalies.[15] Contemporary scholarship has engaged more with questions of literary style and genre. Alter theorized that biblical poetry is designed for "impulse of intensification," or to highlight or summarize a prose narrative, much like the function of a musical chorus in a play.[16] Alter observes that biblical poetry is characterized "by an intensifying or narrative development within the line...the poetry of the bible is concerned above all with the dynamic process moving toward some culmination...."[17]

Based on Alter's theory, one is left to wonder: if the Torah's poetic units were meant to intensify the narrative, why were so many dramatic moments in Israel's history left unsung? The giving of the law at Sinai is a case in point. God's revelation at Sinai, recounted in detail twice within the Torah, is arguably among the most seminal events in Israel's history (Ex. 20, Deut. 5).[18] Whereas there are numerous poems scattered

---

113; Shepherd includes the curse of Adam and Eve in his list of Pentateuchal poems. See Michael Shepherd, *Daniel in the Context of the Hebrew Bible* (Bern: Peter Lang, 2009), 20.

15. Of notable exception is Abarbanel, who discusses the phenomenon of biblical poetry in his commentary on Ex. 15. He understands biblical poetry as having an either liturgical or inspirational/metaphorical purpose.

16. Alter, *Biblical Poetry*, 28, 135. Sailhammer similarly identifies the compositional strategy of the Pentateuch as concluding large units with a poetic epilogue. Cf. John Sailhammer, *The Meaning of the Pentateuch: Revelation, Composition and Interpretation* (Westmont: InterVarsity Press, 2010), 324.

17. Robert Alter, "The Characteristics of Ancient Hebrew Poetry," in *The Literary Guide to the Bible* (ed. Robert Alter and F. Kermode; Cambridge: Harvard University Press, 1987), 611–624, (620).

18. The Ten Commandments themselves do not appear to qualify as poetry.

throughout the Bible which recount and respond to the theophany at Sinai, no celebratory hymns punctuate either of the Torah prose narratives recounting this formative event.[19]

Another approach to biblical poetry is to understand it through a theological prism. Some understand biblical poetry to be part of a larger expostulation against the pagan beliefs prevalent in the ancient world.[20] Shemaryahu Talmon maintains that biblical poetry represented a clear and deliberate divergence from the existing epic poetry style prevalent in the ancient Near East.[21] Whereas epic poetry was used as a tool for relating legends, biblical poetry fails to tell a coherent story. Talmon concludes that biblical poetry is quintessentially polemical and aimed at opposing ancient Near Eastern polytheistic theology.[22]

The conviction that biblical poetry serves a primarily theological purpose was also advanced by Robert Lowth, although he arrived at this understanding purely from a literary perspective.[23] Lowth maintained that the transcendental beauty of biblical poetics contains within it the

---

They are neither written in an elevated or archaic style, nor do they employ parallelism. Whereas parallelism alone may or may not be the sine qua non of biblical poetry, it certainly is one of its distinguishing features.

19. Cf. Deut. 33:1–5; Jud. 5:1–5; Habakkuk 3:1–7; Ps. 68.

20. Cf. W.F. Albright, *Yahweh and the Gods of Canaan: A Historical Analysis of Two Contrasting Faiths* (New York: Doubleday, 1968), 4–5, who writes that whereas there are many points of contact between Israelite and Canaanite poetry, the poetry of the Bible is more sophisticated and complete than Canaanite poetry.

21. Shemaryahu Talmon, "Prose and Poetry in the Mythic and Epic Texts from Ugarit," HTR 67 (1974), 1–15; Cf. U. Cassuto, *Biblical and Canaanite Literatures* (Jerusalem: Magnes, 1972), 16–59 and "The Israelite Epic," in *Biblical and Oriental* Studies (Jerusalem: Magnes, 1975), II 69–109. Cassuto argues that Israel was once in possession of currently lost epic poetry, vestiges of which may be detected in the Bible. No fragments of lost Israelite epic poetry, however, have ever surfaced that might substantiate this assumption. Cassuto maintains that it is the content and spirit of biblical poetry which constitutes the major difference between the two.

22. Shemaryahu Talmon, "Did there exist a national biblical epic?" 91–111 in *Literary Studies in the Hebrew Bible: Form and Content* (Jerusalem: Magnes, 1993).

23. Robert Lowth was an eighteenth-century Anglican clergyman, philologist,

potential to inspire religious fervor (Lowth, *Lectures*, 23). Lowth further submitted that poetry's infusion of feeling and emotion makes it possible for poetry to transcend history, thereby rendering the message of the Bible more accessible (ibid., 4, 8).

The theological approach to biblical poetry is supported by the fact that each of the biblical poems that are specifically introduced with the appellation שירה, "song," feature a call for participation. Nachmanides' commentary on the Song of Moshe or *Haazinu* assumes this approach, where he explains that the term *shirah* implies transmission through oral recitation (Deut. 31:19). The inclusion of the wider community in the declamation of biblical poetry lends support to the supposition of an underlying didactic agenda. In the Song of the Sea, Moshe exhorts all of Israel to sing together with him.

> Then Moshe and the Israelites sang this song to the LORD: "I will sing to the LORD, for He is highly exalted. Both horse and driver He has hurled into the sea." (Ex. 15:1)

The responsive nature of the Song of the Sea is echoed in Miriam's truncated version of the song, in which she calls upon the community of women to join her in song.

> Then Miriam the prophet, Aharon's sister, took a timbrel in her hand, and all the women followed her, with timbrels and dancing. Miriam sang to them: "Sing to the LORD, for He is highly exalted. Both horse and driver He has hurled into the sea." (Ex. 15:20–21)

Israel's Song of the Well also solicits communal participation.

> Then Israel sang this song: "Spring up, O well! Sing about it." (Num. 21:17)

The Song of Moshe in Deuteronomy is introduced with the uncommon instruction that the song be placed "into the mouths" of Israel, שימה בפיהם, ensuring its perpetuity.

---

and professor of literature, famous for his pioneering analysis of biblical poetry.

Now write down this song and teach it to the Israelites and have them sing it, so that it may be a witness for me against them. When I have brought them into the land flowing with milk and honey, the land I promised on oath to their ancestors, and when they eat their fill and thrive, they will turn to other gods and worship them, rejecting me and breaking my covenant. And when many disasters and calamities come on them, this song will testify against them, because it will not be forgotten by their descendants. I know what they are disposed to do, even before I bring them into the land I promised them on oath. So Moshe wrote down this song that day and taught it to the Israelites. (Deut. 31:19–22)

When we consider these Torah songs together, the elements of declamation and communal participation stand out. It should be noted that whereas there is no doubt as to the poetics of units such as the Blessings of Yaakov, Bilam and Moshe, these texts were not intended to be responsive or declarative.[24]

A survey of the way in which the word שירה is used throughout the other books of the Bible confirms our speculation. The Song of Deborah in the Book of Judges features an exhortation for others to sing:

On that day Deborah and Barak son of Abinoam sang this song:
When the princes in Israel take the lead, when the people willingly
    offer themselves
praise the LORD!
Hear this, you kings! Listen, you rulers!
I will sing to the LORD;

---

24. There is an opinion in the scholarship that Gen. 49 should not be viewed as blessings but rather as a compilation of tribal sayings. Cf. J.P. Peters, "Jacob's Blessings," JBL 6 (1886), p. 99–116, esp. 113; J.D. Heck, "A History of Interpretation of Genesis 49 and Deuteronomy 33," BS 147 (1990), 16–31, esp. 17. This approach however is replete with serious drawbacks. Cf. Nahum Sarna, *The JPS Torah Commentary: Genesis* (Philadelphia: JPS, 1989), 331; Gordon J. Wenham, *Genesis 1–15* (WBC 2; Waco: Word, 1994), p. 469–470; Raymond De Hoop, *Genesis 49 in its Literary and Historical Context* (Leiden, Boston: Brill, 1999), 625.

I will praise the LORD, the God of Israel, in song…
Wake up, wake up, Deborah!
Wake up, wake up, break out in song!
Arise, Barak! Take captive your captives, son of Abinoam.
    (Jud. 5:1–3, 12)

King David's Song, which appears with minor variations in both Samuel and in Psalms, is introduced by both texts specifically as שירה. In this valedictory song David vows to praise God among the nations (2 Sam. 22:1, 50; Ps. 18: 1, 50). Unsurprisingly, the entire book of Psalms is filled with numerous examples of the word שיר, in which the exhortation to join in song is implicit. Yeshayahu's and Yechezkel's use of the word שירה is similarly consistent with this approach (Isa. 23:16, 24:9, 26:1, 30:29, 42:10; Ezek. 33:32).

An awareness of the correlation between biblical poetry and responsive declamation paves the way toward a more precise understanding of the unique nature of biblical poetics. While it is undoubtedly true that poetry and prose operate upon opposite ends of a wide continuum, that is not to say that the Bible does not contain clearly discernible poetic selections. In addition to the many poetic stylistic elements enumerated above which contribute to its lyrical beauty, many biblical poems may be identified through their exhortation for others to participate.

Whereas large portions of the Torah are written in poetic style, only three of its songs are explicitly referred to by the text itself as שירה. The inclusion of these poems, the Song of the Sea, the Song of the Well and the Song of Moshe, within the body of the Torah demands our attention. What fundamental theological agenda is advanced through the interruption of the prose retelling of events with these three songs? An analysis of these poems will lead towards an appreciation for the way in which the poetry of the Torah operates harmoniously in its dissemination of theology. In addition to the three core poems of the Torah, the Torah also contains a large corpus of poetic blessing. The forthcoming analysis of the three extended Torah poems will be followed by an examination of Torah blessings, and the way in which these poetic units work together with the songs of the Torah in forming a loosely connected set of lyrical meditations on core Torah theology.

Methodology

Probably the single most important question to consider before approaching any text is *"what is it?"* This deceivingly simple query informs the crux of the methodology which I propose for reading biblical poetry. Mining the poetry of the Torah for its theological gems demands that we acknowledge that the strategies for interpreting poetry and prose aught not be identical. While this may sound self-evident, prevailing practice indicates otherwise. Current biblical scholarship tends to follow the same guidelines for identifying and assessing allusions in biblical poetry as it does in prose. A considerable amount of attention has been devoted to establishing the presence of analogy in prose.[25] Accessing poetry's essence, however, necessitates us to acknowledge poetry as a fundamentally distinct art form.

Recognizing the presence of analogy is critical for being able to interpret the underlying message of any biblical text. To quote Yair Zakovitch, "No literary unit in the Bible stands alone, isolated and independent with no other text drawing from its reservoir and casting it in a new light."[26] When significant new dimensions to the text's meaning result from cross-referencing, it may be attributed to literary allusion.[27] Texts that reinterpret and thereby transform earlier ones are "a mark of ongoing tradition in the homiletical sphere."[28] Nahum Sarna relates to inner biblical allusions as an early stage in the development of Midrash:

> The roots of the midrashic process itself are to be located in the self-conscious patterns of repetition and reinterpretation found in quoted direct speech, and other forms of deliberate repetition in biblical narrative.[29]

---

25. For a broader discussion on the criteria for establishing narrative analogy in biblical prose see Moshe Garsiel, *I Samuel: A Literary Evaluation of Analogies and Parallels* (Ramat Gan: Bar Ilan Univ., 1983), 11–28, (Heb).
26. Yair Zakovitch, "Inner Biblical Interpretation," in *Reading Genesis* (ed. R. Hendel. Cambridge: New York, 2010), 95.
27. Paul R. Noble, "Esau, Tamar and Joseph: Criteria for Identifying Inner Biblical Allusion," *VT* 52 (2002), 219–252.
28. Michael Fishbane, "The Hebrew Bible and Exegetical Tradition," p. 15–30 in *Intertextuality in Ugarit and Israel* (ed. J.C. de Moor. Boston: Brill, 1998), 26.
29. Nahum M. Sarna, *Telling and Retelling: Quotation in Biblical Narrative* (Bloomington: Indiana University Press, 1998), 112.

While there are those who caution against overzealously attributing significance to literary echoes in the biblical text,[30] the compact terseness of biblical poetics leaves little room for the supposition that textual echoes were imbedded into the text for the mere purpose of amusing the perceptive reader.[31] It is critical to stress that the discussion here focuses specifically on the interpretation of poetry. Holding biblical poetry to *a priori* rules is a surefire recipe for its misinterpretation. That being said, a loose set of guidelines for reading poetic texts remains a desideratum. Landy cautions against investing too heavily in a fixed methodology for interpreting biblical poetics:

> Another danger arises from an inflexible methodology, the belief that the strict application of an interpretive formula will automatically provide a complete explication. What is produced however is mystification, not magic, the substitution of the work by scholastic spells.[32]

Landy's interpretation of the Song of Songs employs thematic symmetry alone to interpret analogous texts.[33] The garden motif is enough for Landy to be able to proceed and follow the threads of the parallel text and interpret other elements in the Song of Songs in light of its association with Eden. In my analysis of the poetic texts of the Torah I choose to employ a similar strategy. Determining the presence of analogy begins with the establishment of a pattern of thematic symmetry. When these resonances can be demonstrated to be tools of reinterpretation and transformation, then the assumption of a deliberate correlation is reinforced.

In my analysis of biblical poetry, wordplay will be shown to play a key role in assessing the strength of suggested textual correlations. Absolute rules for establishing the presence of wordplay in poetry, nonetheless,

---

30. Benjamin Sommer, *A Prophet Reads Scripture: Allusions in Isaiah 40–66* (Stanford: Stanford Univ. Press, 1998), 10–18.

31. Cf. Berlin, *Biblical Parallelism*, 6.

32. Francis Landy, "Beauty and the Enigma: An Inquiry into some Interrelated Episodes of the Song of Songs," *JSOT* 17, (1980), 55–106, esp. 62.

33. Landy's analysis of the Song of Songs, in light of its relationship to the Garden of Eden, revolves around the idea of the garden as paradise in both texts. See Francis Landy, "The Song of Songs and the Garden of Eden," *JBL* 98 (1979), 513–28.

remain vexingly elusive.[34] Kabatek cautions against the establishment of fixed rules for identifying wordplay in poetry:[35]

> There seems to be a formal overlap between some forms of poetry and wordplay... But what exactly are the techniques of wordplay on the individual level? Can we establish rules and norms for wordplay? I do not think that this is feasible; we can only establish an open list of possibilities.

The poetry of the Torah alludes to narrative by accessing powerful motifs central to that narrative. Both Torah prose and poetry allude to 'parent' texts by accessing powerful motifs central to that text. Moshe Garsiel proposes three guidelines for establishing literary allusions: (1) if rare words or forms are repeated in the text, (2) if there are many such occurrences, (3) and if other unique stylistic elements are common to both texts.[36]

As noted above, however, given poetry's fundamentally elusive nature, the rules for identifying deliberate intertextuality ought not be identical for poetry and prose. I propose that where Torah poetry is concerned, we adopt the following guidelines. To begin with, when significant motifs are observed to be acting in concert with other critical thematic similarities, the two texts may tentatively be presumed to be related. That is not to say that the analogies ought to be readily perceptible to the unobservant or casual reader. This is especially the case where biblical poetics are concerned. When wordplay is seen to

34. For more on the significance of wordplay in the Bible see S. Gevirtz, "Of Patriarchs and Puns: Joseph at the Fountain, Jacob at the Ford," *HUCA* 46 (1975), 33–54; D.F. Payne, "Characteristic Word-Play in "Second Isaiah": A Reappraisal," *JSS* 12 (1967), 207–229; D. Schmidt, "Critical Note: Another Word-Play in Amos?" *Grace Theological Journal* 8 (1987), 141–142; W.G.E. Watson, "An Example of Multiple Wordplay in Ugaritic," *UF* 12 (1980), 443–444.

35. Johannes Kabatek, "Wordplay and Discourse Traditions," pages 213–228 in *Wordplay and Metalinguistic / Metadiscursive Reflection: Authors, Contexts, Techniques, and Meta-Reflection* (ed. Angelika Zirker, Esme Winter-Froemel; Berlin: Walter de Gruyter, 2015), 223.

36. Moshe Garsiel, *I Samuel: A Literary Evaluation of Analogies and Parallels*, 25.

function within a system of thematic similarities then the assumption of deliberate referencing is strengthened.

Being able to recognize the hidden links between the poems of the Torah and related biblical narratives leads the way to a deeper appreciation for poetry's vital role in the dissemination of Torah theology. An analysis of the poetry of the Torah and its subtle commentary on earlier Torah narratives will reveal Torah poetry to function as a loosely connected network of meditations linking the five books of the Torah, in a broad reflection on God's eternal sovereignty, and Israel's unique role as keepers of the Divine covenant.

Torah Songs

The Song of the Sea

The Song of the Sea, sung in celebration of Israel's miraculous salvation at *Yam Suf*, has traditionally been understood by the classical commentators as a song of thanksgiving. This chapter focuses on the literary style and structure of the Song, leading the way to an understanding of the Song's role as a celebration of God's coronation and an articulation of the Israelite monarchic idea.

שמות פרק טו:א-יח

אָז יָשִׁיר־מֹשֶׁה וּבְנֵי יִשְׂרָאֵל אֶת־הַשִּׁירָה הַזֹּאת לַיקֹוָק וַיֹּאמְרוּ לֵאמֹר אָשִׁירָה
לַיקֹוָק כִּי־גָאֹה גָּאָה סוּס וְרֹכְבוֹ רָמָה בַיָּם: עָזִּי וְזִמְרָת יָהּ וַיְהִי־לִי לִישׁוּעָה זֶה
אֵלִי וְאַנְוֵהוּ אֱלֹהֵי אָבִי וַאֲרֹמְמֶנְהוּ: יְקֹוָק אִישׁ מִלְחָמָה יְקֹוָק שְׁמוֹ: מַרְכְּבֹת פַּרְעֹה
וְחֵילוֹ יָרָה בַיָּם וּמִבְחַר שָׁלִשָׁיו טֻבְּעוּ בְיַם־סוּף: תְּהֹמֹת יְכַסְיֻמוּ יָרְדוּ בִמְצוֹלֹת
כְּמוֹ־אָבֶן: יְמִינְךָ יְקֹוָק נֶאְדָּרִי בַּכֹּחַ יְמִינְךָ יְקֹוָק תִּרְעַץ אוֹיֵב: וּבְרֹב גְּאוֹנְךָ תַּהֲרֹס
קָמֶיךָ תְּשַׁלַּח חֲרֹנְךָ יֹאכְלֵמוֹ כַּקַּשׁ: וּבְרוּחַ אַפֶּיךָ נֶעֶרְמוּ מַיִם נִצְּבוּ כְמוֹ־נֵד נֹזְלִים
קָפְאוּ תְהֹמֹת בְּלֶב־יָם: אָמַר אוֹיֵב אֶרְדֹּף אַשִּׂיג אֲחַלֵּק שָׁלָל תִּמְלָאֵמוֹ נַפְשִׁי אָרִיק
חַרְבִּי תּוֹרִישֵׁמוֹ יָדִי: נָשַׁפְתָּ בְרוּחֲךָ כִּסָּמוֹ יָם צָלֲלוּ כַּעוֹפֶרֶת בְּמַיִם אַדִּירִים:
מִי־כָמֹכָה בָּאֵלִם יְקֹוָק מִי כָּמֹכָה נֶאְדָּר בַּקֹּדֶשׁ נוֹרָא תְהִלֹּת עֹשֵׂה פֶלֶא: נָטִיתָ
יְמִינְךָ תִּבְלָעֵמוֹ אָרֶץ: נָחִיתָ בְחַסְדְּךָ עַם־זוּ גָּאָלְתָּ נֵהַלְתָּ בְעָזְּךָ אֶל־נְוֵה קָדְשֶׁךָ:
שָׁמְעוּ עַמִּים יִרְגָּזוּן חִיל אָחַז יֹשְׁבֵי פְּלָשֶׁת: אָז נִבְהֲלוּ אַלּוּפֵי אֱדוֹם אֵילֵי מוֹאָב
יֹאחֲזֵמוֹ רָעַד נָמֹגוּ כֹּל יֹשְׁבֵי כְנָעַן: תִּפֹּל עֲלֵיהֶם אֵימָתָה וָפַחַד בִּגְדֹל זְרוֹעֲךָ יִדְּמוּ
כָּאָבֶן עַד־יַעֲבֹר עַמְּךָ יְקֹוָק עַד־יַעֲבֹר עַם־זוּ קָנִיתָ: תְּבִאֵמוֹ וְתִטָּעֵמוֹ בְּהַר נַחֲלָתְךָ
מָכוֹן לְשִׁבְתְּךָ פָּעַלְתָּ יְקֹוָק מִקְּדָשׁ אֲדֹנָי כּוֹנְנוּ יָדֶיךָ: יְקֹוָק יִמְלֹךְ לְעֹלָם וָעֶד:

Exodus 15:1–18

Then Moshe and the Israelites sang this song to the LORD: "I will sing to the LORD, for He is highly exalted. Both horse and driver He has hurled into the sea. "The LORD is my strength and my defense; He has become my salvation. He is my God, and I will praise Him, my father's God, and I will exalt Him. The LORD is a warrior; the LORD is His name. Pharaoh's chariots and his army He has hurled into the sea. The best of Pharaoh's officers are drowned in the Red Sea. The deep waters have covered them; they sank to the depths like a stone. Your right hand, LORD, was majestic in power. Your right hand, LORD, shattered the enemy. "In the greatness of Your majesty You threw down those who opposed You. You unleashed Your burning anger; it consumed them like stubble. By the blast of Your nostrils the waters piled up. The surging waters stood up like a wall; the deep waters congealed in the heart of the sea. The enemy boasted, 'I will pursue, I will overtake them. I will divide the spoils; I will gorge myself on them. I will draw my sword and my hand will destroy them.' But You blew with Your breath, and the sea covered them. They sank like lead in the mighty waters. Who among the gods is like You, LORD? Who is like You – majestic in holiness, awesome in glory, working wonders? "You stretch out Your right hand, and the earth swallows Your enemies. In Your unfailing love You will lead the people You have redeemed. In Your strength You will guide them to Your holy dwelling. The nations will hear and tremble; anguish will grip the people of Philistia. The chiefs of Edom will be terrified, the leaders of Moab will be seized with trembling, the people of Canaan will melt away; terror and dread will fall on them. By the power of Your arm they will be as still as a stone – until your people pass by, LORD, until the people You bought pass by. You will bring them in and plant them on the mountain of Your inheritance – the place, LORD, You made for Your dwelling, the sanctuary, Lord, Your hands established. "The LORD reigns for ever and ever."

Introduction

The Song of the Sea (Exodus 15:1–18), which celebrates Israel's miraculous salvation at *Yam Suf*, has traditionally been interpreted as a song of thanksgiving. This chapter focuses on the literary style and overall structure of the Song, in an effort to arrive at an understanding of its precise role. Why was Israel's deliverance at *Yam Suf* singled out by the Torah for rhapsody, while other monumental events in Israel's history such as God's revelation at Sinai, and the dedication of the Tabernacle, to name a few, remained unsung?[1] Some propose that the Song of the Sea serves as a structural marker signaling climactic pause at the precise turning point of the story, the moment at which Israel transitioned from being a motley group of runaway slaves to a free nation.[2] While the Song undoubtedly plays a pivotal role in the Exodus narrative, climactic pause alone doesn't satisfactorily resolve the problem of the interruption of a predominantly prose text with a major poetic interlude. Others have assumed the Song to be a part of a lost Israelite epic poem which predated the written text.[3] No fragments of lost Israelite epic poetry, however, have ever surfaced upon which to substantiate this dubious assumption. Furthermore, it has been convincingly argued that instances of correlation between biblical poetry and ancient Near Eastern epic poetry may be best attributed to the Israelite polemic against ancient Near Eastern polytheism, as opposed to the conjecture of a common

---

1. Songs celebrating these seminal events were recorded in several books of the Bible, most notably Psalms.
2. Cf. James Watts, *Psalm and Story: Inset Hymns in Hebrew Narrative* (Sheffield: Sheffield Academic, 1992), 186–189; David Freedman argues that in the Israelite tradition, poetry and prophecy were essentially part of the same phenomenon. He maintains that the prophecy which is included in the Song justified its inclusion in the text. Cf. David Freedman, *Pottery, Poetry and Prophecy: Studies in Early Hebrew Poetry* (Winona Lake: Eisenbrauns, 1980), 17. While the Song does conclude with a prophetic component, the majority of the text is a historical review of the events at *Yam Suf*.
3. Cf. U. Cassuto, "The Israelite Epic," 80–102 in *Biblical and Oriental Studies* vol. 2 (Jerusalem: Magnes, 1973); W. Albright, *Yahweh and the Gods of Canaan: A Historical Analysis of Two Contrasting faiths* (vol. 7 Jordan Lectures in Comparative Religion; Winona Lake: Eisenbrauns, 1968).

source or influence.[4] In an effort to arrive at an understanding of the precise role that the Song plays within the narration of the Exodus, I will begin with an examination of the Song's genre.

The Genre of the Song

The Song of the Sea's psalm-like quality and celebratory tone led many to view it as a thanksgiving hymn,[5] or a victory song,[6] celebrating God as a holy warrior, איש מלחמה.[7] It has also been suggested that the Song's conclusion upon God's holy mountain points to its role as an enthronement hymn.[8] Neat categorizations, however, tend to become complicated by those stubborn features of the text which fail to conform to *a priori*

---

4. Cf. Shemaryahu Talmon, "Did there exist a national biblical epic?" p. 91–111 in *Literary Studies in the Hebrew Bible: Form and Content* (Jerusalem: Magnes, 1993).

5. F. Crusemann says Moshe's Song is mixed, containing mostly the hymn of the individual. F. Crusemann, *Studien zur Formgeschichte von Hymnus und Danklied in Israel* (WMANT 32; Neukirchen-Vluyn: Neukirchener Verlag, 1969), 19–38; Childs understands Moshe's Song as a hymn. See Brevard S. Childs, *The Book of Exodus: A Critical, Theological Commentary* (OTL; Westminster John Knox Press, 2004), 250; Coats acknowledges that whereas the Song doesn't exhibit a unified genre, it is essentially a hymn of praise. G.W. Coats, "Song of the Sea," CBQ 31 (1969), 1–17, esp. 7–8.

6. J. Muilenburg, *Hearing and Speaking the Word: Selections from the Works of James Muilenburg* (Scholars Press Homage Series; Chico: Scholars, 1984), 151–169, esp. 153. Muilenburg defines the Song as victory liturgy; F.M. Cross and D.N. Freedman, *Studies in Ancient Yahwistic Poetry* (Grand Rapids: Eerdmans, 1975), 45; M.L. Brenner, *The Song of the Sea; Ex. 15:1–21* (BZAW 195; Berlin: de Gruyter, 1991), 36–38; E. Poethig, *The Victory Song Tradition of the Women of Israel* (PhD dissertation, Union Theological Seminary; New York, 1985), 31–68, 85–90, et passim.

7. Patrick D. Miller *The Divine Warrior in Early Israel* (Harvard University Press, 1973), 113; M.C. Lind, *Yahweh Is a Warrior: The Theology of Warfare in Ancient Israel* (Scottdale: Herald, 1980), 49.

8. P. Haupt, "Moses' Song of Triumph," *AJSL* 20 (1904), 149–72; S. Mowinckel, *The Psalms in Israel's Worship* (trans. D.R. Ap-Thomas; 2 vols.; Nashville: Abingdon, 1962), 1:126; Watts supports this approach, noting the strong parallel to Psalms 93–99 and God's enthronement. Cf. J.D.W. Watts, "Song of the Sea – Ex. XV," VT 7 (1957), 371–380, esp. 378; William H. Propp, *Exodus 1–18* (AB 2; New York: Doubleday, 1999), 562. Propp suggests that the Song

assumptions about what elements constitute distinct literary styles. The temporal and stylistic shift in verses 13–18, which alter the orientation of the Song from God's prior salvation to his future deliverance poses such a dilemma.[9] An analysis of the tight structural unity of the Song will demonstrate the fitting placement of verses 13–18 within the larger poetic framework, shedding light on the Song's literary genre, its core message, and its essential role within the narration of the exodus story.[10]

---

should be called the 'Song of the Mountain', due to its climax on God's holy mountain.

9. This dramatic shift in the thrust of the text led many scholars to view the closing verses of the Song as a gloss. Cf. Watts, "Song of the Sea," 378; Coats, "The Song of the Sea," 1–17; E. Zenger, "Tradition und Interpretation in Exodus XV 1–21," 452- 483 in *Congress Volume: Vienna 1980* (ed. J.A. Emerton; VT Sup 32; Leiden: Brill, 1981); T.C. Butler, *Song of the Sea: Exodus 15:1–18: A Study in the Exegesis of Hebrew Poetry* (PhD diss., Vanderbilt, 1971), 102–99; T.B. Dozeman, "Song of the Sea and Salvation History" 94–113 in *On the Way to Nineveh: Studies in Honor of George M. Landes* (eds. Stephen L. Cook and S.C. Winter; ASOR; Atlanta: Scholars Press, 1999).

10. Scholars who support the structural unity of the Song note its transitional genre, its overall conformity with concepts familiar from contemporary mythologies, and its strophe and meter consistencies. Cf. F.M. Cross, *Canaanite Myth and Hebrew Epic: Essays in the History of the Religion of Israel* (Cambridge: Harvard Univ. Press, 2009), 121–144; J. Muilenburg, "A Liturgy of the Triumphs of Yahweh," in *Studia Biblica et Semitica*, ed. W.C. van Unnik and A.S. van der Woude (Wageningen: H. Veenman en Zonen, 1966), 233–251. Muilenburg says there is a transition in genre between the sea material and the conquest material, declarative versus descriptive praise; D.N. Freedman, "Strophe and Meter in Exodus 15," 187–227 in *Potter, Poetry, and Prophecy: Studies in Early Hebrew Poetry* (Winona Lake: Eisenbrauns, 1980); Childs, *Exodus*, 251–252; H. Strauss, "Das Meerlied des Mose: Ein 'Siegeslied' Israels?" ZAW 97 (1985), 106–107; M. Rozelaar, "The Song of the Sea; Exodus XV,1b-18," VT 2 (1952), 221–228; R. Alter, *The Art of Biblical Poetry* (New York: Basic Books, 1985), 50–54; M. Howell, "Exodus 15, 1b-18: A Poetic Analysis," ETL 65 (1989), 9, 34–35, 42; R.J. Tournay, *Voir et entendre Dieu avec les Psaumes ou la liturgie prophetique du second temple a Jerusalem*, (CahRB 24; Paris: J. Gabalda, 1988), 68; and M.L. Brenner, *The Song of the Sea: Ex 15:1–21* (BZAW 195; Berlin: de Gruyter, 1991), 26–34.

The Structure of the Song

Most commentators divide the Song either into two parts (vs. 1–12 and 13–18), separating the Song between past and future events; or into three parts (vs. 1–12, 13–16, and 17–18), further subdividing the forthcoming events between the conquest of the land and God's enthronement.[11] David Zvi Hoffmann proposes that the Song is comprised of seven sections, although he doesn't elaborate any further.[12] I have chosen to focus on the seven-part division proposed by Hoffmann, as each of the sections that he proposes subsumes within them a consistent and meaningful pattern of semantic repetition, pointing to the presence of a chiasmus.

Seven-Part Division of the Song

1. Vs. 1–2 – Statement of intent.
2. Vs. 3–5 – God as holy warrior (third person).
3. Vs. 6–8 – God as holy warrior (second person).
4. Vs. 9–10 – Pharaoh; his hubris and downfall.
5. Vs. 11–13 – Praise of God's feats.
6. Vs. 14–16 – Reaction of Israel's enemies.
7. Vs. 17–18 – Plans for Israel's future and for God's coronation.

In addition to the thematic symmetry and semantic correlation between corresponding units, it will be demonstrated that the Song contains another important stylistic marker pointing to its overall parallel structure. Each of the Song's parallel units contains a repeating word or phrase that reverberates thematically with a repeated word or phrase in the corresponding section. These phrase repetitions will be shown to serve as structural markers meant to draw our attention to the Song's overarching chiastic structure.

---

11. Cf. William Doan, "The Song of Israel: Exodus 15:1–18," *Proceedings, Eastern Great Lakes and Midwest Biblical Society* 25 (2005), 29–41, esp. 29.

12. D.Z. Hoffman brings further support for the unity of the Song with his observation that God's name appears ten times within the song. This is especially significant in light of the importance of the theme of ten in the Exodus narratives. Cf. David Zvi Hoffman, *Exodus* (trans. A. Wasserteil; Jerusalem: Mosad Harav Kook, 2010), 164–165, (Heb.).

Sections One and Seven; Statements of Intent

1. Vs. 1–2	Vs. 17–18
Then Moshe and the Israelites sang this song to the LORD: "I will sing to the LORD, for He is highly exalted. Both horse and driver He has hurled into the sea. "The LORD is my strength and my defense; He has become my salvation. He is my God, and I will glorify Him, my father's God, and I will exalt Him.	You will bring them in and plant them on the mountain of your inheritance, the place, LORD, you made for your dwelling, the sanctuary, Lord, your hands established. "The LORD reigns for ever and ever."

In vs. 1–2 Moshe states his intention to glorify God, and in vs. 17–18 God's plans for Israel's future are specified. The opening and concluding sections of the Song both describe a vision of the future construction of a temple dedicated to God. Verse 17 clearly references the word Temple, מקדש, and verse 2 features the word ואנוהו, stemming from the root נוה, which may relate to "praise,"[13] or "beautification" (Rashi, Ex. 15:2, second interpretation), although it may also refer to a "dwelling place."[14] Onkelos' translation of the word ואנוהו as ואבני ליה מקדש, "I will build Him a Temple," which is corroborated by Ibn Ezra and Bechor Shor,[15] faithfully renders the plain sense of the verse. The Tabernacle, often referred to in the Pentateuch as משכן, or a "dwelling place," functioned as the dwelling place for the Divine Presence. This approach is strongly supported by the only other appearance of the word נוה in the Pentateuch, close by in vs. 13 as part of the term נוה קדשך, "holy dwelling," where the word unmistakably refers to a physical location.

The use of the word נוה can mean one of three things: praise, beautification, or dwelling place. The simple meaning appears to be "dwelling place," based on Onkelos, Ibn Ezra, and Bechor Shor, but since we are dealing with poetry, we can admit multiple simultaneous meanings. In

---

13. Cf. Ibn Shoshan, *New Biblical Concordance*, (Jerusalem: Kiryat Sefer), 1983, 'נוה,' p. 746; HALOT, 'נוה,' p. 678.

14. Ringgren, "נוה," TDOT IX: 273–277.

15. Onkelos and Ibn Ezra, Ex. 15:2. Rashi, ad loc, cites both the approaches to the word.

such a case, the word ואנוהו might refer to two or even all three things at once – it might be a beautified manifestation of God's dwelling where praised is offered to Him.

The parallel position of the words ואנוהו and וארוממנהו, "I will exalt Him," in vs. 2, offers further support for the reading suggesting the erection of a temple. Aside from denoting exultation, the root רום also means "to erect,"[16] and is associated in a variety of sources with temple construction.[17] The roots נוה ,רום, and קדש share a common semantic field, appearing together in Psalm 93 and again within a single verse in Yirmiyahu, where the referent is God's abode (Cf. Ps. 93: 4–5, Jer. 25:30). The juxtaposition of these three terms in the poem's opening and conclusion reinforces the Song's declaration of plans to construct a temple to God.

In addition to conveying a plan to construct a dwelling place dedicated to God, sections one and seven also announce the coronation of God. Vs. 17 clearly references God's enthronement, and vs. 1 describes God in a state of supreme elevation, גאה גאה, a term used throughout the Bible to proclaim God's enthronement, as seen in the following texts:

> The LORD reigns, He is robed in majesty; גאות לבש, the LORD is girded with strength; indeed, the world is established, firm and secure. (Ps. 93:1)

In Psalm 68 the root גאה places God's majesty high above mortal kings:

> Sing to God, you kingdoms of the earth, sing praise to the Lord, to Him who rides across the highest heavens, the ancient heavens, who thunders with mighty voice. Proclaim the power of God, whose majesty גאותו, is over Israel, whose power is in the heavens. (Ps. 68:33–35)

The root גאה is twice used in Deuteronomy 33 to describe God as supreme monarch. Before presenting these verses however, it is relevant to note they are part of an outer hymnal framework encapsulating Moshe's Blessings, which opens with a declaration of God as King:[18]

---

16. *HALOT*, 'רום,' CD-ROM ed., 1204.

17. Firmage, Milgrom, Dahmen, "רום," *TDOT* XIII: 402–412; cf. Gen. 31:45; Jer. 25:30; 31:11; Ezek. 20: 40; 34:14; Ezra 9:9; Sira, (Kahane ed.), 49:12.

18. Cf. A.D.H. Mayes, *Deuteronomy* (NCB 5; Grand Rapids: Eerdmans, 1979),

Then he became King in Jeshurun,
when the heads of the people assembled,
the tribes of Israel together. (Deut. 33:5)

While this verse is ambiguous regarding the referent of "he" –
Moshe or God[19] – we must consider the treaty format of the book of
Deuteronomy. Craige comments that "the treaty-form stresses that the
covenant was made, and renewed, between God as King, on the one hand,
and his vassal people, on the other hand."[20] Furthermore, the suggestion
of Moshe's coronation as king moments before his imminent death would
be anticlimactic, and place Israel's renewed covenant in jeopardy.

The closing verses of Deuteronomy 33, which continue to describe
God's monarchic ascension, stress the root גאה:

There is no one like the God of Jeshurun, who rides across the
heavens to help You – and on the clouds in his majesty, ובגאותו
שחקים (Deut. 33:26).

Blessed are you, Israel! Who is like You, a people saved by the
LORD? He is your shield and helper – and your glorious sword,
חרב גאותך. Your enemies will cower before you, and you will tread
on their heights. (Deut. 33:29)

Job is challenged by God to do the impossible; to raise himself
above all the creation, in effect placing himself on par with God himself,
clothing himself in majesty, גאון, stemming from the root גאה:[21]

396; Ian Cairns, *Deuteronomy, Word and Presence; a Commentary* (ITC; Grand
Rapids: Eerdmans Pub., 1992), 294; D.N. Freedman, "The Poetic Structure
of the Framework of Deuteronomy 33," in *Divine Commitment and Human
Obligation, vol. 2: Poetry and Orthography* (ed. J. Huddlestun; Grand Rapids:
Eerdmans, 1997), 85–107. These scholars contend that the verses of the outer
framework were originally an independent hymn into which the blessings
were inserted. Others have suggested that the hymn was composed in order
to fuse the references to individual tribes in the chapter into one cohesive
story of the entire nation of Israel. Cf. Richard D. Nelson, *Deuteronomy: A
Commentary*, (Louisville: Presbyterian, 2004), 386.

19. Cf. Ibn Ezra, Deut. 33:5, who maintains that Moshe is the king. Nachmanides
and Rashi however agree that God is the referent here.

20. Peter Craige, *The Book of Deuteronomy* (NIC: Grand Rapids: Eerdmans, 1976),
65.

21. *HALOT*, 'גאון,' CD-ROM ed., 169.

Then adorn yourself with glory and splendor, and clothe yourself in honor and majesty, גאון וגבוה. (Job 40:10)

It was noted above that the Song contains another critical stylistic marker critical for identifying its overall parallel structure. Each of the Song's units contains a repeating word or phrase which corresponds thematically with a repeated word or phrase in the parallel section. Section one features the phrase גאה גאה, suggesting God's elevation or enthronement, and section seven features the words מכון and כוננו, both stemming from the root כון, "to be firmly established."[22] These twin concepts, God's enthronement and firm establishment, are fundamentally interconnected, and appear side by side in numerous places throughout the Bible.[23] The phenomenon of twice repeated complementary phrases in parallel subsections will be shown to recur consistently throughout the Song's parallel units.

Sections Two and Six: The Petrification of the Enemy

2. Vs. 3–5

The LORD is a warrior; the LORD is His name. Pharaoh's chariots and his army He has hurled into the sea. The best of Pharaoh's officers are drowned in the Red Sea. The deep waters have covered them; they sank to the depths like a stone.

6. Vs. 14–16

The nations will hear and tremble; anguish will grip the people of Philistia. The chiefs of Edom will be terrified, the leaders of Moab will be seized with trembling, the people of Canaan will melt away; terror and dread will fall on them. By the power of Your arm they will be as still as a stone – until Your people pass by, LORD, until the people You bought pass by.

In verse 5, the Egyptians descend like אבן, "rock," into the deep, and in verse 16, Israel's future enemies are petrified, ידמו כאבן.[24] In verse 3 God is twice declared to be a holy warrior:

---

22. *HALOT*, 'כון,' 465.

23. Cf. Ps. 9:8; 89:5, 15, 37; 93:1, 2; 97: 2; 103:19; Prov. 16:12, 25:5, 29:14, 1 Chron. 17:14, 22:10; 2 Sam. 7:16; 1 Kng. 2:24, 45; Isa. 9:6; 16:5.

24. It is relevant to note that both sections two and six contain the word חיל, albeit

ה׳ איש מלחמה ה׳ שמו

The LORD is a warrior; the LORD is His name.

The second half of this parallel verse, in which it is stated that the Lord is His name, crystallizes what precisely is meant by this description; that God is a holy warrior. Bechor Shor points out that the statement שמו ׳ה echoes God's original message to Moshe at the burning bush, where God introduced himself as "I will be that I will be," in addition to the Tetragrammaton, and concluding "this is my name for all time," זה שמי לעולם (Ex. 3:14–15). Bechor Shor comments there (Ex. 3:14) that the Tetragrammaton, and the name א־היה, "I will be," are two versions of the same name. These names connote God's eternity as well as His role in fighting for Israel in their time of need, as exemplified by the Exodus. The term used here, ה׳ שמו, and the term used there, שמי ה׳, are mirror images; therefore this phrase in the Song of the Sea needs to be understood in light of the phrase's original meaning, i.e., God's actions in the Exodus. This observation accords well with the 'biblical inverted quotation,' documented by P.C. Beentjes. This principle describes the way in which the Bible inverts quotations from earlier canonical texts in a chiastic-like way.[25]

In the corresponding section, in verse 16, Israel is twice declared to be God's nation on a divine warpath:

עד יעבור עמך ה׳ עד יעבור עם זו קנית.

until Your people pass by, LORD, until the people You bought pass by.

---

in two different senses. In vs. 4 it refers to soldiers and in vs. 14 it conveys fear and trembling.

25. P.C. Beentjes, "Discovering a New Path of Intertextuality: Inverted Quotations and Their Dynamics," in L.J. de Regt et al. (eds.), *Literary Structure and Rhetorical Strategies in the Hebrew Bible*, (Van Gorcum: Assen, 1996), 31–50. This phenomenon has been further documented in Yeshayahu's inverted quotations from Psalms. Cf. Moshe Seidl, "Resemblances Between the Book of Isaiah and the Book of Psalms," *Sinai Yarhon* 19 (1955–1956), 149–172, 229–240, 273–280, 333–353, (Heb.).

A key aspect of holy war is the relationship between God and the Israelite army. God fights for Israel, and the nation does not have to worry about the number of its troops or the state of its weapons technology.[26] Deuteronomy conflates God the holy warrior with the Israelite war camp in 23: 10–15, in the laws pertaining to the ritual purity of the war camp:

> For the Lord your God moves about your camp to protect you and to deliver your enemies to you. (Deut. 23:1)

The synthesis between God the holy warrior and the Israelite war camp is also evident in Numbers, where the Ark of the Covenant is described upon the divine warpath in Israel's midst:

> Whenever the ark set out, Moshe said, "Rise up, LORD! May Your enemies be scattered; may Your foes flee before You." Whenever it came to rest, he said, "Return, LORD, to the countless thousands of Israel." (Num. 10: 35–36)

The Song of Deborah also combines the notions of God the holy warrior and Israel, God's blessed warriors:

> Because the chieftains of Israel set themselves out front,
> Because the people offered themselves willingly,
> Blessed be God…
> My heart is with the chieftains of Israel,
> the volunteers among the people.
> Blessed be God! (Jud. 5:2, 9)

The idea of God as holy warrior, mentioned in the opening of the Song, is developed in the Song's closure to include, indeed, to elevate Israel, as His holy warriors. Israel's incarceration in Egypt is described in Deuteronomy as כור הברזל, (Deut. 4:20). Carsten Vang explains that this metaphor refers not to a smelting furnace but rather to a crucible of iron.[27]

---

26. Deut. 7:17–18. Cf. Tremper Longman and Daniel Reid, *God is a Warrior* (Grand Rapids: Zondervan, 2010), 37. Longman and Reid cite examples from the story of Gideon in Judges 17 and the confrontation between David and Goliath in 1 Sam. 17.

27. Carsten Vang, "Israel in the Iron-Smelting Furnace? Towards a New Understanding of the כור הברזל in Deut. 4:20," *HIPHIL Novum* 1(2014), 25–34, 32

This understanding significantly changes the meaning of the metaphor. Instead of describing the hardship of the oppression, it illustrates the sheer impossibility of escape. It is beyond human capacity to extricate oneself from an impenetrable container. The metaphor serves to stress the extraordinary power of God in rescuing Israel from Egypt. Israel's utter vulnerability at *Yam Suf* required God to step in on their behalf in the role of holy warrior, however, the period spent in the wilderness prepared them for what lay ahead, and their future role as warriors in the army of God, under the leadership of Joshua.

Sections Three and Five; God Defeats His Enemies and Redeems Israel

3. Vs. 6–8

Your right hand, LORD,
was majestic in power.
Your right hand, LORD,
shattered the enemy.
In the greatness of Your majesty
You threw down those who
opposed You.
You unleashed Your burning
anger;
it consumed them like stubble.
By the blast of Your nostrils
the waters piled up.
The surging waters stood up like
a wall;
the deep waters congealed in the
heart of the sea.

5. Vs. 11–13

Who among the gods
is like You, LORD?
Who is like You –
majestic in holiness,
awesome in glory,
working wonders?
You stretch out Your right hand,
and the earth swallows Your
enemies.
In Your unfailing love You will
lead
the people You have redeemed.
In Your strength You will guide
them
to Your holy dwelling.

Sections three and five recount the defeat of the Egyptian army and Israel's path to safety. It is noteworthy that the word תבלעמו, "swallowed," in vs. 12 is parallel to the word יאכלמו, "consumed," in vs. 7. Both words end with the poetic מו suffix and together convey the act of consumption.

God is described in both sections as נאדר, "glorious,"[28] and as dispatching His right hand, ימין, in salvation. In verse 6, the reference to God's right hand, a metaphor for His mighty acts, is repeated twice, emphasizing His awesome strength:

ימינך ה' נאדרי בכוח ימינך ה' תרעץ אויב.

In a similar vein, verse 11 twice repeats the complementary assertion that there is no power on par with God.

מי כמוך באלים ה' מי כמוך נאדר בקדש נורא תהילת עשה פלא.

Besides for our chapter, references to "God's arm," and the phrase מי כמוך, "who is like you," appear as a set three more times in the Bible: Deut. 33:29, Ps. 71:19, 89:8–10 (9–11).[29] To begin with, in our text, the question of "who is like God," מי כמוך, is immediately addressed in the ensuing verse in which God's right hand is mentioned, ימינך. In Deuteronomy, the phrase appears together with a description of God's arm in the same verse. The concluding verse of Moshe's Blessings in Deuteronomy 33 states:

Blessed are you, Israel! Who is like you, מי כמוך, a people saved by the LORD? He is your shield and helper and your glorious sword. Your enemies will cower before you, and you will tread on their heights. (Deut. 33:29)

Earlier it was noted that scholars consider the opening and closing verses of Deuteronomy 33 to function as a single framework, forming a hymnal setting to Moshe's Blessings (vs. 2–5 and 26–29).[30] Christensen points out that the two halves of the outer framework form a chiasmus, in which verse 29 and verse 2 are parallel:[31]

---

28. *HALOT*, 'אדר,' 16.
29. The phrase מי כמוך occurs only once more, and that is in Ps. 35:10, with no reference to God's arm.
30. Cf. Mayes, *Deuteronomy*, 396; Ian Cairns, *Deuteronomy*, 294; Freedman, "The Poetic Structure," 85–107; Nelson, *Deuteronomy*, 386.
31. Duane Christensen, "Two Stanzas of a Hymn in Deuteronomy 33," *Biblica* 65 (1984), 382–389.

A. (v. 2) God comes to deliver His people.

　　B. (v. 3–4) God protects and provides for His people.

　　　　C. (v. 5) God is King over Jeshurun.

　　　　C. (v. 26) There is no God like the God of Jeshurun.

　　B. (v. 27–28) Israel is secured in and blessed by God.

A. (v. 29) Israel is delivered by God.

Verse 2 of the outer framework, the parallel of verse 29, references God's right hand:

> He said: The Lord came from Sinai; He shone upon them from Seir; He appeared from Mount Paran, and approached from Ribeboth-kodesh, lightning flashing from His right hand, מימינו.

Even if we choose to reject the suggestion of a chiasmus, the hymn of Deuteronomy 33's outer framework clearly opens and closes with the idea of God's right arm, מימינו, and singularity, מי כמוך.

Psalm 71 discusses God's arm together with the phrase מי כמוך in two consecutive verses:

> Even when I am old and gray, do not forsake me, my God, until I declare Your power to the next generation, Your mighty arm, זרועך to all who are to come. Your righteousness, God, reaches to the heavens, You who have done great things. Who is like You, מי כמוך, God? (Ps. 71:18–19)

The drowning of the Egyptian army is recounted in Psalm 89, with the blending of these two ideas:

> Who is like You, מי כמוך, LORD God Almighty? You, LORD, are mighty, and Your faithfulness surrounds You. You rule over the surging sea; when its waves mount up, you still them. You crushed Rahab like one of the slain; with Your strong arm, בזרוע עזך, You scattered your enemies." (Ps. 89:8/9–10/11)

COSMIC BATTLE

It is widely accepted that the presentation of the Egyptian army at *Yam Suf* shares many parallel features with the slaying of the primordial sea monster from the Ugaritic Baal mythologies.[32] Some of the major correlating themes are: the conflict with watery chaos, kingship, the building of a temple upon a holy mountain, and the defeat of Mot, or death. Brian Russel analyzes the thematic and lexical points of contact between the two corpuses, while enumerating their significant differences. He observes that the Song takes place within "the planes of human history," that the enemy was real, not a mythological monster of chaos, and that those who responded were the Israelites, not an assembly of gods. In the Baal cycle, Baal invites the goddess Anat to his holy mountain, whereas in the Song, it is Israel who is brought there to dwell. Thus it is two gods meeting, rather than God meeting with mere mortals. Russell concludes that the Song's exultation of God's preeminence and singularity in vs. 11 is best understood within the context of the Song's polemic with contemporary polytheistic beliefs:[33]

> Who among the gods is like You, LORD? Who is like You majestic in holiness, awesome in glory, working wonders? (Ex. 15:11)

The Song's polemic with contemporary Baal worship is further supported by the reference to Baal Zephon in the Song's introductory verses (Ex. 14:9). Baal Zephon, also identified with Mount Zephon, played a central role in the cult of Baal.[34] Its striking appearance in such close proximity to the Song raises the suspicion that Baal Zephon's relevance to the Song extends far beyond the function of geographical marker, merely recording the location of the Red Sea crossing. The Song's role as commentary on Baal mythology works well with what we know about the way in which the Bible relates to contemporary mythologies. Sarna writes that "God's decisive overthrow of His mythical primeval enemies is invoked as an assurance of His mighty power for the redemption of

---

32. Cf. Cross, *Canaanite Myth and Hebrew Epic*, p. 112–144; C. Kloos, *Yhwh's Combat with the Sea: A Canaanite Tradition in the Religion of Ancient Israel* (Leiden: Brill, 1986); L.R. Fisher, "Creation at Ugarit and in the Old Testament," *VT* 15 (1965), 313–324.

33. Brian D. Russell, *The Song of the Sea: The Date of Composition and Influence of Exodus 15:1–21* (New York: Peter Lang Pub., 2007), 39–41, 69–70.

34. L. Sinclair, "Baal Zephon," *Eerdmans Dictionary of the Bible* (ed. D. Freedman and A. Myers; Amsterdam: Amsterdam University Press, 2000), 137.

Israel through a like victory over the present historical enemies of the nation."[35]

The Song of course isn't the only biblical text which preserves the tradition of God's cosmic battle and supremacy over a mythological sea monster.[36] Scattered references in the Bible refer to the primordial monster by a variety of names.[37] One of the names used by Yeshayahu is *tanin* (Isa. 27:1). Elsewhere in the prophets, we find that the *tanin* was a nickname used to describe Egypt, and even Pharaoh himself (Ezek. 32). Amos Hakham suggests that the *tanin* – or snake of Aharon which swallowed the staffs of Pharaoh's magicians at the introduction to the ten plagues – foreshadows the splitting of *Yam Suf*, and was in and of itself a poetic slaying of the *tanin* – or Egypt.[38] Hakham interprets the Rabbinic homily in which the Egyptians are represented and defended by an official heavenly agent who is subsequently defeated by God, as reflective of this mythological struggle and demonstrative of the Bible's unequivocal stance on God's supremacy over all earthly and cosmic forces.[39]

---

35. Nahum Sarna, *Understanding Genesis: The Heritage of Biblical Israel* (New York: Schocken, 1970), 23.

36. Cf. the following biblical texts which reference God's victory over a primordial sea monster: Gen. 1:21, Isa. 27:1; 51:9, Ps. 74:13; 89:11; 148:7, Job 7:12; 13:13, 21:12. On the comparison between the divine battle against the primordial sea monster in the Bible and in Ugarit, see J. Day, *God's Conflict with Dragon and Sea* (Cambridge: Cambridge University Press, 1985); S. Loewenstamm, "Anat's Victory over the Tunnanu," *Journal of Semitic Studies* 20 (1975), 22–27; idem, "The Ugaritic Myth of the Sea and its Biblical Counterparts," pages 96–101 in *Eretz-Israel: Archaeological, Historical and Geographical Studies* (Jerusalem: Israel Exploration Society, 1969); H. Niehr, "Tannîn," pages 715–720 in G.J. Botterweck, H. Ringgren, H. Fabry (eds.), *TDOT*, vol. 8; Mary K. Wakeman, *God's Battle with the Monster: A Study in Biblical Imagery* (Leiden: Brill, 1973).

37. Names used in the Bible to refer to the sea monster include *taninim*, *tanim*, *tanin*, *rahav*, *leviatan*, *nahash briah*, and *nahash akalaton*.

38. Amos Hakham, *Exodus* (vol. 1, Daat Mikra; Jerusalem: Mosad harav Kook, 1991), (Heb.), 282–283. Cf. Isa. 27:1; 51:9. Elsewhere, the primordial sea monster is referred to as *Rahav*. Cf. Ps. 74:12–15; 89:10–11; Job 26:12–13. Cf. Ezek. 32, where Pharaoh is referred to as a *tanin* or sea monster.

39. *Midrash Vayosha* in Eisenstein, *Otzar HaMidrashim*, 148; Cf. the following

Within the broader context of the Song's analogy with and commentary on ancient Mesopotamian cosmologies, it is noteworthy that both sections three and five in the Song describe the defeat of the Egyptian army in terms uniquely associated with the slaying of serpents and sea-monsters.[40] Vs. 6 employs the unusual term רעץ meaning "vanquish."[41] The word רעץ appears only once more in the Bible, where it is parallel to the root רצץ (Jud. 10:8):

> God became angry with them. He sold them into the hands of the Philistines and the Ammonites, who that year shattered and crushed them, וירעצו וירצצו. For eighteen years they oppressed all the Israelites on the east side of the Jordan in Gilead, the land of the Amorites. (Jud. 10:7–8)

Both רעץ and רצץ stem etymologically from the common root רעע, meaning "to shatter or crush" as well as "to do evil."[42] The close association of the root רצץ with the vanquishing of the primordial sea-monster is of particular interest:[43]

> It was You who crushed, רצצת, the heads of Leviathan, לויתן, and gave it as food to the creatures of the desert. (Ps. 74:14)

The snake/primordial sea monster was the biblical symbol of cosmic evil, ער:[44]

Rabbinic sources for the war fought between God and the mythological sea monster: BT *Bava Batra* 74b, *Exodus Rabbah* 15:22, BT *Hagigah* 12a, BT *Sanhedrin* 97b.

40. The close relationship and seeming interchangeability between the serpent and the mythological sea monster may be observed in Isa. 27:1; 51:9; Ps. 74:13–14.

41. *HALOT*, 'רעץ,' 1271.

42. Ringgren, "רצץ," *TDOT* XIII:641–643; *HALOT*, 'רעע,' 1269–1270.

43. The act of crushing as a means for vanquishing the primordial sea monster, this time referred to as *Rahav*, is again witnessed in the book of Job 26:12: "By His power the sea grew calm. By His skill He crushed, מחץ, the great sea monster." Cf. *HALOT*, 'מחץ,' 571.

44. Cf. also Job 7:12; C.H. Gordon, "Leviathan: A Symbol of Evil," in *Biblical Motifs* (ed. A. Altmann, Studies and Texts 3; Cambridge: Harvard Univ. Press, 1966), 1–9.

On that day, the LORD will punish with his sword, his fierce, great and powerful sword, Leviathan the gliding serpent, Leviathan the coiling serpent; he will slay the monster of the sea. (Isa. 27:1)

The roots רצץ, רעץ, and רעע, are lexically and thematically interrelated. All three convey notions of smashing as well as evil. It is salient to add that according to the Ugaritic texts, Baal challenges the sea monster Yamm specifically by smashing its head.[45] It is important to stress that the mere presence of the root רעע alone doesn't prove an association with the slaying of the primordial sea dragon; however, its appearance opposite the swallowing up of the enemy in the parallel section of the Song subtly adds to the Song's suggestions of Baal's defeat.

The parallel section of the Song, in vs. 12, describes the Egyptians as having been swallowed up, תבלעמו. The verbs בלע and רצץ come together in Job in a discussion of the futility of evil, suggesting a fundamental correlation between the two ideas:

What he toiled for he must give back uneaten, ולא יבלע; he will not enjoy the profit from his trading. For he has oppressed רצץ the poor and left them destitute; he has seized houses he did not build. (Job 20:18–19)

Contemplating the significance of the root בלע within the context of the Exodus narrative conjures images of Aharon's staff swallowing up the snakes produced by Pharaoh's magicians; an episode noted above for its role in portending Egypt's defeat at *Yam Suf*. The theme of snakes being swallowed up was a significant motif in Ancient Egypt. By way of example, an Egyptian spell depicts a mottled knife representing a snake which "goes forth against its like" and swallows it.[46] The Pyramid text of the 12th dynasty priest Senwosret Ankh reads "Unis is the nau snake, the leading bull. He swallows his seven snakes," meaning that Unis becomes the primary serpentine life force.[47] In ancient Egypt, the

45. Cf. CTA, 2, esp. 4.24ff; M.K. Wakeman, *God's Battle with the Monster: A Study in Biblical Imagery* (Leiden: Brill, 1973), 37–38.

46. *Ancient Near Eastern Texts Relating to the Old Testament*, (ed. James B. Pritchard; Princeton: Princeton Univ. Press, 1969), 326c.

47. Susan Morrow, *The Dawning Moon of the Mind: Unlocking the Pyramid Texts* (New York: Farrar, Straus and Giroux, 2015), 54.

snake represented the life force, and the swallowing of snakes is akin to the swallowing up of that life force.[48] The swallowing up of Pharaoh and his army in the Song further subtlety augments Pharaoh's portrayal as a mythical serpent.[49]

Intimations of the vanquishing of serpents in parallel verses of the Song serve as a fitting encasement of section four, verses 9–10, the Song's climax, which focuses on the ultimate downfall of Pharaoh, whom Yechezkel later described as the sea-monster incarnate (Cf. Ezek. 32).

Section Four – The Center of the Chiasmus: Pharaoh's Hubris and Downfall

Vs. 9–10

The enemy boasted,
"I will pursue, I will overtake them.
I will divide the spoils;
I will gorge myself on them.
I will draw my sword
and my hand will destroy them."
But You blew with Your breath,
and the sea covered them.
They sank like lead
in the mighty waters.

Vs. 9 and 10, which highlight Pharaoh's hubris and downfall, are the fulcrum upon which the Song pivots. Vs. 9 features remarkably extensive alliteration, meant to grab the listener's ear as it focuses attention on Pharaoh's arrogance. The first five words of the verse begin with the letter *aleph*, connoting self,[50] and the final three phrases conclude with the letter *yud*, also signifying the self:

---

48. Gillian Alban, *Melusine the Serpent Goddess in A.S. Byatt's Possession and in Mythology* (Lanham: Lexington Books, 2003), 141.

49. The presentation of the Egyptian army throughout the Song in the singular form reinforces their subtle portrayal as a single monstrous creature.

50. While the first two *alephs* which appear at the beginning of the first two words of the opening clause don't function as a first-person prefix, the role of the

אמר אויב ארדוף אשיג אחלק שלל תמלאמו נפשי אריק חרבי תורישמו ידי.

This poetic device has the combined effect of shining a spotlight on Pharaoh's egocentrism, as it vividly portrays him to be a myopic military commander with delusions of grandeur.

The Song's epicenter focuses the attention on Pharaoh's overconfident vaunt that he would fill his נפש, his very being, with plunder. Pharaoh's pretensions are swiftly dashed in vs. 10 in a metathetic twist, where God rearranges the letters of Pharaoh's נפש to read נשף, causing him and his army to be blown effortlessly into the sea.

Whereas Pharaoh is unmistakably the object of God's wrath at the nucleus of the Song, his title there is curiously and uncharacteristically omitted. By referring to Pharaoh as "the enemy," אויב, the Song emasculates Pharaoh, stripping him of his identity and diminishing his prestige. In a single literal and figurative blow, Pharaoh, the insuperable monarch of Egypt, is reduced to an anonymous foe. Pharaoh's metamorphosis in the Song's climax casts him in the role of archetype, the personification of evil. The Song of the Sea emerges as the celebration of nothing less than the triumph of good, or God, over evil.

Summary of the Chiasmus

A. Vs. 1–2 – Statement of intent, focus on the future (ישיר, אשירה).

    B. Vs. 3–5 – God as holy warrior.

        C. Vs. 6–8 – God's right hand defeats the enemy.

            D. Vs. 9–10 – Pharaoh; his hubris and defeat

        C. Vs. 11–13 – God's right hand defeats the enemy.

    B. Vs. 14–16 – Israel as God's holy army.

A. Vs. 17–18 – Future plans for Israel and God's coronation.

A. GOD'S ENTHRONEMENT IS ANNOUNCED TOGETHER WITH PLANS FOR THE BUILDING OF A TEMPLE.

Parallel temple-related terminologies include ואנוהו, stemming from נוה,

---

    aleph prefix in the subsequent three words has the overall effect of casting a self-absorbed thrust upon the entire clause.

abode, and מקדש, temple. The repetitive phrase גאה גאה, supreme elevation, and מכון־כוננו, firm establishment, together suggest enthronement.

B. GOD IS A HOLY WARRIOR AND ISRAEL REPRESENTS GOD IN BATTLE.

The parallel phrases comparing Israel's enemies to a rock, אבן, link the two sections. The repetition of God as holy warrior, ה' איש מלחמה ה' שמו, is complemented by Israel twice being referred to as God's fighting force,

עד יעבור עמך ה' עד יעבור עם זו קנית.

C. GOD IS THE ULTIMATE MASTER OF ALL EARTHLY AND COSMIC FORCES.

Parallel lexemes referring to God's right hand, ימין, and his gloriousness, נאדר, connect the two sections. Corresponding themes of eating and swallowing topped with the poetic מו ending further link the two. The repetitive phrases concerning God's arm and his singular feats suggest a correlation between the two sections.

D. GOD EFFORTLESSLY ELIMINATES PHARAOH, DASHING HIS DELUSIONS OF GRANDEUR.

Extended alliteration highlighting Pharaoh's boast and the metathetic twist of נפש־נשף set this section apart from the rest, pointing to its place in the Song's epicenter.

Conclusion

The chiasmus which unifies the Song equips it with form as well as function. The outer layer of the Song of the Sea celebrates God's coronation and future enthronement, while its inner strata centers on the eradication of evil. The Song's celebration of God's vanquishing of evil is the theological underpinning of the Israelite monarchic idea. Whereas ancient Near Eastern gods demonstrated their prowess through military triumph in a cosmic struggle, the biblical notion of monarchy is inexorably linked with rooting out evil. The core of the chiasmus of the Song features the arrogant rantings of Pharaoh, who is portrayed in terms that conjure images of the primordial sea-monster – evil incarnate. Pharaoh's struggle for self-deification leaves him eternally embalmed in a literary tomb at the heart of the Song of the Sea, the song of the God of Israel's enthronement. Pharaoh's defeat at *Yam Suf* is an eternal reminder of the possibility that good may yet triumph of over evil. The defeat of evil, momentary as it was, is the context for – indeed the climax of – God's enthronement at *Yam Suf*. This triumph explains why Israel's deliverance there was rhapsodized. The theme of the struggle between the forces of good and evil, which informs the book of Genesis from its opening chapters, culminates in the book of Exodus. Genesis opens with the story of creation and its tree of good and evil at the center of the Garden of Eden. The story of the struggle against evil continues its development in the flood story, the tower of Babel, and later again with the destruction of Sodom. The theme of the struggle against evil continues its development in the book of Exodus with Israel's subjugation in Egypt, where it ultimately reaches its climax with God's coronation in the Song of the Sea.

The Song of the Well

The Song of the Well appears in the Book of Numbers nestled between the recounting of Israel's journey around Moab and the defeat of Amorite kings, Sihon and Og. This brief song celebrates the miraculous well that quenched Israel's thirst along their desert sojourn. The Song's appearance between two other brief enigmatic poems adds to its mysterious air. In order to unpack the Song's mysterious message, this chapter of the book temporarily shifts attention to the poem's larger poetic context before returning to the meaning and theological implications of the Song of the Well. The Song of the Well emerges as an exultation of Israel as the beneficiaries of God's lovingkindness; an alternative yet complementary perspective on the divine monarchy as presented in the Song of the Sea.

במדבר פרק כא:יז-כ

אז ישיר ישראל, את־השירה הזאת עלי באר ענו־לה. באר חפרוה שרים כרוה נדיבי העם במחוקק במשענותם וממדבר מתנה. וממתנה נחליאל ומנחליאל במות. ומבמות הגיא אשר בשדה מואב ראש הפסגה ונשקפה על פני הישימון.

Numbers 21:17–20

Then Israel sang this song: "Spring up, O well! Sing about it, about the well that the princes dug, that the nobles of the people sank – with scepters and staffs." Then they went from the wilderness to Mattanah, from Mattanah to Nahaliel, from Nahaliel to Bamoth, and from Bamoth to the valley in Moab where the top of Pisgah overlooks the wasteland.

The Song of the Well

A remarkably brief poem known as the Song of the Well appears in the Book of Numbers nestled between the recounting of Israel's journey around Moab and the defeat of the two Amorite kings, Sihon and Og.[1] The Song celebrates the miraculous well that quenched Israel's thirst along their desert sojourn. This seemingly minor poem harbors far greater theological significance than meets the eye. The Song states:

> Then Israel sang this song: "Spring up, O well! Sing about it, about the well that the princes dug, that the nobles of the people sank, the nobles with scepters and staffs (Num. 21:17–18).

One of the many outstanding features of this poem is its striking brevity. Ibn Ezra's suggestion that the full text of the original song was not included in the Torah accentuates the enigma (on Num. 21:17). Additional conundrums presented by the Song are the glaring absence of any direct references to God or Moshe, and its seemingly achronological redaction at the tail end of Israel's desert journey. Even if we accept, as has been argued by some, that the Song of the Well relates to earlier events, its sequential misplacement remains problematic.[2] The Song's

---

1. The original version of much of this chapter appears in Geula Twersky, "Song of the Well," *Tradition*, 51.4 (2019), 173–180.
2. See Hizkuni on Numbers 21:17 who suggests that whereas the Song of the Well was sung earlier, it is recorded here in order to avoid drawing negative attention to Moshe and Aharon. *Baal HaTurim* addresses the problem of the Song's appearance here by arguing that it is a valedictory song celebrating the defeat of Moab, sung not about a well, but in close proximity to one. *Ohr*

appearance nestled between two other brief enigmatic poems adds to its mysterious air. These cryptic poems, the Song of Waheb, and the Song of Heshbon, harbor valuable insight into the opaque message of the Song of the Well. In the interest of garnering clues that will aid in unpacking the Song of the Well, we will temporarily turn our attention to the poem's larger context.

Like the Song of the Well, the Song of Waheb that precedes it relates to miracles performed on Israel's behalf along the way to the promised land.[3]

> That is why the Book of the Wars of the Lord says: . . . Waheb in Suphah and the ravines, the Arnon and the slopes of the ravines that lead to the settlement of Ar and lie along the border of Moab (Num. 21:14–15).

The Song of Waheb seems to be missing a verb. What event took place there?[4] Rashi (v. 17) suggests that we should not assume the *vav* in the word *v-h-v*, the root of Waheb, serves as a conjunction, but rather as part of the root *y-h-v*, or *h-v*, meaning "to give."[5] He interprets the poem as a song of thanksgiving for Israel's miraculous military victory over the Amorites. Steiner reinforces this approach with his suggestion that the word *et* (את), which is usually omitted in biblical poetry, does not function here in its usual role as a direct object marker, but as a

---

HaHayyim suggests that Torah, which the Rabbis famously say is analogous to water, is the real subject of the Song.

3. See Rashi, Numbers 21:16, who understands the Song of the Well to be directly related to the miraculous victory against Moab, as Israel only became aware of their salvation with the appearance of blood and slain body parts in their water supply.

4. Driver suggests that the phrases *et vahav* and *ve-et ha-nehalim* are the subjects of *va-yomer* and that *eshed ha-nehalim* is the opening phrase of a new sentence, or the quotation, which is left incomplete. He understands the poem to mean "Wherefore Vaheb in Suphah and the ravines are mentioned 'in the book of the Wars of the Lord (saying): '(O' Arnon and (thou) watershed of the ravines.'" This approach however creates more problems than it solves. See G.R. Driver, "Geographical Problems," *Eretz-Israel: Archaeological, Historical and Geographical Studies Dedicated to Professor Benjamin Mazar on his Fiftieth Birthday* (Bialik Institute, 1958), 16–20.

5. *Hebrew and Aramaic Lexicon of the Old Testament* (HALOT), s.v. "hv," 236.

shortened form of the poetic verb *ata*, meaning "to come."[6] Steiner supports this hypothesis by citing the poetic preamble to the Blessings of Moshe which opens similarly, with God coming, *ata*, in a storm (Deut. 33:2), and the Song of Heshbon (the third of the songs quoted in this chapter), which opens with the words *bo'u Heshbon*, "come to Heshbon" (Num. 21:27). Steiner surmises that this formulation may have once been a standard poetic opening.[7] Additional correspondences between the Song of Waheb and the Song of Heshbon reinforce the assumption of a correlation between the two.

The Song of Heshbon reads:

> That is why the poets say: "Come to Heshbon and let it be rebuilt; let Sihon's city be restored. Fire went out from Heshbon, a blaze from the city of Sihon. It consumed Ar of Moab, the citizens of Arnon's heights (Num. 21:27–28).

Both the Heshbon poem and the Song of Waheb relate to Amorite battles. In addition, they both open with nearly identical phrases indicating quotation from earlier poets or poetry (*al ken yomru* / *al ken ye'amar*). Both poems refer to the Arnon Stream and may be interpreted to be recounting a great conflagration. The latter point is based on the Septuagint's translation of the word *sufa* (Num. 21:14) as "firestorm" as opposed to a place name.[8] Whereas the word *sufa* is generally understood to be a "whirlwind," it connotes a "firestorm" in several biblical sources.[9] The many resonances between these two poems reinforce the preference for this reading.

---

6.   *HALOT*, s.v. "*ata*," 102.

7.   Richard C. Steiner, "The Book of the Wars of the Lord (Num 21:14–20): Philology and Hydrology, Geography and Ethnography," *Journal of the American Oriental Society* 140.3 (2020), 565–591. Steiner cites *Midrash Lekach Tov* on our passage and Duane L. Christensen, "Num 21:14–15 and the Book of the Wars of Yahweh," *Catholic Biblical Quarterly* 36 (1974), 359–60.

8.   The Septuagint reads: "Therefore it is said in a book: a war of the Lord has set on fire Zoob"; see Joel Hoffman, *In the Beginning: A Short History of the Hebrew Language* (NYU Press, 2004), 93.

9.   Cf. Isa. 29:6; 66:15; Amos 1:14; Onkelos on Numbers 21:14 who understands the word *sufa* to be referring to the miracle at the Red Sea (*Yam Suf*).

In considering the possible association between the three poems which comprise this brief unit, the placid, pastoral tone which characterizes the Song of the Well seems to be conspicuously out of place sandwiched between two poems celebrating war victories.[10] Do the Song of the Well and the two victory songs which encase it recount a string of disparate, miraculous events which coincidentally transpired along the way to the promised land? Or possibly, do the three songs share a more integrated literary association? A closer examination of the Song of the Well suggests the latter.

The closing word of the Song's initial verse, *matana*, which may be interpreted to mean "a gift," is immediately followed by the same word's reappearance in the opening of the ensuing verse, where it functions as a place name. Understanding the word's initial use as a place name as well is reinforced by the continued listing of Israel's encampments through v. 20.[11]

> And from Bamoth, to the valley in Moab where the top of Pisgah, *rosh ha-pisgah*, overlooks the wasteland, *ve-nishkefah al pnei ha-yeshimon* (Num. 21:20).

Interestingly, the very same place names listed in the final verse of the Song are mentioned again in the same order in the ensuing chapters (22–23) within the context of Bilam's Blessings. Bilam's initial blessing is described as having transpired upon *bamot ba'al* (22:41), the heights of Baal. The second blessing was uttered atop a tall mountain, referred to as *rosh ha-pisgah* (23:14), and the third blessing took place at a location "overlooking the wasteland," *ha-nishkaf al pnei ha-yeshimon* (23:28). The repetition of the site names in these neighboring texts suggests a correlation between the Song of the Well and the Blessings of Bilam. While the first two Blessings of Bilam feature a partial view of Israel, the third blessing climaxes with Bilam's unobstructed view of the entire nation:

---

10. This may have been the reason why Rashi reads the Song of the Well as relating to a military victory against the Amorites.

11. Rashbam and Ibn Ezra (v. 18) agree that the verses here are listing place names. Ibn Ezra explains the omission of these locations from the itinerary in Numbers 33, as the place name *Almon Divletaima* is used in v. 41 in reference to the general area or region encompassing the specific locales.

How beautiful are your tents, Yaakov, your dwelling places, Israel!
Like valleys they spread out, like gardens beside a river, like aloes
planted by the Lord, like cedars beside the waters. Water will flow
from their buckets; their seed will have abundant water. Their
king will be greater than Agag; their kingdom will be exalted.
God brought them out of Egypt; they have the strength of a wild
ox. They devour hostile nations and break their bones in pieces;
with their arrows they pierce them. Like a lion they crouch and
lie down, like a lioness – who dares to rouse them? May those
who bless you be blessed and those who curse you be cursed!
(Num. 24:5–9).

In his third oration, Bilam praises Israel's encampment upon a body
of fresh water, *alei nahar… alei mayim*, upon the river… upon the water
(24:6). Interestingly, the Song of the Well makes striking use of a nearly
identical expression, *alei be'er*. Whereas this phrase has generally been
interpreted to mean "rise up, well" it may also be understood as "upon
the well," or "upon fresh water."[12] Bilam's third oration also praises Israel
for its strong leadership, and unrivaled war victories, (Num. 24:7–8).
These three elements, the life-giving qualities of water, Israel's exalted
leadership, and military prowess, form the crux of Bilam's final blessing.
They also parallel the very same themes which form the core of the
tripartite poem cluster in chapter 21. The war song from the "Book of the
Wars of the Lord" praises Israel's overwhelming military victory over the
Amorites, and the Song of the Well offers pastoral praise focusing upon
flowing water, while paying tribute to Israel's leadership:

About the well that the princes dug, that the nobles of the people
sank – the nobles with scepters and staffs (Num. 21:18).

We may add that the third song of the cluster, the Song of Heshbon,
attributed to the *moshlim* or poets (Num. 21:27), is assumed by the Sages
to have been uttered by Bilam, whose orations are referred to by the text
itself as a *mashal*, a parable (Num. 23:7, 18; 24:3, 15).[13] The Sages further

---

12. The Septuagint reads "over the well"; see also Bechor Shor, ad loc.
13. See *Bamidbar Rabbah* 19:30, *Midrash Tanchuma* 24, *Midrash Aggadah Bamidbar* 21:30.

relate Bilam to the Song of the Well by thematically grouping the entire song cluster in chapter 21 together with Bilam's orations, in a Midrash enumerating God's acts of lovingkindness.[14]

Bilam's orations, like the songs in chapter 21 which precede them, also blend pastoral metaphors with military imagery. This mix of poetic motifs recurs throughout the Bible, notably in Psalm 23:

> The Lord is my shepherd, I lack nothing. He makes me lie down in green pastures, he leads me beside quiet waters, he refreshes my soul, for His name's sake. Even though I walk through the darkest valley, I will fear no evil, for You are with me; your rod and your staff, they comfort me. You prepare a table before me in the presence of my enemies. You anoint my head with oil; my cup overflows. Surely Your goodness and love will follow me all the days of my life, and I will dwell in the house of the Lord forever.

Like Israel's depiction in the Blessings of Bilam, the Song of the Well mixes pastoral water imagery together with military imagery. This is achieved through the Song's proximity to and close association with the Song of Waheb which precedes it. In this way, the Song of the Well portrays Israel as the beneficiaries of God's military protection as well as His loving and gentle embrace. Another primary theme of the Bilam story is that God's plan for Israel is not subject to change:

> But God said to Bilam: Do not go with them. You must not put a curse on those people, because they are blessed (Num. 22:12).

> How can I curse those whom God has not cursed? How can I denounce those whom the Lord has not denounced? (Num. 23:8).

> I have received a command to bless; He has blessed, and I cannot change it (Num. 23:20).

> I see it, but not now; I behold it, but not near. A star will come out of Yaakov; a scepter will rise out of Israel…" (Num. 24:17).

---

14. *Midrash Aggadah Bamidbar 25.*

The Song of the Well, when viewed as a part of its larger poetic context, like the Blessings of Bilam which it foreshadows, is a celebration of God's steadfast and unflinching devotion to Israel. This may explain why neither Moshe nor any other leader is named by the Song. By making only a generic reference to Israel's leadership, much like what we find in Bilam's Blessings, the Song of the Well conveys a timeless message: Israel's relationship with God is neither limited to nor defined by any single charismatic leader. Whereas God's name is hidden from plain view in the Song of the Well, the Song's proximate and literary connection to the Song of Waheb preceding it, which clearly references God, effectively suggests God's presence, as it reinforces the ongoing need to seek Him out.[15]

The more democratic contour of the Song of the Well is aptly suited to the larger context of the book of Numbers and its subtle shift away from centralized charismatic leadership.[16] The Rabbinic name for the book, *Pekudim*, Numbers, based on the census that is conducted in the opening chapters, reflects the book's emphasis on the significance of the individual. Nachmanides points out that the words *bemispar shemot*, "enumerated by name" (Num. 1:2), indicate that each individual who was counted first stated his name, thereby elevating his status, as opposed to being reduced to a mere number (Num. 1:2). Already in the opening of Numbers it is the tribal heads, *Nesi'im*, as opposed to Moshe and Aharon, who are introduced as the central players. Rashi draws attention to this fundamental shift by noting Aharon's dismay on account of having been marginalized at the Tabernacle's dedication ceremony (Num. 8:2). Moshe's characterization of his role as one who must carry a suckling infant highlights Israel's need to foster greater personal responsibility (Num. 11:12). Eldad and Medad's subsequent prophetic episode apart

---

15. It is not clear what "The Book of the Wars of the Lord" is. Nachmanides and Ibn Ezra assume it to be a lost Israelite book (see their commentaries on Exodus 21:14). Shadal on Num. 21:4 argues that the Torah does not need to rely on external source material. He understands the verse to be referring to a "telling" or an oral tradition.

16. For a broader discussion on the shifting focus from charismatic leader to the individual in the book of Numbers, see Yitzchak Twersky, *Amittah shel Torah*, vol. 2 (Targum, 2007), 125–136.

from Moshe and the appointed elders is welcomed by Moshe as a harbinger of continued and increased religious leadership (Num. 11:29). The
notion of the elevated role of the individual is later co-opted by Korach,
who cunningly anchors himself on this very principle, in a distorted
attempt to discredit and depose Moshe and Aharon. While it may be
noted that Yehoshua is appointed as leader in the end of Numbers
(27:12–23), that appointment is counterbalanced by his being both a
man of God as well as a man of the people, "a man of spirit."[17] Numbers
does not reject the institution of leadership, rather it embraces a more
down-to-earth model.

In addition to the Song's resonances with leitmotifs from throughout
Numbers, it also resonates strongly with the themes of the Song of the
Sea found in Exodus. This is made apparent through its distinctive
opening, *az yashir*, as well as through the common motif of miracles
performed on Israel's behalf involving water. The combination of the
pastoral description of Israel in the Song of the Well together with the
military theme of the Song preceding it, harkens back to the convergence
of the very same ideas which inform the concluding verses of the Song of
the Sea. It is there that Israel's role as an integral part of God's covenantal
plan was formally articulated:

> By the power of Your arm they [the enemies] will be as still as
> a stone until Your people pass by, Lord, until the people You
> bought pass by. You will bring them in and plant them on the
> mountain of your inheritance the place, Lord, You made for your
> dwelling, the sanctuary, Lord, Your hands established. The Lord
> reigns for ever and ever. (Ex. 15:16–18)

God appears in the Song of the Sea as a holy warrior (Ex. 15:3), but in
the Song of the Well, His attribute of lovingkindness is emphasized. The
narrative framework of the book of Exodus is liberation from Egyptian
bondage, and Israel's dedication to God's service beginning at Sinai and
continuing within the Tabernacle.[18] God in effect establishes his identity

---

17. Onkelos (Numbers 27:18) understands "a man of spirit" to refer to Joshua's
    prophetic abilities, whereas Rashi explains the phrase to reference Joshua's
    ability to relate to each individual.
18. Cf. Nachmanides' introduction to Exodus, where he discusses the Tabernacle
    as an extension of God's revelation at Sinai.

in Exodus as King (Ex. 15:18). Numbers, on the other hand, focuses on God's manifest presence in Israel's midst on their way to the promised land. The book's opening chapters describe Israel's careful arrangement around the Tabernacle, and God's palpable presence guiding the nation (ch. 1–10). The Book of Numbers, then, is dedicated to exploring how God's role as king is expressed though His day-to-day involvement and care for His people. The Song of the Well's portrayal of God as Israel's benefactor along their desert sojourn, despite the numerous pitfalls along the way, is aptly set in the Book of Numbers.

The Song of the Well is an inseparable part of its broader poetic setting. Its appearance against the backdrop of the Songs of Waheb and Heshbon, places the Song at the center of a larger military framework. The Song's exultation of Israel as the beneficiaries of God's lovingkind-ness offers an alternative yet complementary message to that proposed by the Song of the Sea. The main thrust of the Song of the Sea is God's military victory over the Egyptians; the Song of the Well emphasizes Israel as the object of God's benevolence.[19] Nachmanides points out that a fundamental confusion arose following Israel's salvation at *Yam Suf* (on Ex. 14:10).

> It is possible that the people believed in God and prayed to Him for salvation, however they were unsure if Moshe had acted out of a desire to rule over them. Even though they themselves had witnessed the open miracles, they presumed that Moshe had performed them through his wisdom, or that God had brought the plagues upon the Egyptians because of their [Egypt's] evil; for if God had intended to save them then Pharaoh surely would not have chased after them.

Israel entertained the erroneous belief that God's primary goal may have been the military defeat of His enemies as opposed to devotion to His people. This fallacious assumption is ultimately put to rest with the Song of the Well. Both the Song of the Sea and the Song of the Well feature a combination of the military and the pastoral, albeit with a

---

19. While the Song of the Sea certainly praises God for Israel's salvation, its opening – and indeed the majority of its passages – relates most directly to the drowning of the Egyptian army.

different emphasis. The Song of the Sea's presentation of Israel's salvation is ancillary to God's military victory; the Song of the Well stresses Israel as the eternal object of God's love, devotion, and commitment.

Parshat Massei and the Song of the Well

Parshat Massei, the final Torah portion in the book of Numbers, contains a laconic review of Israel's forty-two desert encampments (ch. 33). Whereas critical events that transpired during Israel's desert sojourn – such as the splitting of the sea at Yam Suf, the giving of the law at Sinai, and the dispatching of the spies at Kadesh, to name a few – are curiously omitted from the list, several incidents of seemingly lesser consequence are included in the itinerary. The events that are recounted together with Israel's journeys include the Egyptian's preoccupation with the burying of their dead at the time of Israel's overt departure from Raamses (vs. 4), the providential encounter at Elim with its seventy date palms and twelve springs (vs. 9), the lack of water at Rephidim (vs. 14), the death of Aharon at Mount Hor (vs. 38–39), and the subsequent news of Israel's imminent approach reaching the Canaanite king of Arad (vs. 40).

Moskovitz, in his commentary on Numbers,[20] suggests that the list's sustained refrain, ויסעו... ויחנו, "and they travelled... and they encamped," gives the unit a poetic quality similar to the list of the thirty-one vanquished Canaanite kings in Joshua 12,[21] which is traditionally transcribed in poetic format, in accordance with its role as a victory ballad.[22] In that text, each of the Canaanite kings are introduced with the word "king" and are followed by the word "one" in poetic refrain. The poetic quality of these verses is reinforced by the section's reverberations with chapter 21, the setting of the Song of the Well. In that chapter we read of Israel's skirmish with the king of Arad, who is similarly described as having "heard" of Israel's approach (vs. 1). The story of Israel's battle against the Canaanite king is followed by the repercussions of Israel's complaint over

---

20. Y. Moskovitz, *Numbers* (Daat Mikra; Jerusalem, Mosad Harav Kook, 1988), 396, (Heb.).

21. I would like to thank my dear friend, Beth Prebore, for bringing this interpretation to my attention.

22. See *Midrash Pitron Torah*, Ohrbach ed., *Parshat Haazinu*, 321.

the lack of provisions after having departed Mount Hor where Aharon had been laid to rest (vs. 4–9). The string of verses that follow echo the refrain formula from *Parshat Massei*, "and they travelled…and they encamped," (vs. 10–13).

The unmistakable reverberations between the opening section of *Parshat Massei* and the larger literary framework of the Song of the Well joins these two units together. Furthermore, the particular events listed together with Israel's desert encampments in *Parshat Massei*, like the Song of the Well and its poetic context, mix pastoral water imagery together with military imagery. To review, the events recounted in chapter 33 reflect on both Egypt's and Arad's military defeat, in addition to key instances featuring either a providentially abundant supply of fresh water and provisions (at Elim), or a lack thereof (at Rephidim). The recounting of Aharon's death at Mount Hor among Israel's travels further signifies the laying to rest of the generation that had left Egypt, and the ushering in of the new era, which was meant to bring with it the entry into the land.

Aharon's death is paradigmatic of the death of the high priest, which allows for the re-entry into society of the accidental murderer after his forced exile to a city of refuge.[23] Israel's imminent entry into the land, however, was tragically derailed by Israel's worship of Baal Peor, a de facto rejection of the covenant. The reframing of *Parshat Massei*, and its poetic return to the events surrounding the Song of the Well, further highlight God's readiness to forgive Israel's folly and restore them to their land, in a supreme act of love, devotion, and commitment.

---

23. For more on the connection between the death of Aaron at Mount Hor and the laws pertaining to the city of refuge see Yitzchak Twersky, *Amittah shel Torah*, vol. 2 (Targum, 2007), 221–226.

The Song of Moshe

The Song of Moshe has been noted for its many resonances throughout the books of the prophets. In this chapter, the Song will also be shown to contain subtle references to several earlier biblical narratives, namely: The stories of creation, Adam's expulsion from Eden, the flood, the destruction of Sodom and Gomorrah, the Yehudah and Tamar narrative, and the sin of the golden calf. The Song's allusions to these foundational texts bridge formative events from the past with those yet to unfold, as part of its broader meditation on God's relationship with Israel throughout history. The Song of Moshe emerges as a meditation on Israel's irrevocable bond with God the Divine Monarch in an amalgamation of the core ideas championed in the Songs of the Sea and the Well.

דברים פרק לב:א-מג

הַאֲזִינוּ הַשָּׁמַיִם וַאֲדַבֵּרָה וְתִשְׁמַע הָאָרֶץ אִמְרֵי־פִי: יַעֲרֹף כַּמָּטָר לִקְחִי תִּזַּל כַּטַּל אִמְרָתִי כִּשְׂעִירִם עֲלֵי־דֶשֶׁא וְכִרְבִיבִים עֲלֵי־עֵשֶׂב: כִּי שֵׁם ה' אֶקְרָא הָבוּ גֹדֶל לֵאלֹקֵינוּ: הַצּוּר תָּמִים פָּעֳלוֹ כִּי כָל־דְּרָכָיו מִשְׁפָּט אֵל אֱמוּנָה וְאֵין עָוֶל צַדִּיק וְיָשָׁר הוּא: שִׁחֵת לוֹ לֹא בָּנָיו מוּמָם דּוֹר עִקֵּשׁ וּפְתַלְתֹּל: הֲ־לַה' תִּגְמְלוּ־זֹאת עַם נָבָל וְלֹא חָכָם הֲלוֹא־הוּא אָבִיךָ קָּנֶךָ הוּא עָשְׂךָ וַיְכֹנְנֶךָ: זְכֹר יְמוֹת עוֹלָם בִּינוּ שְׁנוֹת דּוֹר־וָדוֹר שְׁאַל אָבִיךָ וְיַגֵּדְךָ זְקֵנֶיךָ וְיֹאמְרוּ לָךְ: בְּהַנְחֵל עֶלְיוֹן גּוֹיִם בְּהַפְרִידוֹ בְּנֵי אָדָם יַצֵּב גְּבֻלֹת עַמִּים לְמִסְפַּר בְּנֵי יִשְׂרָאֵל: כִּי חֵלֶק ה' עַמּוֹ יַעֲקֹב חֶבֶל נַחֲלָתוֹ: יִמְצָאֵהוּ בְּאֶרֶץ מִדְבָּר וּבְתֹהוּ יְלֵל יְשִׁמֹן יְסֹבְבֶנְהוּ יְבוֹנְנֵהוּ יִצְּרֶנְהוּ כְּאִישׁוֹן עֵינוֹ: כְּנֶשֶׁר יָעִיר קִנּוֹ עַל־גּוֹזָלָיו יְרַחֵף יִפְרֹשׂ כְּנָפָיו יִקָּחֵהוּ יִשָּׂאֵהוּ עַל־אֶבְרָתוֹ: ה' בָּדָד יַנְחֶנּוּ וְאֵין עִמּוֹ אֵל נֵכָר: יַרְכִּבֵהוּ עַל־בָּמֳותֵי אָרֶץ וַיֹּאכַל תְּנוּבֹת שָׂדָי וַיֵּנִקֵהוּ דְבַשׁ מִסֶּלַע וְשֶׁמֶן מֵחַלְמִישׁ צוּר: חֶמְאַת בָּקָר וַחֲלֵב צֹאן עִם־חֵלֶב כָּרִים וְאֵילִים בְּנֵי־בָשָׁן וְעַתּוּדִים עִם־חֵלֶב כִּלְיוֹת חִטָּה וְדַם־עֵנָב תִּשְׁתֶּה־חָמֶר: וַיִּשְׁמַן יְשֻׁרוּן

וַיִּבְעָט שָׁמַנְתָּ עָבִיתָ כָּשִׂיתָ וַיִּטֹּשׁ אֱלוֹהַּ עָשָׂהוּ וַיְנַבֵּל צוּר יְשֻׁעָתוֹ: יַקְנִאֻהוּ בְּזָרִים
בְּתוֹעֵבֹת יַכְעִיסֻהוּ: יִזְבְּחוּ לַשֵּׁדִים לֹא אֱלֹהַּ אֱלֹהִים לֹא יְדָעוּם חֲדָשִׁים מִקָּרֹב בָּאוּ
לֹא שְׂעָרוּם אֲבֹתֵיכֶם: צוּר יְלָדְךָ תֶּשִׁי וַתִּשְׁכַּח אֵל מְחֹלְלֶךָ: וַיַּרְא ה׳ וַיִּנְאָץ מִכַּעַס בָּנָיו
וּבְנֹתָיו: וַיֹּאמֶר אַסְתִּירָה פָנַי מֵהֶם אֶרְאֶה מָה אַחֲרִיתָם כִּי דוֹר תַּהְפֻּכֹת הֵמָּה בָּנִים
לֹא אֵמֻן בָּם: הֵם קִנְאוּנִי בְלֹא אֵל כִּעֲסוּנִי בְּהַבְלֵיהֶם וַאֲנִי אַקְנִיאֵם בְּלֹא עָם בְּגוֹי
נָבָל אַכְעִיסֵם: כִּי אֵשׁ קָדְחָה בְאַפִּי וַתִּיקַד עַד שְׁאוֹל תַּחְתִּית וַתֹּאכַל אֶרֶץ וִיבֻלָהּ
וַתְּלַהֵט מוֹסְדֵי הָרִים: אַסְפֶּה עָלֵימוֹ רָעוֹת חִצַּי אֲכַלֶּה בָּם: מְזֵי רָעָב וּלְחֻמֵי רֶשֶׁף
וְקֶטֶב מְרִירִי וְשֶׁן בְּהֵמֹת אֲשַׁלַּח בָּם עִם חֲמַת זֹחֲלֵי עָפָר: מִחוּץ תְּשַׁכֶּל חֶרֶב
וּמֵחֲדָרִים אֵימָה גַּם בָּחוּר גַּם בְּתוּלָה יוֹנֵק עִם אִישׁ שֵׂיבָה: אָמַרְתִּי אַפְאֵיהֶם
אַשְׁבִּיתָה מֵאֱנוֹשׁ זִכְרָם: לוּלֵי כַּעַס אוֹיֵב אָגוּר פֶּן יְנַכְּרוּ צָרֵימוֹ פֶּן יֹאמְרוּ יָדֵינוּ
רָמָה וְלֹא ה׳ פָּעַל כָּל זֹאת: כִּי גוֹי אֹבַד עֵצוֹת הֵמָּה וְאֵין בָּהֶם תְּבוּנָה: לוּ חָכְמוּ
יַשְׂכִּילוּ זֹאת יָבִינוּ לְאַחֲרִיתָם: אֵיכָה יִרְדֹּף אֶחָד אֶלֶף וּשְׁנַיִם יָנִיסוּ רְבָבָה אִם לֹא
כִּי צוּרָם מְכָרָם וַיהוָה הִסְגִּירָם: כִּי לֹא כְצוּרֵנוּ צוּרָם וְאֹיְבֵינוּ פְּלִילִים: כִּי מִגֶּפֶן
סְדֹם גַּפְנָם וּמִשַּׁדְמֹת עֲמֹרָה עֲנָבֵמוֹ עִנְּבֵי רוֹשׁ אַשְׁכְּלֹת מְרֹרֹת לָמוֹ: חֲמַת תַּנִּינִם
יֵינָם וְרֹאשׁ פְּתָנִים אַכְזָר: הֲלֹא הוּא כָּמֻס עִמָּדִי חָתֻם בְּאוֹצְרֹתָי: לִי נָקָם וְשִׁלֵּם
לְעֵת תָּמוּט רַגְלָם כִּי קָרוֹב יוֹם אֵידָם וְחָשׁ עֲתִדֹת לָמוֹ: כִּי יָדִין ה׳ עַמּוֹ וְעַל
עֲבָדָיו יִתְנֶחָם כִּי יִרְאֶה כִּי אָזְלַת יָד וְאֶפֶס עָצוּר וְעָזוּב: וְאָמַר אֵי אֱלֹהֵימוֹ צוּר
חָסָיוּ בוֹ: אֲשֶׁר חֵלֶב זְבָחֵימוֹ יֹאכֵלוּ יִשְׁתּוּ יֵין נְסִיכָם יָקוּמוּ וְיַעְזְרֻכֶם יְהִי עֲלֵיכֶם
סִתְרָה: רְאוּ עַתָּה כִּי אֲנִי אֲנִי הוּא וְאֵין אֱלֹהִים עִמָּדִי אֲנִי אָמִית וַאֲחַיֶּה מָחַצְתִּי
וַאֲנִי אֶרְפָּא וְאֵין מִיָּדִי מַצִּיל: כִּי אֶשָּׂא אֶל שָׁמַיִם יָדִי וְאָמַרְתִּי חַי אָנֹכִי לְעֹלָם:
אִם שַׁנּוֹתִי בְּרַק חַרְבִּי וְתֹאחֵז בְּמִשְׁפָּט יָדִי אָשִׁיב נָקָם לְצָרָי וְלִמְשַׂנְאַי אֲשַׁלֵּם:
אַשְׁכִּיר חִצַּי מִדָּם וְחַרְבִּי תֹּאכַל בָּשָׂר מִדַּם חָלָל וְשִׁבְיָה מֵרֹאשׁ פַּרְעוֹת אוֹיֵב:
הַרְנִינוּ גוֹיִם עַמּוֹ כִּי דַם עֲבָדָיו יִקּוֹם וְנָקָם יָשִׁיב לְצָרָיו וְכִפֶּר אַדְמָתוֹ עַמּוֹ:

Deuteronomy 32

Listen, you heavens, and I will speak; hear, you earth, the words
of my mouth. Let my teaching fall like rain and my words descend
like dew, like showers on new grass, like abundant rain on tender
plants. I will proclaim the name of the LORD. O, praise the greatness of our God! He is the Rock, His works are perfect, and all His
ways are just. A faithful God who does no wrong, upright and just
is He. They are corrupt and not His children; to their shame they
are a warped and crooked generation. Is this the way you repay
the LORD, you foolish and unwise people? Is He not your Father,
your Creator, who made you and formed you? Remember the

days of old; consider the generations long past. Ask your father and He will tell you, your elders, and they will explain to you. When the Most High gave the nations their inheritance, when He divided all mankind, he set up boundaries for the peoples according to the number of the sons of Israel. For the LORD's portion is His people, Yaakov his allotted inheritance. In a desert land He found him, in a barren and howling waste. He shielded him and cared for him; He guarded him as the apple of His eye, like an eagle that stirs up its nest and hovers over its young, that spreads its wings to catch them and carries them aloft. The LORD alone led him; no foreign god was with him. He made him ride on the heights of the land and fed him with the fruit of the fields. He nourished him with honey from the rock, and with oil from the flinty crag, with curds and milk from herd and flock and with fattened lambs and goats, with choice rams of Bashan and the finest kernels of wheat. You drank the foaming blood of the grape. Jeshurun grew fat and kicked; filled with food, they became heavy and sleek. They abandoned the God who made them and rejected the Rock their Savior. They made Him jealous with their foreign gods and angered him with their detestable idols. They sacrificed to false gods, which are not God – gods they had not known, gods that recently appeared, gods your ancestors did not fear. You deserted the Rock, who fathered you; you forgot the God who gave you birth. The LORD saw this and rejected them because He was angered by his sons and daughters. "I will hide My face from them," He said, "and see what their end will be; for they are a perverse generation, children who are unfaithful. They made Me jealous by what is no god and angered Me with their worthless idols. I will make them envious by those who are not a people; I will make them angry by a nation that has no understanding. For a fire will be kindled by My wrath, one that burns down to the realm of the dead below. It will devour the earth and its harvests and set afire the foundations of the mountains. I will heap calamities on them and spend My arrows against them. I will send wasting famine against them, consuming pestilence and deadly plague; I will send against them the fangs

of wild beasts, the venom of vipers that glide in the dust. In the
street the sword will make them childless; in their homes terror
will reign. The young men and young women will perish, the
infants and those with gray hair. I said I would scatter them and
erase their name from human memory, but I dreaded the taunt
of the enemy, lest the adversary misunderstand and say, 'Our
hand has triumphed; the LORD has not done all this.'" They are
a nation without sense, there is no discernment in them. If only
they were wise and would understand this and discern what their
end will be! How could one man chase a thousand, or two put
ten thousand to flight, unless their Rock had sold them, unless
the LORD had given them up? For their rock is not like our Rock,
as even our enemies concede. Their vine comes from the vine
of Sodom and from the fields of Gomorrah. Their grapes are
filled with poison, and their clusters with bitterness. Their wine
is the venom of serpents, the deadly poison of cobras. "Have I
not kept this in reserve and sealed it in My vaults? It is Mine to
avenge; I will repay. In due time their foot will slip; their day of
disaster is near and their doom rushes upon them." The LORD will
vindicate His people and relent concerning His servants when
He sees their strength is gone and no one is left, slave or free. He
will say: "Now where are their gods, the rock they took refuge
in, the gods who ate the fat of their sacrifices and drank the wine
of their drink offerings? Let them rise up to help you! Let them
give you shelter! "See now that I Myself am He! There is no god
besides Me. I put to death and I bring to life, I have wounded and
I will heal, and no one can deliver out of my hand. I lift My hand
to heaven and solemnly swear: As surely as I live forever, when I
sharpen My flashing sword and My hand grasps it in judgment, I
will take vengeance on My adversaries and repay those who hate
Me. I will make My arrows drunk with blood, while My sword
devours flesh: the blood of the slain and the captives, the heads
of the enemy leaders." Rejoice, you nations, with His people, for
He will avenge the blood of His servants; He will take vengeance
on His enemies and make atonement for His land and people.

Introduction

The admonitions of the book of Deuteronomy conclude with the Song of Moshe. While the Song is unique in a variety of respects, one of its outstanding features is the Divine directive which precedes it, instructing Moshe to "place it in their (Israel's) mouths," שימה בפיהם:

> Now write down this song and teach it to the Israelites and have them sing it, so that it may be a witness for Me against them. (Deut. 31:19)

The popular translation rendering the awkward phrase, שימה בפיהם, "place it in their mouths," as "have them sing it,"[1] implies that the Song should be recited. This approach is suggested by many of the classical commentators.[2] The seemingly innocuous placing of words into the mouth is in fact a technical term for the initiation of prophecy, or the sanctification of the prophet. In Exodus, God instructs Moshe to place God's word into Aharon's mouth (Ex. 4:15), and Aharon is later referred to as Moshe's prophet (Ex. 7:1). In the Bilam narrative, Bilam describes God as though placing the prophecy into his mouth (Num. 22:38; 23:12). In Deuteronomy, God assures Moshe that a prophet will be appointed in his stead, who will receive the Divine word into his mouth (Deut. 18:18). God literally places His prophetic word into the mouths of Yeshayahu (Isa. 51:16) and Yirmiyahu (Jer. 1:9). In Yeshayahu's case, the initial prophecy is likened to burning coals upon the prophet's lips (Isa. 6:6–9). Later, Yeshayahu describes God's word as being placed directly into the mouths of future members of the Jewish nation (Isa. 59:21). In the book of Yechezkel, God feeds Yechezkel a scroll containing a written prophecy, which becomes sweet in his mouth (Ezek. 2:9–10; 3:1–3). All of these episodes share the common denominator of relating to God's initial contact with the prophet, or their consecration as a prophet.[3]

Jacob Arlow, psychoanalyst and student of the Bible and its psychoanalytic interpretation, in an essay on the mystical experiences accompanying the sanctification of the biblical prophets, observes that

---

1. Cf. NIV translation ad loc.
2. Cf. Onkelos, Ibn Ezra and Nachmanides on Deut. 31:19.
3. Isa. 51:16 reflects upon Yeshayahu's career as a prophet.

the initial confrontation in the Bible between God and the prophet is frequently accompanied by an oral component through which the prophet acquires his prophetic authority.[4] God's instruction to Moshe, that he should place the Song into the mouths of the people, implies far more than the imperative to instruct Israel in its recitation. The act of placing the Song into Israel's mouth consecrates the Nation of Israel as a nation of prophets.[5] The sweeping historical perspective which informs the framework of the Song confirms Israel's role as God's representatives and the prophetic bearers of His eternal word.

The prophetic authority bestowed upon Israel through the Song helps to explicate the immeasurable influence which the Song had on the breadth of the prophetic literature. There is hardly a book of the Bible which does not echo the language and imagery of the Song. Its profound influence has been documented in the books of Yeshayahu,[6] Yechezkel,[7]

---

4. Jacob A. Arlow, "The Consecration of the Prophet," *Psychoanalytic Quarterly* 20 (1951), 374–397.

5. Cf. *Kuzari* 1:26 in which Yehudah Halevi suggests that Israel is deemed a nation of prophets.

6. Cf. S.R. Driver, *Deuteronomy*, (ICC 21; Edinburgh: T & T Clark, 1978) 348; Moshe David Cassuto, "Hosea and the Book of the Torah," *Memorial for Zvi Perez Chiyot* (Vienna: Alexander Kahat Memorial Foundation, 1933), 262–78, (Heb.); L.G. Rignell, "Isaiah Chapter 1: Some Exegetical Remarks with Special Reference to the Relationship between the Text and the Book of Deuteronomy," ST 11 (1957), 140–58; O. Kaiser, *Isaiah. 1.1–12, II. 13–39* (OTL, 2 vols.; Philadelphia: Westminster Press, 1983), 1:1–2; Harold Fisch, *Poetry with a Purpose: Biblical Poetics and Interpretation* (Bloomington and Indianapolis: Indiana Univ. Press, 1990), 69–71; Dov Rappel, *The Song of Moses*, 35–40. Ronald Bergey, "The Song of Moses and Isianic Prophecies: A Case of Early Intertextuality?" *JSOT* 28, 1 (2003), 33–54; Paul Kim Hyun Chul, "The Song of Moses in Isaiah 40–55," in *God's Word for Our World: Biblical Studies in Honor of Simon John De Vries* (2 vols.; Deborah L. Ellens et al. eds.; London, New York: T & T Clark, 2004), 1:147–71; Thomas A. Keiser, "The Song of Moses: A Basis for Isaiah's Prophecy," *VT* 55, 4 (2005), 486–500; C.A. Ginzburg, "The End of the Song of Moses," *Tarbitz* 24 (1954), 1–3, (Heb.).

7. Cf. Cassuto, "Hosea and the Book of the Torah," 262–78; Von Rad, *Deuteronomy*, 200; Jason Gile, "Ezekiel 16 and the Song of Moses: A Prophetic Transformation?" *JBL* 130, 1 (2011), 87–108.

Yirmiyahu,[8] Hosea,[9] Micah,[10] Amos,[11] Zephaniah,[12] Job,[13] the Psalter,[14] Kings,[15] and Maccabees.[16] It has furthermore been suggested that references to the awesome 'יום ה, "day of the Lord," which appear throughout the prophetic literature, trace their origin back to the Song, where God's

---

8. Cf. Cassuto, "Hosea and the Book of the Torah," 262–78; William L. Holladay, "Jeremiah and Moses: Further Observations." *JBL* 85, 1 (1966), 17–27; Driver, *Deuteronomy*, 348; Rappel, *The Song of Moses*, 35–40; Jack R. Lundbom, *Jeremiah 1–20: A New Translation with Introduction and Commentary* (AB 21A; New York: Doubleday 1999), 109–17.

9. Driver, *Deuteronomy*, 348; Cassuto, "Hosea and the Book of the Torah," 262–78; M. Lana, quoted by Paul Sanders in *The Provenance of Deuteronomy 32* (Leiden, New York: Brill, 1996), 64.

10. Driver, *Deuteronomy*, 348.

11. Lana, "Deuteronomio," 188, quoted by Sanders, *Provenance*, 64.

12. Oral comments by A. Ho, quoted by Mark Leuchter in "Why Is the Song of Moses in the Book of Deuteronomy," *VT* 57 (2007), 295–317, 296.

13. Cf. Ed Greenstein, "Parody as a Challenge to Tradition: The Use of Deut. 32 in the Book of Job," pages 66–78 in *Reading Job Intertextually* (ed. Katharine Dell and Will Kynes; New York: Bloomsbury Academic, 2012).

14. Mordecai Lahav discusses *The Song's* relationship with Psalm 81 in his article, "The Historical Background of the Song of Moses," in *Memorial Volume for Niger: Articles on Bible Research* (ed. Arthur Brom; Jerusalem: The Israel Society for Bible Research, 1959), 80–7, (Heb.); Aage Bentzen in his *Introduction to the Old Testament* (Copenhagen: G.E.C. Gad, 1952), 164, notes *The Song's* relationship with Ps. 50, 78, 81, 95 and 106; Alexander Rofe notes *The Song's* relationship with Ps. 82 in his *Introduction to the Book of Deuteronomy* (Jerusalem: Akadmon, 1988), 216–33, (Heb.); Rappel, *The Song of Moses*, 37–40, discusses the relationship with a wide range of Psalms; Tigay notes the relationship with Ps. 78 in *Deuteronomy*, 511; David Emanuel notes the relationship with Ps. 81 in "An Unrecognized Voice: Intra-Textual and Intertextual Perspectives on Psalm 81," *HS* 50 (2009), 85–120.

15. Shemaryahu Talmon and Weston Fields, "The Collocation 'משתין בקיר ועצור ועזוב' and its Meaning," *ZAW* 101 (1989), 85–112.

16. Daniel R. Schwartz, "From Mattathias' Speech: On 'Zeal for the Law' and Heilsgeschichte in the Second Century BCE," in *Heil und Geschichte: Die Geschichtsbezogenheit des Heils und das Problem der Heilsgeschichte in der Biblischen Tradition und in der Theologischen Deutung* (Jö Jörg Frey, Stefan Krauter and Hermann Lichtenberger, eds.; Tübingen, Germany: Mohr Siebeck, 2009), 185–93.

day of vengeance was first invoked.[17] Echoes of the Song reverberating throughout nearly every book of the prophetic literature confirm its significance as the foundation of biblical prophecy.

In addition to the echoes from the Song of Moshe which resonate throughout the prophetic literature, the Song contains subtle references to several foundational biblical narratives. The Song will be shown to access the stories of creation, Adam's expulsion from Eden, the flood, the destruction of Sodom and Gomorrah, the Yehudah and Tamar narrative, and the sin of the golden calf. The Song's allusions to these texts bridge formative events from the past with those yet to unfold, as part of its broader meditation on God's relationship with Israel throughout history.

1 The Genesis-Song of Moshe Connection

The Song's resonances with the Genesis creation narrative, and the Sodom narrative, have been noted by several commentators.[18] Rappel

---

17. Moshe Frank, "The Song of Moses," *Tarbitz* 18 (1946), 129–38 (Heb.). The Song's influence on the books of the apocrypha, pseudepigrapha, and other sectarian writings is also well documented. See Richard H. Bell, *Provoked to Jealousy: The Origin and Purpose of the Jealousy Motif in Romans 9–11* (Tubingen: Mohr Siebeck, 1994), 200–285.

18. Cf. Bachya Ibn Paquda Gen. 32:4, Seforno Deut. 32:7 and R. Avraham Yaakov Sabba, (fifteenth-century Verona Italy, also known as *Tzror Hamor*) on Deut. 32; Cf. *Midrash Tannaim* (Hoffman) 32:1. Cf. The article of Beeri Amitai, "An Eternal Love for His Nation," *Hashira Hazot* (eds. Uri Arman and Yonatan Krauss; Jerusalem: Old City Press, 2003), 52–74, (Heb.). Beeri notes the terms; *esh kadcha, hashchet and dor tahapuchot*; Jan-Pierre Sonnet, *The Book within the Book; Writing in Deuteronomy* (eds. R. Alan Culpepper and Rolf Rendtorff; Leiden, New York, Koln: Brill, 1997), 176; Harold Fisch, *Poetry with a Purpose: Biblical Poetics and Interpretation* (Bloomington and Indianapolis: Indiana Univ. Press, 1990), 72; Cf. the following scholars who comment on the relationship between sections of the Yaakov narratives and *The Song*; S.R. Driver, *Deuteronomy* (ICC 21; Edinburgh: T & T Clark, 1978), 355; Yair Zakovitch, "Inner Biblical Interpretation," pages 429–453 in *Biblical Literature: Foreword and Studies* (ed. Ziporah Talshir; Jerusalem: Yad Yitzchak Ben Zvi, 2011), (Heb.).

reads the opening sections of the Song as a general overview of the
history of the Genesis creation narrative:

> Listen, you heavens, השמים and I will speak; hear, you earth,
> והארץ the words of my mouth. Let my teaching fall like rain and
> my words descend like dew, like showers on new grass, דשא like
> abundant rain on tender plants עשב. I will proclaim the name of
> the LORD. O, praise the greatness of our God! (Deut. 32:1–3)

Rappel cites the words דשה and עשב, grasses, השמים והארץ, heaven and
earth, together with the Tetragrammaton, as a fundamental constellation
of ideas supporting the parallel nature of the two texts.[19] Fisch remarks,
"As the Song of Moshe proceeds, we seem to move chronologically
through the early chapters of Genesis."[20] The geographical partitioning
of nations in Gen. 10, and the occurrence of the verb פרד,[21] in both texts,
has also been noted to suggest a further relationship between Genesis
and the Song.[22] Sonnet elaborates on the resonances to Genesis in the
backdrop of the Song:

---

19. Dov Rappel, *The Song of Moses; with an Introduction and Interpretation* (Tel
    Aviv: Yediot Acharonot, 1996), 24.

20. Fisch, *Poetry with a Purpose*, 72; Christensen also observes that "The original
    creation event in Gen. 1:1 began with the creation of heavens and earth,
    which is where The Song of Moses begins as well." Duane L. Christensen,
    Deuteronomy (WBC 6B; Nashville: Thomas Nelsen Pub., 2002), 793; Fried-
    man comments on the terms תהו, "wasteland," and רחף, "hovering," which
    both appear exclusively in these two places in the Pentateuch. He draws a
    further connection between the "the venom of serpents which slither upon
    the dust," in the Song (Deut. 32:24), and the curse of the serpent in Genesis:
    "You will crawl on your belly and you will eat dust all the days of your life."
    (Gen. 3:14). See Richard E. Friedman, "Parshat Haazinu: Does the Torah
    End with 'The End'? Traditional and Critical Perspectives on the Ending of
    the Torah," http://thetorah.com/the-end-of-the-torah/.

21. *HALOT*, "פרד," 962.

22. W.F. Albright, "Some Remarks on the Song of Moses in Deuteronomy 32,"
    VT 9, 4 (1959), 339–346, esp. 343–344; Moshe D. Cassuto, *A Commentary on
    the Book of Genesis* (trans. Israel Abrahams; 2 vols.; Jerusalem: Magnes Press,
    1984), 174–178; Michael S. Heiser, "Deuteronomy 32:8 and the Sons of God,"
    BS 158 (2001), 52–74, esp. 53; Eugene Merrill, *Deuteronomy* (NAC; Nashville:

The Song first revisits the lexical and metaphoric universe of creation.... Next come the flood and the phase of corruption, (expressed through the word *shachet*), and the immediate aftermath of the flood story.... A further greater disaster in the Genesis record, namely the overthrow of Sodom and Gomorrah, is then echoed.[23]

The Song's allusions to the creation narrative opens the door to the possibility that other key elements of the Genesis creation story may be waiting to be discovered beneath the surface layer of the text. This leads us to consider echoes of the creation of mankind, and the Song's systematic suggestion of Israel in comparison with Adam.

11 Israel in Comparison with Adam[24]

Numerous significant themes leading up to and following the sin of Adam also play a prominent role in the Song:

LIFE-GIVING WATERS

The creation of Adam in Genesis is heralded by life-giving waters which rise and quench the parched land:

> This is the account of the heavens and the earth when they were created, when the LORD God made the earth and the heavens. Now no shrub had yet appeared on the earth and no plant had yet sprung up, for the LORD God had not sent rain on the earth and there was no one to work the ground, but streams came up from the earth and watered the whole surface of the ground. Then the LORD God formed a man from the dust of the ground and breathed into his nostrils the breath of life, and the man became a living being. (Gen. 2:4–7)

Broadman and Holman Pub., 1994), 413; Christopher Wright, *Deuteronomy* (NIBC; Peabody: Hendrickson Pub., 1996), 299; Rappel, *The Song of Moses*, 24.

23. Sonnet, *The Book within the Book*, p. 176; Cf. Yitzchak A. Twersky, *Amittah Shel Torah* (2 vols.; Southfield: Targum, 2007), 2:347–8.

24. This perspective on the use of the Adam image to represent Israel is a refinement and development of an analysis first presented in my master's thesis, for which Dr. Joshua Berman served as faculty adviser.

In like manner, the Song's teachings are introduced through the metaphor of life-promoting precipitation upon the land:

Listen, you heavens, and I will speak; hear, you earth, the words of my mouth. Let my teaching fall like rain and my words descend like dew, like showers on new grass, like abundant rain on tender plants. (Deut. 32:1–2)

AGRICULTURAL BOUNTY

Man is placed in an environment of abundant agricultural bounty prepared for him by God. In Eden, God creates a beautiful garden for Adam:

The LORD God made all kinds of trees grow out of the ground – trees that were pleasing to the eye and good for food. (Gen. 2:9)

Adam is not only warned to abstain from the fruit of the tree of knowledge; he is directed to eat from all the other trees in the garden (Gen. 2:16). In the Song, Israel is placed in a choice location where all their material needs will be met:

He made him ride on the heights of the land and fed him with the fruit of the fields. He nourished him with honey from the rock, and with oil from the flinty crag, with curds and milk from herd and flock and with fattened lambs and goats, with choice rams of Bashan and the finest kernels of wheat. You drank the foaming blood of the grape. (Deut. 32:13–14).

DISOBEDIENCE

Man abuses the bounty provided by God. Man's failure to realize the obligation of obedience is epitomized in both accounts through the act of eating. In Genesis, God charges Adam with the crime of having eaten from the fruit of the tree of knowledge of good and evil (Gen. 3:11), and in Deuteronomy we read:

Jeshurun grew fat and kicked; filled with food, they became heavy and corpulent. They abandoned the God who made them and rejected the Rock their Savior. (Deut. 32:15)

The act of eating presents mankind with both opportunity for growth as well as a moral challenge. Deuteronomy 8 warns that food consumption ought to lead to expressions of gratitude and blessing, while overeating constitutes a real and present danger:

> When you have eaten and are satisfied, praise the Lord your God for the good land he has given you. Be careful that you do not forget the Lord your God, failing to observe his commands, his laws and his decrees that I am giving you this day. Otherwise, when you eat and are satisfied, when you build fine houses and settle down, and when your herds and flocks grow large and your silver and gold increase and all you have is multiplied, then your heart will become proud and you will forget the Lord your God, who brought you out of Egypt, out of the land of slavery… You may say to yourself, "My power and the strength of my hands have produced this wealth for me" (Deut. 8: 10–14, 17).

God's abundant gifts can easily be misconstrued as evidence of self-sufficiency and lead to self-aggrandizement. The Song affords us insight into the potentially dangerous spiral of unrestrained consumption. Adam's paradigmatic partaking of the forbidden fruit, although perhaps a perceived minor indulgence, contained within it the seeds of moral excess.

MORTAL MAN AND IMMORTAL GOD

The fundamental parameters of the distinction between God and humankind are explored in the Song of Moshe. Adam's desire to partake of the forbidden fruit stemmed from his aspiration to "be like God…" (Gen. 3:4). After God expels Adam from Eden, He also blocks his path back, lest he "become like one of us" and proceed to "reach out his hand and take also from the tree of life and eat and live forever" (Gen. 3:22). In like manner, the Song concludes with God's declaration of His singularity:

> See now that I Myself am He! There is no god besides Me! I put to death and I bring to life, I have wounded and I will heal, and no one can deliver out of My hand. I lift My hand to heaven and solemnly swear: As surely as I live forever (Deut. 32:39–40).

Interestingly, whereas Adam's re-entry into the Garden of Eden is proscribed, lest he eat from the tree of life, in the Song, after having descended to the abject depths of utter hopelessness and despair, ואפס עצור ועזוב,[25] Israel, in the ultimate expression of Divine grace, is restored to life and the land.

NEED FOR INTROSPECTION

God enjoins man to reflect upon his actions. When Adam crosses the threshold of sin, God probes Adam with the rhetorical question איכה, "where are you?" (Gen. 3:9), encouraging introspection. God continues to interrogate Adam whether he ate from the forbidden fruit (Gen. 3:11), further prodding him to evaluate his behavior. Similarly, in the Song, God implores Israel to evaluate their behavior:

> If only they were wise and would understand this and discern what their end will be! How could one man chase a thousand, or two put ten thousand to flight, unless their Rock had sold them, unless the LORD had given them up (Deut. 32:29–30).

Israel needs to assess how it is that they sank so low.[26] In both texts, God summons man to contemplate the consequences of their actions. In Genesis, Adam responds to God's inquiry by declaring that he hid on account of his nakedness.

> He answered, "I heard you in the garden, and I was afraid because I, אנכי, was naked; so I hid" (Gen. 3:10).

---

25. Cf. P.P. Saydon, "The Meaning of the Expression 'עצור ועזוב'," *VT* 2 (1952), 371–374.

26. These verses can be interpreted either as referring to Israel (Ibn Ezra), or to their enemies (Nachmanides). Fullerton comments on these passages; "There are few passages in the Old Testament in which a purely exegetical attack upon meaning yields less satisfying results." Cf. Kemper Fullerton, "On Deuteronomy 32:26–34," *ZAW* 46 (1928), 138–55. If we read the verses as referring to Israel, then it is alluding to the past, when God's providence protected Israel from their enemies. If we read the verses as referring to Israel's current enemies, then the verses are addressing the disturbing fact that Israel is being persecuted with God's approval. Either way, Israel must evaluate how it is that their relationship with God has spiraled so terribly out of control.

Adam uses the formal word אנכי here, expressing more than the colloquial refence to self, אני. The term אנכי is an expression of existential identity.[27] Adam's sudden need to hide from God and clothe himself marks the very moment at which he developed an awareness of self. This existential awakening is dramatized in the text by an opening of the eyes (Gen. 3:7). The price of Adam's individuation in the Garden of Eden is rupture from God. God does not inquire *where* Adam is to be found physically, איפה אתה, but where he is spiritually, איכה. Similarly, in the Song, Israel's abandonment of God is symptomatic of a broad spiritual estrangement.

EXECRATIONS

Both texts feature execrations which integrate a constellation of unique elements. Eve's curse, "With pain shall you bear offspring" (Gen. 3:16), although commonly understood as referring to the pain of childbirth, may alternatively be referring to the suffering associated with infant/child mortality. This reading is supported by the similar syntax found in the parallel curse of Adam, which speaks repeatedly of "eating food" (Gen. 3:17–19), when the meaning is certainly the opposite. Adam's curse portends famine and death, not abundance.

This interpretation of Eve's curse is interesting in light of the subsequent murder of Hevel in ch. 4. The Song also warns Israel that their children will die in their lifetime: "In the street the sword will make them childless, תשכל," (Deut. 32:25).[28] Like Adam who is cursed with famine and starvation, Israel is cursed in the Song, "I will send wasting famine against them" (Deut. 32:24).

In addition to the curses of hunger and mortality, snakes play an especially prominent role in both texts. The Genesis account revolves around the machinations of the serpent, which continues to occupy the limelight in the curse of man.

---

27. Cf. R. Yochanan's statement in BT *Shabbat* 105a, in which he explains the word אנכי to be an acronym for אנא נפשי כתיבת יהבית, "I Myself made this writing."

28. *HALOT* 'שכל,' CD-ROM ed., 1491.

And I will put enmity between you and the woman, and between your offspring and hers; he will crush your head, and you will strike his heel. (Gen. 3:15)

The Song makes three separate poetic references to snakes; vipers (*zochalei afar*), serpents (*tanninim*), and cobras (*petanim*) (Deut. 32:24, 33), all within the context of execrations. The phenomenon of the invocation of snakes in an execration is unique to these two biblical narratives. Both texts also highlight the snakes' distinctive characteristic of crawling in the dust. This is especially interesting considering that we do not find this attribute mentioned in any other biblical text featuring snakes:

You will crawl on your belly and you will eat dust all the days of your life. (Gen. 3:14)

The venom of vipers that slither in the dust. (Deut. 32:24)

Curiously, the Song uses a variety of poetic terms when referencing snakes, ie. זוחלי עפר, creatures that slither in the dust, תנינים, serpents,[29] and פתנים, horned vipers,[30] instead of utilizing the most familiar word for "snake," namely נחש, a ubiquitous word in the Bible, and a central word in the Genesis account. The omission of the term נחש in a text which stands out for its plethora of snake lexemes serves to intensify its absence. Oftentimes in poetry it is the unspoken yet blatantly implied word which points to its elusive presence.

The Russian literary critic Viktor Shklovsky coined the term "defamiliarization" to describe this poetic device:

We find material obviously created to remove the automatism of perception; the author's purpose is to create the vision which results from that de-automatized perception. A work is created "artistically" so that its perception is impeded and the greatest possible effect is produced through the slowness of the perception.[31]

---

29. *HALOT* 'תנין,' CD-ROM ed., 1764.

30. *HALOT* 'פתן,' CD-ROM ed., 990.

31. Victor Shklovsky, *Art as Technique. Literary Theory: An Anthology* (ed. Julie Rivkin and Michael Ryan; Malden: Blackwell, 1998), 19; Defamiliarization may be found throughout the Bible. For example, throughout the Exodus

Through its use of defamiliarization, the Song forces the reader to slow down and in so doing, recognize that the text is drawing upon allusions to the familiar. By echoing the themes of the creation of Adam while deliberately relying on poetic terminology not found in that story, the reader is forced to avoid the automatism inherent in the observation of things common. The reference to snakes is abundantly clear in the Song, as is the unspoken image of the נחש.

EXILE

Man is denied the privilege of continuing to enjoy the fruits of the land. Whereas Adam was formerly free to feed upon the fruits of Eden, the land itself is now cursed (Gen. 3:17). Adam is exiled from the garden where he will need to toil for his daily bread (Gen. 3:17–19). In the Song, Israel is also denied access to the bounty of the land and its produce, which has been devastated by fire (Deut. 32:22).

GOD'S UNSHEATHED SWORD

Both texts conclude with God's sword poised and ready for meting out punishment. In Genesis, God places a flaming sword along the path back to Eden to block Adam's re-entry (Gen. 3:24), and in the Song, God sharpens his flashing sword, אִם־שַׁנּוֹתִי בְּרַק חַרְבִּי, ready to take vengeance upon his enemies, (Deut. 32:41). The word used to describe the flashing of God's sword is ברק. The only other text of the Bible in which the words חרב and ברק are brought together in a discussion of God's arsenal is in

---

story God's redemptive role is repeatedly referred to as his hand, יד: (Ex. 3:19, 20; 6:1; 7:4, 5; 9:3, 15; 13:3, 9, 14, 16). In Moshe's song at the Red Sea, while there is no mention of God's יד in reference to Israel's redemption from Egypt, there is reference to His arm, זרוע, (Ex. 15:16), and to His right hand, ימין (Ex. 15:6, 12). (The reference to God's יד in Exodus 15:17 refers to the *future* building of the Temple, not the Exodus from Egypt). The words זרוע and ימין in Moshe's song are clearly references to God's redemptive hand, יד, the same hand which played a central role in Israel's salvation from Egypt. Another clear example of defamiliarization in the Bible may be observed in Hos. 11:8, where Hosea compares Israel to Adma and Zeboim instead of the infamous twin cities Sodom and Gomorrah, ironically, in order to emphasize their correlation with those very cities.

the book of Yechezkel. Like the Song, Yechezkel speaks of God's sword of destruction, חרב, as gleaming with lightning, ברק:

> Son of man, prophesy and say, "This is what the Lord says: 'A sword, a sword, חרב, sharpened and polished, sharpened for the slaughter, polished to flash like lightning, ברק!'" (Ezek. 21:14–15)

This image is reminiscent of Yechezkel's vision of the chariot in ch. 1, where a fire from between the *keruvim* gleams with a flashing light, ברק:

> The appearance of the living creatures was like burning coals of fire or like torches. Fire moved back and forth among the creatures; it was bright, and lightning, ברק, flashed out of it. (Ezek. 1:13)

Yechezkel's vision of the chariot in the opening chapter foreshadows the message of his ensuing prophecies. The menacing *keruvim* in Yechezkel's initial vision portend the destruction that informs the thrust of his prophecies. We may infer that Yechezkel's description of God's fiery sword of destruction in chapter 21 is an elaboration on his initial prophecy of a gleaming fire, ברק, between the *keruvim*. Ezek. 21 goes on to depict the fiery sword of God's imminent destruction being brandished from side to side:

> Slash to the right, you sword, then to the left, wherever your blade is turned (Ezek. 21:16).

When we combine all the basic elements that we have observed, images of the *keruvim* stationed on the path to Eden, and the fiery sword that they brandished, come to mind:

> After he drove the man out, he placed on the east side of the Garden of Eden cherubim and a flaming sword flashing back and forth to guard the way to the tree of life. (Gen. 3:24)

To review, the end of the Song portrays God as brandishing his fiery sword, אִם־שַׁנּוֹתִי בְּרַק חַרְבִּי. The recurrence in Yechezkel of God's burning sword of destruction, in the same lexical terms as those found in the

Song, matches what we already know about Yechezkel's reinterpretation of the Song.[32] Yechezkel adds the dimension of menacing *keruvim* to the description of the destruction provided by the Song. Yechezkel's fire-brandishing *keruvim*, which play such a critical role in his vision of the impending exile, conjure images of the menacing *keruvim* of Eden fame. Yechezkel's vision is the missing link for understanding the implications of God flashing sword of destruction in the Song. God's threatening sword which is brandished at the conclusion of the Song is a device meant to invoke images of the *keruvim* and the flashing sword stationed along the path to the Garden of Eden.

WORDPLAY

The relationship between the Eden narrative and the Song is further enhanced by word play. The verbs יצר and בנה, "to form" and "to build," play a critical role in the creation of Adam and Eve in Gen. 2:7, וייצר ה' אלקים את האדם, and in Gen. 2:22, ויבן ה' אלקים את הצלע, where God is observed engaging in the act of creating man and woman.[33] Deut. 32:10 describes God's role vis-à-vis the nascent Nation of Israel as יְבוֹנְנֵהוּ יִצְּרֶנְהוּ, deriving from the verbs בין and נצר, "to consider and to guard." Whereas יִצְּרֶנְהוּ derives from נצר, the truncated verb form evokes יצר, meaning "to form." Wordplay suggestive of both נצר and יצר can be observed in Yeshayahu's reflection on God's relationship with Israel (Isa. 42:6):

אני ה' קראתיך בצדק ואחזק בידך **ואצרך** ואתנך לברית עם לאור גויים.

Pseudo-Johnathan renders the word וְאֶצֶּרְךָ here to mean "I established you," whereas Ibn Ezra and Kimchi translate the word as "I guarded you" (Cf. Targum, Ibn Ezra, Kimchi, ad loc.) Here, like in the Song, the context is God's involvement in Israel's nascent development.

---

32. Cassuto, "Hosea and the Book of the Torah," 262–78; Von Rad, *Deuteronomy*, 200; Jason Gile, "Ezekiel 16 and the Song of Moses: A Prophetic Transformation?" *JBL* 130, 1 (2011), 87–108.

33. Cf. *HALOT*, 'בנה,'; 428 'יצר' 139, CD-ROM ed. It is noteworthy that the Sages suggest a play on words by the creation of woman. They read ויבן as deriving from בנה as well as בין meaning intelligence, suggesting that God outfitted women with superior intelligence. Cf. *Niddah* 45b.

Word play of this variety, wherein two similar sounding words are evoked, is termed paronomasia.[34] A clear example of paronomasia in the Bible can be observed in Amos 8:1–2, where Amos sees קַיִץ, "summer fruit," in a prophetic vision, and understands that the intended message is that the קֵץ, "the end," is near. When taken together with the numerous thematic similarities between the two texts, these word plays point to a deliberate echo from the Eden narrative.

To recap, all the dominant themes of the Eden narrative resurface in the Song, and they do so in the same order:

1. Gentle rain quenches the land
2. The creation of man/Israel
3. Placement in a lush garden
4. The directive to eat divinely provided foods
5. Sin through the act of eating
6. Man's/Israel's rejection of God
7. God demands that man evaluate his own actions
8. Curses which include childhood mortality, famine and dangerous snakes that "slither in the dust"
9. Man's mortality contrasted with God's immortality
10. The land is rendered uninhabitable; exile is inevitable
11. God's flaming sword is readied for meting out justice
12. Elaborate wordplays employing defamiliarization and paronomasia hint at the roots נחש and יצר, which are central to the Genesis creation narrative.

The casting of Israel in the role of Adam in the Song brings a message of comfort and hope. Adam's violation of the Divine command not to eat the forbidden fruit ought to have resulted in his immediate death

---

34. Cf. C.G.E. Watson, *Classical Hebrew Poetry* (Sheffield: JSOT Supplement Series 26, 1984), 242–243. Watson describes paronomasia in the Bible as "the deliberate choice of two or more different words which sound nearly alike"; I. Casanowicz, *Paronomasia in the Old testament* (PhD diss., Johns Hopkins Univ., 1894); A. Guillaume, "Paronomasia in the Old Testament" *Journal of Semitic Studies* 9 (1964), 282–290; S.B. Noegel ed., *Puns and Pundits: Word Play in the Hebrew Bible and Ancient Near Eastern Literature* (Sheffield: JSOT Supp. Series 26, 1984).

(Gen. 2:17). Adam's mitigated punishment left open the possibility of repentance. God, in a gesture of lovingkindness, further provided for Adam and Eve in the aftermath of their sin by clothing them.[35] Likewise, the Song's conclusion with the promise of atonement, כפרה, even in the absence of any repentance on the part of Israel, is a gesture of God's infinite compassion and eternal commitment to His nation.

III The Genesis Flood Narrative and The Song

We will begin our analysis of the Song in light of possible references to the Genesis flood narrative by focusing our attention on the semantic field of the five initial verses of each respective text. There are ten common terms between Deut. 32:1–5 and Gen. 6:9–12, and they are (1) righteousness (צדיק), (2) blamelessness (תמים), (3) speaking (אמר), (4) way, path (דרך), (5) corruption (שחת), (6) land (ארץ), (7) God (א-לקים), (8) generation (דור), (9) name (שם), and (10) son/sons (בן, בנים).

It may be argued that when considered individually these terms are not distinctive enough to suggest analogy. However, we must also consider the lexical cohesion of the text – the unique way in which each text uses this particular set of words.[36] In both texts, words of warning are offered to an entire generation that has become corrupted and that has been singled out for destruction. The word שחת stands out as a strong marker linking the two narratives. It is critical to note that these are the only two biblical texts which implicate an entire generation, דור, in corruption, שחת, and sentence them to destruction, also שחת. The word שחת is being used in two capacities – to imply both the sin and the punishment. The identical wordplay in both texts substantiates the theory of deliberate referencing. We will now turn our attention to the significant thematic resemblances between the two texts.

---

35. Gen. 3:21. Cf. *Midrash Aggadah*, Gen. 3:21.
36. Adele Berlin explores "lexical cohesion"; the way in which words are connected in a sequence, and the role that this plays in interpretation. Cf. Adele Berlin, "Lexical Cohesion and Biblical Interpretation," *Hebrew Studies* 30 (1989), 29–40.

THE CORRUPTION/ DESTRUCTION OF AN
ENTIRE GENERATION (שחת)

In both the flood story and the Song, the word שחת is used to insinuate
the irreparable corruption of an entire generation, דור. In considering
the parallel sematic field which these texts share, and the unique combination of the terminologies שחת and דור used together in precisely the
same way in both texts, all within the opening verses; the effect upon
the reader is a return to the literary mindset of the flood; its causes and
aftermath. It is noteworthy that the word שחת is used in precisely the
same idiosyncratic way in both texts, expressing a tension between
corruption and destruction.

The Song's proclamation of Israel's guilt is ambiguous:

> His degenerate children have treated him basely (שחת), a twisted
> and crooked generation! (Deut. 32:5)

If the children are corrupt, then the singular word שחת ostensibly
doesn't modify them. If the word שחת refers to God then the syntax
remains unclear.[37] Many of the classical commentators combine the
word לא with בניו, thereby altering the meaning. God's 'not-children'
have sinned against him, and brought destruction upon themselves
(Cf. Targum Onkelos, Rashi, Nachmanides, Ibn Ezra, Hizkuni and
Sforno). This interpretation leaves the number of the subject and the
verb mismatched, although there are other cases in which a singular
verb precedes a plural subject.[38] The opacity of vs. 5 contributes to the
ambiguity of the word שחת, which can indicate either corruption or
destruction.[39] The word שחת as an indicator of both corruption and
destruction also plays a prominent role in the flood text, appearing

---

37. The Samaritan Pentateuch reads *shachatu lo lo banav mumam*, meaning "not
    in Him did the blemished children bring ruin/destruction," probably to
    eliminate the difficulty of the lack of correspondence between the singular
    word *shichet* and the plural *banav*. The Masoretes placed a *tifha* under the
    word *lo* marking the division of the colon, in agreement with the rendering
    of the LXX, and Peshitta. Cf. Sanders, *Deuteronomy 32*, 145.

38. Sanders, *Deuteronomy 32*, 146 nt. 212.

39. HALOT, 'שחת,' 1471.

there a total of seven times; four times indicating destruction, and thrice connoting corruption (Cf. Gen. 6:11, 12, 13, 17; 9:11, 15). There is a progression from the people's actions being corrupt which transitions to the world becoming corrupt and finally to God's destruction of the land. Sarna comments on the transition observed in the usage of the word שחת in the flood narrative:

> The idea is that humankind cannot undermine the moral basis of society without endangering the very existence of its civilization. In fact, through its corruption, society sets in motion the process of inevitable self-destruction.[40]

The ambiguity of the word שחת in the Song also harbors a self-destructive connotation.

GUILT AND INNOCENCE

Deut. 32 juxtaposes Israel's corruption with God's perfection in two consecutive, antithetically parallel verses:

4a He is the Rock, His works are perfect, (תמים) and all His ways (דרכיו) are just.

4b A faithful God who does no wrong, upright and just (ישר – straight) is He.

5a They are corrupt and not His children; to their shame, (מומם).

5b They are a warped and crooked generation.

Vs. 4a and 5a contrast תמים, blamelessness, with מום, meaning blemish, and 4b and 5b contrast straight with crooked.[41] The implication of the juxtapositioning of these verses is that God's 'ways – דרכיו' in vs. 4a are being contrasted with Israel's 'way', or דרכו. While vs. 5 doesn't use the word דרכו, it is strongly hinted at by the clear and deliberate contrast between the two verses. This analogy brings to mind the unique description of the generation of the flood; a generation whose 'way', דרכו, became corrupt:

---

40. Nahum Sarna, *The JPS Torah Commentary: Genesis* (Philadelphia: JPS, 1989), 51.

41. While *tamim* and *mum* derive from different roots, there is a clear play on words in their deliberate juxtapositioning.

God saw how corrupt the earth had become, for all the people
on earth had corrupted their ways, השחית דרכו. (Gen. 6:12)

HEAVEN AND EARTH

The original creation event in Genesis that begins with the creation of
heavens and earth is also the starting point of the Song of Moshe. The
praise of God as creator and his ways in history is the central focus of
the Song's opening section. Heaven and earth also play a crucial role in
the Genesis flood narrative:

> And, behold, I, even I, do bring a flood of waters upon the earth, to
> destroy all flesh, wherein is the breath of life, from under heaven;
> and everything that is in the earth shall die (Gen. 6:17).[42]

PROTECTED SPACE

Deuteronomy 32 compares God's protection over Israel to a mother bird
hovering over her nest, קן:

> Like an eagle that stirs up its nest, (קנו), and hovers over its
> young, that spreads its wings to catch them and carries them
> aloft (Deut. 32:11).

The Genesis flood account describes the ark as having been constructed with individual compartments, קנים, a peculiar choice of words
for describing human habitation (Gen. 6:14).[43] The only other instance
of the Bible using the word קן to connote a space intended for human
beings is in in Job, where it references a coffin (29:18). What makes the
word's appearance in the Genesis flood narrative all the more striking
is that, whereas we are informed that all manner of animal species were
brought aboard the ark, the only animals delineated are birds: a raven
and a dove (Cf. Gen. 8:6–12). In contrast with the dove which Noah
thrice releases to test the inhabitability of the land, Noah's motivation
for releasing the raven remains a mystery.[44] The role of Noah here

---

42. Cf. Gen. 7:11–12, 23; 8:1–2.
43. Cf. *HALOT*, 'קן,' 1109.
44. Rashi, Radak, and Hizkuni on Gen. 8:7 agree that Noah sent the raven out
    of the protection of the ark as a means of determining the habitability of the

appears to be analogous to a mother-bird nudging her fledglings out of the safety of the nest. God's protection over Noah during the Flood may aptly be described "Like an eagle that stirs up its nest (קנו), and hovers over its young, that spreads its wings to catch them and carries them aloft" (Deut. 32:11).

THE RAINBOW, קשת

The rainbow, קשת, the symbol of God's everlasting pledge to never again-destroy mankind by flood, is mentioned three times in the Genesis flood narrative (Gen. 9:13, 14, 16). All of the remaining seventy-two references to the קשת in the Bible reference the warrior's might and archery skill.[45] Nachmanides suggests that the rainbow represents the idea of God's inverted military bow, suggesting Divine disarmament (Gen. 9:12). The correlation between the rainbow and the archer's bow is reinforced by Hosea who recounts God's covenant with His creation, together with a promise that in the future there will be no more threats of violence from either a bow or a sword, קשת וחרב (Hosea 2:20). The notion of a symbolic relationship between the rainbow and the archer's bow is reinforced by ancient Babylonian astronomical records which describe rainbows as "stretching."[46] Interestingly, the Sumerian bow-wielding warrior god Ninurta was depicted with a crown, which was referred to as a *Manzat*, Akkadian for "rainbow."[47] It is striking that the rainbow, קשת, fashioned after the concept of the archer's bow, a symbol of aggression, acquires

---

land. In the Epic of Gilgamesh flood story, Utnapishtim is instructed to take the seed of all living creatures onto his boat, although the creatures are not identified in the story. The epic later recounts how Utnapishtim released three birds, a dove, a swallow and a raven, to test if the land was inhabitable. Cf. *The Epic of Gilgamesh*, (trans. N. Sanders; London: Penguin, 1973), ch. 5.

45. HALOT 'keshet,' 1155.
46. Abraham J. Sachs and Hermann Hunger, *Astronomical Diaries and Related Texts from Babylonia Vol. 1; Diaries from 652 B.C. to 262 B.C.* (Vienna: Verlag der Osterreichischen Akademie der Wissenschaften, 1988), 45, 47, 69, 141, 171, 183, 479.
47. Jeremy Black and Anthony Green, *Demons and Symbols of Ancient Mesopotamia: An Illustrated Dictionary* (Austin: Univ. of Texas Press, 1992), p. 153. *Manzat* was also the name of a goddess and a star in the constellation of

a peaceful connotation in the biblical flood story. The bow, a symbol of military might, functions in Genesis as a symbol of strength through self-restraint. The theme of God's self-restraint throughout history is another dominant leitmotif in the Song, in which God overcomes His jealous rage over Israel's vexing provocations. Instead of wiping Israel out at the Song's conclusion, God restores them (Cf. Deut. 32:7, 27, 35–36).

Although the text in the Song doesn't specify the term קשת, its latent presence is suggested within the discussion of God's military arsenal. Gen. 9:13 uses the word קשתי, "My bow." The Song refers to God's sword, חרבי, "My sword," and arrows, חצי, "My arrows" (Deut. 32:42). The description of God's arrows, חצי, in the Song a priori presumes God's bow as well. The possessive form used to describe God's weapons in the Song, חרבי וחצי, suggests the possessive קשתי, 'my bow', the term used for the rainbow in Genesis.

Whereas we are naturally inclined to examine the words that appear in the text, we are less disposed to consider words hinted at – but curiously omitted by – the text. This was noted above in the discussion involving the *presence of absence*, or the literary term "defamiliarization," (specifically regarding the snake and the absence of the word נחש). While God's "bow" is hinted at in the Song, its omission from the text requires investigation. The word קשת is entirely omitted, but replaced by the less familiar relatives חצי and חרבי. The Genesis flood narrative imbues God's personal קשת with a peaceful significance. While the Song ultimately closes with a message of peace and hope, the overall tenor of the Song is overwhelmingly one of reproach. The bulk of the Song and its terrifying descriptions of God's jealous wrath is inconsistent with the peaceful symbolism of the rainbow. Perhaps this is the reason that the Song relegated all hints to the קשת to the opaqueness of the subtext.

THE COVENANT

The covenant between God and man, which is central to the Genesis flood narrative, plays a significant role in the introduction to the Song,

Andromeda. This star may be illustrated as a rainbow arching over a horse's head, a symbol for the sun-god in the Neo-Assyrian Period. Cf. Ibid, p. 104.

where it is mentioned twice (Deut. 31:16, 20). The Song itself functions
as a witness to the covenant:

> Now write down this song and teach it to the Israelites and have
> them sing it, so that it may be a witness for Me against them.
> When I have brought them into the land flowing with milk and
> honey, the land I promised on oath to their ancestors, and when
> they eat their fill and thrive, they will turn to other gods and
> worship them, rejecting Me and breaking My covenant. And
> when many disasters and calamities come on them, this song
> will testify against them, because it will not be forgotten by their
> descendants. I know what they are disposed to do, even before
> I bring them into the land I promised them on oath. So Moshe
> wrote down this song that day and taught it to the Israelites
> (Deut. 31:19–22).

The Song's paradoxical conclusion in which God restores Israel to
their former status despite their failure to repent reinforces God's eternal
commitment to the covenant.[48] God's covenant with the patriarchs
was also fundamentally unilateral in nature, without any stipulations
regarding reciprocal obligations.[49] An indication of the one-sided nature
of the patriarchal covenant may be observed in the covenant between
the parts. It would have been expected that Avraham pass between the
parts, in accordance with the ancient custom in which both parties
demonstrated their commitment. Instead, God alone swears and it is
only His fire that passes through the parts.[50]

---

48. The paradoxical conclusion of Deut. 32 led Frank to conclude that the Song's
    primary theological purpose is to be an expression of God's unmitigated love
    and compassion for Israel. Cf. Moshe Frank, "The Song of Moses," *Tarbitz*
    18 (1946), 129–138 (Heb.).

49. Cf. God's covenant with Avraham in Gen. 12:1–3 and 15:18–21, affirmed later
    with Yitzchak in Gen. 17:21 and Yaakov in Gen. 35:9–13.

50. Cf. Gen. 15:9–21; Merrill suggests that God's unconditional covenant with
    Avraham took the form of an ancient Near Eastern royal land grant which
    was also fundamentally unilateral in nature. Eugene Merrill, "A Theology of
    the Pentateuch," pp. 7–87 in *Biblical Theology of the Old Testament* (ed. Roy
    Zuck; Chicago: Moody, 1991), 26.

Like God's unilateral covenant with the patriarchs, God's vow to Noah never to allow a deluge to wipe out mankind again, together with His failure to exact any obligations from mankind in return, reinforces the unconditional nature of the covenant. The Song's paradoxical conclusion with Israel's restoration, despite the nation's failure to repent, reinforces the idea of the Song as an eternal witness to the covenant.

REVIEW OF THE EVIDENCE

1. Heaven and earth are central motifs in both the Genesis flood narrative, and in the dramatic opening of the Song.

2. The shared semantic field and lexical cohesion of the first five verses of both the Song and the first five verses of the Genesis flood narrative draw the reader into the literary mindset of the flood.

3. The ambiguity of the word שחת in the Song, meaning both "destruction" and "corruption," suggests the same self-destructive connotation found in the flood narrative.

4. The parallelism between verses 4 and 5 in the Song indicates that God's "ways," דרכיו, from vs. 4 are being contrasted with Israel's "way," דרכו, in vs. 5, recalling the Genesis flood narrative's unique description of that generation as a generation whose "way," דרכו, became corrupted.

5. The openings of both texts set up a contrast between blame and blamelessness.

6. The Song compares God's protection over Israel to a mother-bird hovering over her nest, קן. The Genesis flood account describes the ark as being made of individual compartments, or קנים. Noah's sending off of the dove and the raven from the safety of the ark evokes the image a mother-bird nudging her fledglings out of the safety of the nest.

7. The קשת functions in the flood story as a symbol of God's self-restraint. God's self-restraint in His relationship with Israel throughout their history is at the crux of the Song. While the Song does not contain the word קשת it does strongly suggest it, with its emphasis on God's military arsenal, especially His arrows.

8. The covenant between God and man is central to the Genesis flood narrative and is at the crux of the Song as well, even with the absence of any blatant references to the בְּרִית. The paradoxical conclusion of the Song, in which God's eternal bond with Israel is restored, recalls the unilateral nature of God's covenant with mankind after the flood.

THE SIGNIFICANCE OF THE THEMATIC LINKS BETWEEN THE SONG AND THE GENESIS FLOOD NARRATIVE

The Genesis flood narrative, like the Song, chronicles the moral degeneration and self-destruction of an entire generation. God's compassion for mankind and His unilateral covenant with Noah after the flood story serves as the theological blueprint for the Song, in which God's compassion prevails over His wrath in affirmation of the covenant. The paradigmatic relationship between God's covenant with mankind in the days of Noah and God's relationship with Israel throughout history is also at the heart of Yeshayahu's message of comfort to Israel. Yeshayahu 54 speaks of God's covenant in the days of Noah, comparing it to the covenant with Israel. Yeshayahu emphasizes that God's fury towards Israel does not abrogate His eternal love:[51]

> "In a surge of anger I hid My face from you for a moment, but with everlasting kindness I will have compassion on you," says the LORD your Redeemer. "To Me this is like the days of Noah, when I swore that the waters of Noah would never again cover the earth. So now I have sworn not to be angry with you, never to rebuke you again. Though the mountains be shaken and the hills be removed, yet My unfailing love for you will not be shaken nor My covenant of peace be removed," says the LORD, who has compassion on you" (Isa. 54:8–10).

---

51. Cf. Gary V. Smith, *The New American Commentary: Isaiah 40–66* (Nashville: B&H, 2009), p. 484. While Targum and 1QIs. have the two words *ki* and *Noah* appearing together as one, *kimei*, "like the days of Noah," which agrees with the LXX, as opposed to the Masoretic text's "for the waters of Noah," this does not alter our understanding of Yeshayahu's comparison between God's covenant in the time of Noah and his covenant with Israel.

Yeshayahu was not the only prophet to compare God's covenant with Noah to the covenant with Israel. Yechezkel also draws upon the paradigm of Noah, together with Daniel and Job, as exemplars of righteous men who lived through great calamities yet were incapable of rescuing others (Cf. Ezek. 14:12–20). Yechezkel's catalogue of calamities includes famine, wild animals, enemy attack, and pestilence. Even though Noah is clearly referenced in the text, the possibility of a devastating flood is glaringly absent from Yechezkel's list of potential disasters. This is likely due to God's promise that He would never again devastate the land with a flood the likes of which destroyed mankind in Noah's generation. Like Yechezkel, the Song also leaves floodwaters out of its list of potential disasters. Yechezkel's catalogue of devastations is concentrated in the short span of two verses, matching the calamities enumerated in the Song:

famine	"I will send wasting famine against them" (The Song, v. 24).
wild animals	"I will send against them the fangs of wild beasts" (The Song, v. 24).
enemy attack	"In the street the sword will make them childless; in their homes terror will reign" (The Song, v. 25).
pestilence	"Consuming pestilence and deadly plague" (The Song, v. 24).

The one-to-one correlation between Yechezkel's text and the Song reinforces the assumption of a correlation between the Song and the Genesis flood narrative, despite the Song's failure to directly reference a flood.

The prophetic tradition of linking God's covenant with Noah with His covenant with Israel is also present in Hosea, who describes the role of the beasts of the field and the bow, קשת, in God's everlasting covenant with Israel:

In that day I will make a covenant for them with the beasts of the field, the birds in the sky and the creatures that move along the ground. Bow, קשת, and sword and battle I will abolish from the land, so that all may lie down in safety (Hos. 2:20).

The Song's subtle allusions to the Genesis flood narrative are part of a broad phenomenon within Israel's prophetic tradition linking God's covenant with Noah and Israel. The analogy between these two covenants rests upon the notion of the flood story as archetype for God's commitment to the seemingly incompatible ideals of justice and compassion. Whereas the Song articulates the terrible consequences of breach of covenant, its conclusion guarantees God's everlasting love and commitment towards His people.

IV The Song's Suggestion of Israel in Comparison with Sodom

The Song sets up a comparison between Israel on one side and Sodom and Gomorrah on the other, although it remains unclear if the referent is Israel or their enemies:[52]

> Theirs is the vine of Sodom and the fields of Gomorrah. Their grapes are filled with poison, and their clusters with bitterness[53] (Deut. 32:32).

The ambiguous nature of this verse is typical of the general ambiguity of the surrounding text.[54] Many commentators take the position that vs. 32 is referencing Israel's enemies, as the verse's message appears to reach its climax in vs. 35, where God declares that He will deliver His ultimate vengeance. On the face of things, this verse seems to refer to Israel's enemies.[55] However, the verse may alternatively be read as expounding on the reference to "the enemy," אויבנו, from the previous verse.[56] Rashi and Rashbam understand our verse to be a continuation

---

52. Beeri suggests that the Song invokes Sodom and Gomorrah as these cities are the classical biblical archetype of evil and destruction. Cf. the article of Beeri Amitai, "An Eternal Love for His Nation," 52–74.

53. *Merorot* is rendered "bitter grapes" by Bauer, "*marar*," HALOT, CD-ROM ed., 638.

54. Fullerton comments on our verse, "There are few passages in the Old Testament in which a purely exegetical attack upon meaning yields less satisfying results." See Kemper Fullerton, "On Deuteronomy 32:26–34," ZAW 46 (1928), 138–55.

55. Cf. Sanders, *Deuteronomy 32*, 225.

56. Driver, *Deuteronomy*, 372–373; Zakovitch writes that when poetic verses

of the thread that began in vs. 26–30, in which the third person pronoun refers to Israel.[57] This approach is probably inferred from Yeshayahu, who draws upon the Song in his opening words, invoking heaven and earth as witnesses:

> Hear me, you heavens! Listen, earth! For the LORD has spoken: "I reared children and brought them up, but they have rebelled against me" (Isa. 1:1).

An analogy between Israel and Sodom soon follows.

> Unless the LORD Almighty had left us some survivors, we would have become like Sodom, we would have been like Gomorrah (Isa. 1:9).

Further support for Israel's being cast in the Song as the infamous twin cities derives from the explicit comparison to Sodom and Gomorrah in the text leading up to the Song in ch. 29. There, Israel's sins bring about a destruction reminiscent of the overturning of Sodom and Gomorrah:

> The LORD will never be willing to forgive them; his wrath and zeal will burn against them. All the curses written in this book will fall on them, and the LORD will blot out their names from under heaven. The LORD will single them out from all the tribes of Israel for disaster, according to all the curses of the covenant written in this Book of the Law. Your children who follow you in later

---

appear to invite a dual meaning then both implied meanings may be assumed to have been intended. See Yair Zakovitch, *I Will Utter Riddles from Ancient Times: Riddles and Dream – Riddles in Biblical Narrative* (Tel Aviv: Am Oved Pub., 2005) 88–172, esp. 89 (Heb.); Christenson agrees that the ambiguity of the text here is intentional. See Duane L. Christensen, *Deuteronomy* (WBC 6B; Nashville: Thomas Nelsen Pub., 2002), 808; Fokkelman assumes the referent of the third person pronouns between vs. 26–34 to change from verse to verse. See Fokkelman, *Major Poems of the Hebrew Bible: At the Interface of Hermeneutics and Structural Analysis* (4 vols.; Assen, The Netherlands: Van Gorcum 1998), 1:74.

57. Rashi and Rashbam on Deut. 32:32; Boston also understands vs. 32 to be referring to Israel. See Boston, "The Song of Moses: Deuteronomy 32:1–43," (Ph.D. diss., Union Theological Seminary, 1966), 113–115.

generations and foreigners who come from distant lands will see
the calamities that have fallen on the land and the diseases with
which the LORD has afflicted it. The whole land will be a burning
waste of salt and sulfur – nothing planted, nothing sprouting,
no vegetation growing on it. It will be like the destruction of
Sodom and Gomorrah, Admah and Zeboyim, which the LORD
overthrew in fierce anger (Deut. 29:19–23).

Reversed metaphor strategy, a rhetorical device intended to convey
dramatic irony, plays a prominent role in the Song, in which the life-
supporting forces of nature quickly transform into instruments of God's
wrath.[58] The prominence of this compositional strategy in the Song
points to Israel as the referent of the wine analogy in vs. 32, as opposed
to their enemies. The blood of grapes, דם ענב, that Israel enjoyed in vs.
14, which is a positive image, morphs into poisonous grapes, ענבי רוש, in
vs. 32. This metaphor reversal is evocative of the refreshing dew which
sustains plant life in the opening of the poem, and which gives way to a
scorched earth and the obliteration of all plant life in vs. 22. Similarly, in
vs. 10, God surrounds Israel to protect them from danger, while in vs. 30
He hands them over to the hostile forces that seek their destruction.

In a desert land He found him, in a barren and howling waste. He
shielded him and cared for him; He guarded him as the apple of
His eye (Deut. 32:10).

How could one man chase a thousand, or two put ten thousand
to flight, unless their Rock had sold them, unless the Lord had
given them up? (Deut. 32:30)

In vs. 13 Israel is described as an infant suckling from the hand of
God, וינקהו, while in vs. 25 God destroys Israel's suckling infants, יונק. In
vs. 23 and 25 God uses his sword and arrows to attack Israel, חצי אכלה בם,
מחוץ תשכל חרב whereas later in vs. 42, these same weapons are used in
Israel's defense, אשכיר חצי מדם וחרבי תאכל בשר. In the beginning of the
Song of Moshe, God's loving care toward the fledgling nation of Israel
is described as a mother-bird that cares for and protects her young:

---

58. Tremper Longman, Leland Ryken and James Wilhoit eds., *Dictionary of
Biblical Imagery* (Westmont: InterVarsity Press, 1998), 206.

Like an eagle that stirs up its nest and hovers over its young, that spreads its wings to catch them and carries them aloft. The Lord alone led him; no foreign god was with him (Deut. 32:11–12).

Later in the Song, blessings are transformed into execrations, and God's eagle-like protection of his fledgling nation gives way to Resheph, a force of death and destruction associated with flying creatures:[59]

I will send wasting famine against them, consuming pestilence, לחמי רשף and deadly plague; I will send against them the fangs of wild beasts, the venom of vipers that glide in the dust (Deut. 32:24).

The Song's suggestion of an analogy between Israel and Sodom and Gomorrah, especially in light of the reversed metaphor strategy that operates throughout the Song, underscores the need to compare Israel with these two inversely parallel and infamous cities. As we shall see, the themes and motifs which pervade the Sodom narrative resurface throughout the Song.

BOUNTY

Both the inhabitants of Sodom and Israel enjoyed the bountiful produce of the land:

Lot looked around and saw that the whole plain of the Jordan toward Zoar was well watered, like the garden of the LORD, like the land of Egypt. This was before the LORD destroyed Sodom and Gomorrah) (Gen. 13:10).

---

59. Cf. Job 5:7; The LXX translates Resheph in Job as *gypos*, meaning "vultures." See Mulder, "רשף," *TDOT* 16:10–16 esp. 16; The Vulgate renders the word to mean *avis*, meaning "bird." See *HALOT*, "רשף," 1298; Gesenius, in an attempt to streamline the biblical definitions of Resheph, renders Resheph in Job 5:7 as "sparks." See Wilhelm Gesenius, *A Hebrew and English Lexicon of the Old Testament: Including the Biblical Chaldee* (trans. Edward Robinson; Boston: Crocker and Brewster, 1849), 418 nt. 128v; Sira 43:14 and 17 poses a challenge to this assumption: "Through this the treasures are opened: and clouds fly forth as *fowls* ... The noise of the thunder maketh the earth to tremble: so doth the northern storm and the whirlwind: *as birds flying* he scattereth the snow and the falling down thereof is as the lighting of grasshoppers."

He made him ride on the heights of the land and fed him with the fruit of the fields. He nourished him with honey from the rock, and with oil from the flinty crag, with curds and milk from herd and flock and with fattened lambs and goats, with choice rams of Bashan and the finest kernels of wheat. You drank the foaming blood of the grape (Deut. 32:13–14).

CORRUPTION

Sodom and Gomorrah are described in Genesis as a profoundly corrupt society.

Then the LORD said, "The outcry against Sodom and Gomorrah is so great and their sin so grievous (Gen. 18:20).

Israel is described with similar imagery in the Song:

They are corrupt and not His children; to their shame they are a warped and crooked generation. (Deut. 32:5)

Fisch comments that the depiction of Israel in the Song invokes the word שחת in vs. 5, which is highly reminiscent of the description of Sodom, where it is found a total of nine times.[60] In both cases, a nation is depicted by the text as having become morally corrupted and faces divine retribution as a result. The theme of corruption breeding destruction was noted above in the discussion on the flood narrative.

THE PERFECTION OF GOD'S JUSTICE

Both the Sodom narrative and the Song emphasize God's attribute of justice:

For I have chosen him, so that he will direct his children and his household after him to keep the way of the LORD by doing what is right and just, לעשות צדקה ומשפט so that the LORD will bring about for Avraham what He has promised him (Gen. 18:19).

He is the Rock, His works are perfect, and all His ways are just. A faithful God who does no wrong, upright and just is He, כי כל דרכיו משפט... צדיק וישר הוא. (Deut. 32:4)

---

60. Gen. 13:10, 18:28, 31, 32, 19:13, 14, 29.

God's choice of Avraham is explained by the text in Genesis as having been designed by God in order to promote His mission and the dissemination of divine justice. Foreknowledge of God's decision to destroy Sodom prompts Avraham's declaration, "Will the Judge of all the land not judge righteously?" (Gen. 18:25). At the conclusion of the dialogue, Divine justice is ultimately vindicated at the expense of human reasoning, when Avraham concedes defeat (Gen. 18:33). The Song also advances an elaborate defense of God's impeccable justice prior to its exposition on His impending retribution.

SEEING THE EVIL

In both the Sodom and Gomorrah narrative, and in the Song, God is described as "seeing" the evil: "I will go down and see" (Gen. 18:21), "and God saw" (Deut. 32:19). Sarna comments, "This stated intention is an element in the motif of theodicy, or the vindication of divine justice, that is essential to the Sodom narrative."[61] God is described in a similar vein before His decision to bring the Flood (Gen. 6:12), at the dispersal of mankind in the Tower of Babel narrative (Gen. 11:5), and prior to the punishing of the Egyptians in Exodus (Ex. 2:25). In each of these cases, God's first-hand verification of the evil report is understood to be a prerequisite for Divine justice – meaning that God will not mete our punishment until He Himself "sees" or witnesses the evil.[62]

CONFLAGRATIONS

Both accounts describe a conflagration of massive proportions. The destruction of Sodom and Gomorrah was absolute.

> And He overthrew the cities, and the entire area and all of the inhabitants of the cities, and what grew on the ground" (Gen. 19:25).

---

61. Sarna, *Genesis*, 132.
62. God's immediate presence, *penei Hashem*, among man is specified in both texts: "For we are about to destroy this place, because the outcry before God's presence, has become too great...", *ki gadlah tzaakatam et penei Hashem* (Gen. 19:13). The Song's description of God hiding his face in reaction to Israel's sin in Deut. 32:20, *astira panai mehem*, also indicates that His presence among them was formerly more readily apparent.

The Song also describes an all-encompassing destruction intended
to wipe out the land, people, and plant life.

The destruction of Sodom takes place by means of fire (Gen. 19:24).
In the Song, the land is also destroyed by a wild conflagration.

> For a fire will be kindled by My wrath, one that burns down
> to the realm of the dead below. It will devour the earth and its
> harvests and set afire the foundations of the mountains. I will
> heap calamities on them and spend My arrows against them. I
> will send wasting famine against them, consuming pestilence and
> deadly plague; I will send against them the fangs of wild beasts,
> the venom of vipers that glide in the dust. In the street the sword
> will make them childless; in their homes terror will reign. The
> young men and young women will perish, the infants and those
> with gray hair (Deut. 32:22–25).

Sonnet reads the images of fire in the Song and the use of the word
הפך, "overturn," in תהפוכות דור (Deut. 32:20), as echoes of the Sodom
narrative in Genesis.[63] In both narratives, the overarching context is
one of a fiery Divine retribution. We may understand אספה from Deut.
32:23 as another example of shared lexical terminologies between the
two texts. ספה, meaning "swept away," is a central word in the Sodom
narrative, appearing there four times.[64] BDB explains אספה to mean that
God will sweep Israel away because of their iniquity.[65] This reading is
supported by the second half of the verse where the word אכלה, meaning
"I will destroy," appears parallel to אספה.

The Song's thematic reverberations of the Sodom narrative in Genesis
provide a context for us to be able to observe both their commonalities
and disparities. While Israel is likened to Sodom in a variety of ways, they
are unlike Sodom in one critical respect. Whereas Sodom's destruction
is absolute, Israel is ultimately restored at the conclusion of the Song.

---

63. Sonnet, *The Book Within the Book*, 176.

64. Gen. 18:23, 24; 19:15, 17. Cf. Fisch, *Poetry with a Purpose*, 72.

65. BDB, "ספא," 705a; The LXX, Vulgate and Peshitta read "I shall gather," which
     derives from אסף, meaning to gather. Cf. Sanders, *Deuteronomy 32*, 193.
     Sanders understands אספה to derive from יסף, meaning "to add, or heap on."

Rejoice, you nations, with His people, for He will avenge the blood of His servants; He will take vengeance on His enemies and make atonement for His land and people (Deut. 32:43).

In the Song, Israel sinks to unprecedented depths, yet unlike the Sodomites, they are not beyond redemption. This variance is made even more stark by Israel's complete absence to repent. What theological mechanism might explain this glaring anomaly? We will be in a better position to revisit this question after completing our survey of the allusions to earlier biblical narratives in the Song.

v The Relationship between the Yehudah and Tamar Affair and The Song

A close reading of the Song indicates that allusions to Yaakov's family, specifically to the Yehudah and Tamar narrative in Gen. 38, lie beneath the surface layer of the Song. These allusions are concentrated within the short span of eleven consecutive verses (Deut. 32: 4–14). Gen. 38 chronicles the moral and mortal demise of the family of Yehudah. Crimes of self-interest, exploitation, and treachery threaten the lineage of Yehudah with annihilation. Yehudah's saving grace is his ultimate admission of guilt, which he himself contrasts with Tamar's moral superiority.

Yehudah recognized them and said, "She is more righteous than I, since I wouldn't give her to my son Shelah" (Gen. 38:26).

The Song also tells the story of the moral breakdown and near destruction of the nation of Israel.

Like the story of Yehudah and Tamar, the Song contrasts guilt with righteousness:

He is the Rock, His works are perfect, and all His ways are just. A faithful God who does no wrong, upright and just is He. They are corrupt and not His children; to their shame they are a warped and crooked generation (Deut. 32:4–5).

Both the Yehudah and Tamar affair and the Song come to their respective conclusions with the promise of restoration. The reverberations of the Yehudah and Tamar story in the Song transmit the message that the privileges of election are accompanied by covenantal responsibility, and that the consequence of infidelity is self-destruction. These literary echoes from the Yehudah and Tamar episode in the Song also convey a powerful and timeless message of hope; though Israel may falter, restoration is their destiny.

CORRUPTION AND THE PROBLEM OF 'NO SONS'

The Song opens with a description of Israel's abject perfidy:

> Yet his degenerate children have treated him basely, שחת לו לא בניו מומם a twisted and crooked generation! (Deut. 32:5)

Gen. 38, like our verse, uses the term שחת together with the word play לו and לא in a single verse, in describing Onan's birth control strategy. The similarity is striking since these two verses are the only two biblical texts where these phrases converge:[66]

> But Onan knew that the child would not be his, לא לו; so when-ever he slept with his brother's wife, he spilled וׁשחת his semen on the ground to keep from providing offspring for his brother (Gen. 38:9).

Instead of fulfilling their conjugal responsibilities, Er and Onan reduced Tamar to an object of their pleasure. In the Song, Israel – like Er and Onan – is guilty of infidelity. In both cases, treachery results in the consequence of לא בנים, or a lack of sons. A close examination of the word יעיר, in v. 11, may reveal a veiled reference to Er, ער:

> As an eagle protects, יעיר, its nestlings, hovering over its young, so He spread His wings, took them, bore them upon His pinions (Deut. 32:11).

The etymology of the name "Er" likely derives from the root ער, meaning "to protect," although some understand יעיר to derive from the root עור, "to stir up."[67] The Ugaritic word gr, signifying protection,

---

66. *HALOT* 'שחת,' 1471.
67. *HALOT*, "ער," 876.

supports the former definition.[68] This understanding of the word is confirmed by Job:

> If you were pure and upright, surely now He would protect you, יָעִיר אֵלֶיךָ, and make the habitation of your righteousness prosperous (Job 8:6).

The definition "to protect" works much better in explaining the sense of the text in the Song, where God's hovering over His young is most certainly an act of guarding, not stirring. In failing to fulfill his marital responsibility, Er goes from being a guardian to an agent of harm. The ironic twist in Er's role is confirmed by his very name, and the verse's deliberate metathesis of the letters in Er's name to read "evil," רַע:

> But עֵר, Yehudah's firstborn, was wicked, רַע, in the LORD's sight; so the LORD put him to death. (Gen 38:7)

Onan's demise echoes the account of Er's death, with the repetition of the word רַע, and in the comparison drawn between the two brothers:

> What he (Onan) did was wicked, וַיֵּרַע, in the LORD's sight; so the LORD put him to death also. (Gen 38:10)

By extension, the analogy to Israel's infidelity, as described in the Song, may be understood as an allusion simultaneously to both Er and Onan.

THE COVENANT OF MARRIAGE AND ITS PERVERSION

In the Song, God's protection is compared to a mother-bird hovering over her young:

> As an eagle protects its nestlings, hovering over its young, so He spread His wings, took them, bore them, יִפְרֹשׂ כְּנָפָיו יִקָּחֵהוּ יִשָּׂאֵהוּ, upon His pinions. (Deut. 32:11)

God is described here as performing three actions: spreading His wings, יפרוש כנפיו, taking, יקחהו, and carrying, ישאהו. These terms share

---

68. Cf. Sanders, *Deuteronomy 32*, 163–164.

the uncanny distinction of being the three biblical phrases for marriage.[69] The presence of all three biblical terminologies for marriage, appearing consecutively within a single verse, is undoubtably deliberate. The appearance of the rare root ער within the same verse adds further support to the suggested allusion to the biblical Er, about whom the Bible tells us exceedingly little, save for the fact that he failed to fulfill his marital obligations.

The Song's blending of the parental and marital motifs is similar to Ezek. 16, where Israel is described as an abandoned baby girl in the wilderness whom God discovers, adopts, and ultimately marries.[70] Modern scholars have noted a common motif of the foundling, and by extension drawn a literary connection between these two texts.[71] Gile's comments on a key lexical parallel strengthen the presumption of deliberate association between the two texts:[72]

> The most fascinating verbal parallel between these two passages is found at this point in the story in Deut. 32:11 and Ezek. 16:8, namely, the phrase *paras kanaf*. In Deuteronomy 32, YHWH's care for Israel is portrayed as an eagle spreading *paras* its wings *kanaf* over its young; in Ezekiel 16, when YHWH enters into a marriage covenant with Jerusalem, he spreads *paras* his garment *kanaf* over her. While spreading a garment over a woman undoubtedly refers

---

69. Cf. Ezek. 16:8; Ruth 3:9; Deut. 22:13; 2 Chron. 11:21. For a discussion on the phrase פרש כנף as a metaphor for marriage in the bible cf. Paul A. Kruger, "The Hem of the Garment in Marriage: The Meaning of the Symbolic Gesture in Ruth 3:9 and Ezek 16:8," *JNSL* 12 (1984), 79–86.

70. Hosea, which also mixes the marriage and parenthood metaphors, has likewise been noted for being deep influenced by the Song. Cf. Moshe David Cassuto, "Hosea and the Book of the Torah," *Memorial for Zvi Perez Chiyot* (Vienna: Alexander Kahat Memorial Foundation, 1933), 262–278, (Heb.).

71. Moshe Greenberg, *Ezekiel 1–20: A New Translation with Introduction and Commentary* (vol. 22, Anchor Yale Bible Commentaries; New York: Doubleday, 1983), 299–300; Gile broadens the discussion, enumerating the many parallels between the two texts by focusing primarily on patterns of thematic links and plot structures. Cf. Jason Gile, "Ezekiel 16 and the Song of Moses: A Prophetic Transformation?" *JBL* 130. 1 (2011), 87–108.

72. Ibid, p. 92.

to acquiring her in marriage (cf. Ruth 3:9), if Ezekiel is drawing
from Deuteronomy 32, then the phrase also represents an allusion
to Deut. 32:11 – a double entendre of sorts.

Er and Onan's refusal to father children with Tamar is the catalyst
for Yehudah's unwitting fulfillment of levirate marriage. Following Er
and Onan's death, Yehudah's refusal to allow his youngest son Shelah to
perform levirate marriage leaves Tamar with little choice. She disguises
herself as a prostitute and manipulates Yehudah into fulfilling his filial
obligations. As the story progresses, Yehudah's parental and marital roles
become intertwined, much like they do in the Song.

Yehudah's payment to Tamar was guaranteed by a collateral consisting
of three items: his seal, his פתיל (which BDB defines as the cord from
which the seal was hung), and his staff.[73] These items, the symbols of
Yehudah's identity and stature, ultimately turn into the symbols of his
perversion. Verse 5 in the Song compares Israel to a twisted cord, פתלתל,
a hapax stemming from the rare root פתיל.[74]

Yet his degenerate children have treated him basely, a twisted and
crooked, עיקש ופתלתל, generation! (Deut. 32:5)

The roots עקש and עשק, are both related to oppression, violence, and/
or rape.[75] In considering the story of Yehudah and Tamar, the nature of
the crimes committed against Tamar are probably best described by this
very word. Tamar was objectified, sexually violated, and oppressed by a
string of men who were morally obligated to have been her protectors.
The Song's insinuation of sexual perversion is further enhanced by the
ensuing verse:

---

73. BDB, "פתל," 836b.

74. There are only four other verses in the bible which use the root *p-t-l* to convey
    perversion. Two of the verses are near duplicates of each other (Ps. 18:27 and
    2 Sam. 22:27). Three of the verses share other unique commonalities with
    v. 5 in the Song, and are likely referencing our verse. Cf. Ps. 18:27, Pr. 8:8, Job
    5:13, 2 Sam. 22:27.

75. Warmuth, TDOT, "עשק," 11:326; Kaiser, HALOT, "עשק," p. 897. The word עשק
    connotes rape in Is. 23:12, Hos. 12:8.

Is this the way you repay the LORD, you foolish, נבל, and unwise people? (Deut. 32:6)

The word נבל used here to describe Israel's lack of wisdom, is also noted for its connotation of sexual perversion.[76]

ADMISSIONS OF GUILT CONTRASTED WITH RIGHTEOUS CONDUCT

Yehudah's affair with Tamar concludes with his bold admission of guilt:

Yehudah recognized them and said, "She is more righteous than I, צדקה ממני, since I wouldn't give her to my son Shelah." And he did not sleep with her again. (Gen 38:26)

In confessing his guilt and affirming her righteousness, Yehudah contrasts his disloyalty with Tamar's steadfastness. In the Song, Israel's guilt is contrasted with God's righteousness:

The Rock – how faultless, are His deeds, how right all His ways! A faithful God, without deceit, just and upright is He! Yet His degenerate children have treated Him basely, a twisted and crooked generation! (Deut. 32:4–5)

The description of God as blameless, תמים, is contrasted by the verse with the description of Israel as blemished, מומם. The phrase א-ל אמונה ואין עול צדיק וישר הוא conveys a straight and unwavering steadfastness, in contradistinction to Israel's twisted perfidy.

POWERFUL SYMBOLS OF DIVINE ELECTION

The patriarchal blessing to Yehudah ultimately reaffirms his absolution and bestows upon him a tangible symbol of divine favor, the "blood of grapes":

Binding his donkey to the vine, and his donkey's colt to the choice vine, He washed his garments in wine, And his clothes in the blood of grapes, דם ענב (Gen 49:11).

---

76. Marbock, TDOT, "נבל," 9:157–171, esp. 163; Cf. 2 Sam. 13:12–13 and Job 2:10, where the word נבל clearly indicates sexual perversion.

In the Song, the "blood of grapes" is also used as a potent symbol
of God's blessing:

> Butter from cows and milk from sheep, with the best of lambs;
> Bashan bulls and goats, with the cream of finest wheat; and the
> foaming blood of grapes, ודם ענב, you drank (Deut. 32:14).

These are the only two texts in the Bible where this unique phraseol-
ogy occurs. Furthermore, both texts use the phrase דם ענב in precisely the
same way, as symbols of election and blessing. This lexical allusion conjures images of Yehudah, as it points to the presence of a constellation of
allusions relating to various aspects and phases of his moral development.

RESTORATION

Both the Song and Gen. 38 conclude with the triumph of grace and
restoration. Yehudah is absolved of his iniquity, and Tamar bears him
twin sons, in effect replacing Er and Onan. Restoration is the stated
purpose of Levirate marriage:

> Then Yehudah said to Onan, "Sleep with your brother's wife and
> fulfill your duty to her as a brother-in-law to raise up offspring
> for your brother, והקם זרע לאחיך (Gen. 38:8).

Like the story of Yehudah and Tamar, Israel's sins are forgiven in the
Song, which concludes with the promise of their ultimate restoration.

THEMATIC REVIEW OF THE RELATIONSHIP BETWEEN
THE YEHUDAH AND TAMAR STORY AND THE SONG

Whereas a straightforward reading of the Song does not overtly conjure
images of the story of Yehudah and Tamar, the concentration of the
allusions to that narrative in the Song within a span of a mere eleven
verses (Deut. 32:4–14), reinforces the deliberate presence of a delicate
system of allusions beneath the surface layer.

Review of the Thematic Resonances

1. Descriptions of endemic corruption featuring the word שחת.
2. Marriage as an expression of covenantal responsibility.
3. Covenantal infidelity.

4. Entangling of marital and parental motifs.
5. Problem of לא בנים, or a lack of sons together with the play on words לא לו.
6. Undertone of sexual perversion (נבל, פתלתל, עקש).
7. Irony reflected in the word ער; protectors becoming agents of harm and disaster.
8. Abuse of potent symbols of blessing; the "blood of grapes," דם ענב.
9. Heavy stress on the contrast between righteousness and treachery.
10. Restoration.

The story of Yehudah and Tamar serves as a remarkably fitting paradigm for Israel's relationship with God throughout history. Yehudah's admission of guilt and ultimate commitment to the marriage covenant through levirate marriage with Tamar serves as the foundation of his ascendancy. Similarly, Israel's crimes of infidelity threaten to undermine their relationship with God. God's eternal love and commitment towards Israel expressed in the Song offer a similar message of promise and hope for future reconciliation.

VI The Sin of the Golden Calf and the Song

The Song's recounting of the idol-worshipping proclivities of an entire nation recalls the sin of the golden calf, paradigmatic in Deuteronomy for Israel's idolatrous tendencies (Cf. Deut. 9). Sforno understands the use of the word שחת in the Song to be a lexical indicator pointing towards the sin of the golden calf.[77] Drawing upon these observations, I will present a fuller picture of the convergent themes and terminologies which bind the sin of the golden calf together with the Song.

THE CORRUPTION OF AN ENTIRE NATION

A significant factor strengthening the presumption of a correlation between the sin of the golden calf and the Song is the corruption of the entire nation, עם. In the golden calf affair, the entire nation is implicated in the crime of corruption:

---

77. Sforno, Deut. 32:5; Tigay also points out that the word שחת, "corruption," resonates with the same term found in the golden calf affair. See Tigay, *Deuteronomy*, 301.

Then the LORD said to Moshe, "Go down, because your people, whom you brought up out of Egypt, have become corrupt, שחת" (Ex. 32:7).

Then the LORD told me, "Go down from here at once, because your people whom you brought out of Egypt have become corrupt, שחת. They have turned away quickly from what I commanded them and have made an idol for themselves" (Deut. 9:12).

The Song also incriminates the entire nation in the sins of idolatry and corruption:

They are corrupt, שחת, and not His children; to their shame they are a warped and crooked generation. Is this the way you repay the LORD, you foolish and unwise people? Is He not your Father, your Creator, who made you and formed you? (Deut. 32:5–6)

THE CULT OF THE BULL

The Song's account of Israel's idolatrous offenses includes their worship of שדים:

They sacrificed to false gods, שדים, which are not God – gods they had not known, gods that recently appeared, gods your ancestors did not fear (Deut. 32:17).

Most commentators understand the word שדים to derive from the Akkadian word for "demons," šēdu. This word had a dual meaning: either referencing a malevolent demon, or a protective spirit.[78] The etymology of the word שדים may alternatively derive from the Assyrian šēdu, "protective spirits," which were represented by the bull-colossus, often found at the entrance of Assyrian palaces.[79] These two approaches

---

78. HALOT, 'שד,' 1417. The word occurs once more in the Bible, in Ps. 106:37.

79. Driver, Deuteronomy, 362; BDB 'shed,' 993b; William James Beale, Divine Causation: A Critical Study of 'Intermediaries' (London: Macmillan, 1937), 185; William Alexander, Demonic Possession in the New Testament: Its Historical, Medical, and Theological Aspects (Eugene: Wipf and Stock, 2001), 18–19; F.H.W. Gesenius, Gesenius' Hebrew and Chaldee Lexicon of the Old Testament

to the word שדים both reference the same cognate root indicative of a protective spirit. It is likely that the Song deliberately chose the word שדים due to its unique semantic versatility. It simultaneously connotes a broad range of foreign practices of worship, while pointing specifically to Israel's treachery in the context of the sin of the golden calf.

ISRAEL'S REJECTION

God's rejection of Israel is a critical component in the narration of the golden calf affair. Israel, formerly God's special people, עם סגולה,[80] suddenly become Moshe's charge, עמך, "your (Moshe's) nation":

> Then the LORD said to Moshe, "Go down, because your people, עמך, whom you brought up out of Egypt, have become corrupt" (Ex. 32:7).

> Then the LORD told me, "Go down from here at once, because your people whom you brought out of Egypt have become corrupt, שחת עמך. They have turned away quickly from what I commanded them and have made an idol for themselves (Deut. 9:12).

Similarly, in the Song, God appears to suspend His relationship with the nation of Israel, referring to them as "non-children":[81]

> They are corrupt and not His children. לא בניו; to their shame they are a warped and crooked generation (Deut. 32:5).

RESTORATION

In the golden calf narrative, God regrets His decision to destroy Israel and reinstates them as His people:

Scriptures (tr. S.P. Tregelles;), p. DCCCV. Gesenius relates the root *shed* to the root *shoor*, to rule.

80. Ex. 19:5, Deut. 7:6, 14:2, 26:18. See *HALOT*, 'סגלה,' 742.

81. The syntax of this verse is problematic. While the Masoretes placed a *tifha* beneath the word "no," separating it from the word *banav*, "His children," others combine the two. Cf. Sanders, *Deuteronomy 32*, p. 145–146; Ibn Ezra and Nachmanides on Deut. 32:5 read the phrase as "non-children."

Then the LORD relented וינחם and did not bring on His people
לעמו the disaster He had threatened (Ex. 32:14).

The rare combination of these two roots, נחם together with עמו, also
appears in the Song, where it expresses God's change of heart and Israel's
restoration as God's special nation:[82]

> The LORD will vindicate His people עמו and relent concerning
> His servants when He sees their strength is gone and no one is
> left, He will have a change of heart, ויתנחם (Deut. 32:36).

EAGLE'S WINGS

God is compared to a נשר, an eagle, in only two places in the Bible; in
Exodus' introduction to God's revelation at Sinai, prior to the sin of the
golden calf, and in the Song's description of God's loving protection
over Israel prior to their apostasy:

> Then Moshe went up to God, and the LORD called to him from
> the mountain and said, "This is what you are to say to the descen-
> dants of Yaakov and what you are to tell the people of Israel: 'You
> yourselves have seen what I did to Egypt, and how I carried you
> on eagles' wings and brought you to Myself" (Ex. 19:3–4).

> Like an eagle that stirs up its nest and hovers over its young, that
> spreads its wings to catch them and carries them aloft (Deut.
> 32:11).

Both of these texts relate to the protection offered to Israel by
eagles' wings. In Exodus, Israel rides in safety atop the wings, and in
Deuteronomy, they are protected beneath them.

A STIFF-NECKED PEOPLE

Israel is referred to as a stiff-necked people, עם קשה עורף, seven times
in the Bible; six of these instances appear within the literary context

---

82. Ps. 135:14 contains a direct quote of Deut. 32:36. In a similarly fashion, Isa.
49:13 and 52:9 paraphrase our verse.

of the sin of the golden calf.[83] The seventh occurrence appears in the introduction to the Song in ch. 31:

> For I know how rebellious and stiff-necked you are, ואת ערפך הקשה. If you have been rebellious against the LORD while I am still alive and with you, how much more will you rebel after I die? (Deut. 31:27)

ATONEMENT, כפרה

In Exodus' account of the sin of the golden calf, Moshe attempts to atone for Israel's sin, אכפרה (Ex. 32:30). The root כפר has four different basic definitions, (to ransom, to cover, to propitiate/atone/avert, to pitch), although they are not all necessarily considered to be etymologically related.[84] Nonetheless, the similarities between the various definitions seem to have prompted word play in the Bible, often making it difficult to pin down which meaning should be applied in a particular context. The Song's closing words feature the root כפר, although the difficult syntax of the verse has challenged interpreters:[85]

---

83. Ex. 32: 9; 33:3, 5; 34:9; Deut. 9: 6, 13. Isa. 48:4 states that Israel is hard, *kashe*, and that their neck, *orpecha*, is made of iron tendons. While the phrase is highly reminiscent of the similar phrase, "a stiff-necked people," used in the Pentateuch, it appears in Yeshayahu in an entirely reconstructed format.

84. BDB, "kaphar" 497a–499a. BDB on our vs. translates the word *kaphar* to mean "propitiate."

85. 4QDt reads *vayechaper*, but this probably reflects a later stage of verbal syntax. Cf. Patrick W. Skehan, "A Fragment of the Song of Moses from Qumran," BASOR 133 (1954), 12–15. The word *vechiper* may be understood to be past, present and future tense. Cf. Paul Sanders, *Deuteronomy 32*, 253; 4QDt reads *admat ammo*, but this reading is highly suspect. The Samaritan Pentateuch agrees with 4QDt. It is possible that the LXX does as well but this is unclear. The Peshitta and Onkelos support the Masoretic reading. Cf. Sanders, *Deuteronomy 32*, 254. Most scholars believe the Qumran scribes to have modernized the form *vechiper* to read *vayechaper*. Cf. Sanders, *Deuteronomy 32*, 253. By the same token it is possible that they amended the problematic word 'admato' to read 'admat.' The phrase *admato ammo* appears to either be missing a *vav*, or to contain an extra *vav*. In other words, had it said 'admato ve-ammo' or 'admat ammo' it could either be read as 'his land and his people' or alternatively, 'the land of his people.'

Rejoice, you nations, with His people, for He will avenge the blood of His servants; He will take vengeance on His enemies and make atonement for His land and people, וכפר אדמתו עמו (Deut. 32:43).

Tur-Sinai proposes an explanation for the unusual placement of the *vav* at the end of the word אדמת.[86] He notes that the Aramaic word *adma* means "red blood," as does *dāmu* in Akkadian. The term אדמתו עמו employs an archaic poetic suffix, like that found in the Psalms 50:10, חיתו יער, beasts of the forest. In this way the verse fuses the blood and the land into one word. With this reading in mind, both the Exodus account of the golden calf affair and the Song conclude with the promise of Israel's atonement and their restoration to their land.[87]

Allusions to the sin of the golden calf in the Song are robust. The sin of the golden calf serves as archetype of Israel's idolatrous proclivities and breach of covenant on a national scale. Its inclusion in the Song's subtext underscores the dangers inherent in Israel's recidivist tendencies. The precedent that the sin of the golden calf sets for the possibility of national atonement even in cases of breach of covenant, infuses Moshe's parting words with a message of hope.

REFLECTION ON THE COMBINED EFFECT OF THE SONG'S NARRATIVE ALLUSIONS

The Song, aptly described by Fokkelman as "an extremely complex edifice,"[88] employs a cryptic compositional strategy and near inscrutable language that generate a literary smokescreen, obscuring the intricate allusions that lie beneath the surface. Quarrying the Song reveals a subtext evoking narratives of Israel's nascent development spanning the books of Genesis and Exodus; the story of creation, Adam's expulsion from Eden, the flood, the destruction of Sodom and Gomorrah, the

---

86. Cf. nt. 42.

87. The conclusion of the golden calf affair in Ex. 34:10–16 reaffirms God's commitment to instating Israel in Canaan.

88. J.P. Fokkelman, *Major Poems of the Hebrew Bible: At the Interface of Hermeneutics and Structural Analysis* (4 vols.; Assen, The Netherlands: Van Gorcum 1998), 1: 54–149, 58.

Yehudah and Tamar affair, and the sin of the golden calf. It is somewhat surprising, given the Song's extended recounting of Israel's history, that the foundational stories of the patriarchs and matriarchs are neither mentioned outright nor do they appear to be alluded to. This lacuna is further accentuated by Deuteronomy's many outright references to Israel's patriarchs.[89] What were the criteria for the incorporation of reference texts in the Song? The biblical stories that have been shown to inform the Song's subtext share a constellation of common themes which in broad strokes include the chronicling of sin, the enduring nature of God's covenant, the parameters of divine justice and the promise of restoration. The Song's systematic allusions to formative events contribute to the Song's thematic development of the evolution of sin. A close reading of Moshe's parting words prior to the Song lends insight. Deut. 29 warns lest any individual, family, or tribe succumb to the temptation of sin:

> Make sure there is no man or woman, clan or tribe among you today whose heart turns away from the Lord our God to go and worship the gods of those nations; make sure there is no root among you that produces such bitter poison. When such a person hears the words of this oath and they invoke a blessing on themselves, thinking, "I will be safe, even though I persist in going my own way," they will bring disaster on the watered land as well as the dry. The Lord will never be willing to forgive them; His wrath and zeal will burn against them. All the curses written in this book will fall on them, and the Lord will blot out their names from under heaven. The Lord will single them out from all the tribes of Israel for disaster, according to all the curses of the covenant written in this Book of the Law." (Deut. 29:17–20)

The sinners and instigators delineated in this passage range from the individual, to the clan, to the tribe, and ultimately to the entire nation. This set is directly relevant to the Song's choice of narrative allusions. Adam's sin represents the transgression of an individual while the collective sin of Yehudah, Er, and Onan, constitute the collusion of a clan.

---

89. Cf. Deut. 1:8; 6:10; 9:5, 27; 29:12; 30:20; 34:4.

Sodom and Gomorrah serve as a paradigm for the corruption of a city, while the sin in the days of Noah implicated an entire generation. The references in the Song to the sin of the golden calf broaden the focus to include the entire nation of Israel. The allusions woven into the fabric of the Song represent the full spectrum of paradigms for breach of covenant. The Song presents an overview of Israel's serial abandonment of God, alongside a portrayal of God's indefatigable love and steadfast commitment to them despite their infidelities. The Song's allusions to an array of Torah narratives recounting the evolution of sin and the possibility of repentance reinforce the Song's role as both a warning against future transgression as well as a harbinger of hope.

VII What Precisely *Is* the Song?

The Song is as majestic as it is mysterious.[90] It echoes Israel's tempestuous past as it portends their turbulent future. This however does not satisfactorily answer the question of why the Torah concludes with a recounting of past events chronicling sin, nor does it resolve our initial query; what precisely *is* the Song? If the Song is intended to be a condensed history, as has been suggested, why then were so many seminal events in Israel's history omitted from the events recounted by the text?[91]

Many scholars have noted affinities between the Song and ancient Near Eastern suzerain/vassal covenantal lawsuits, prompting them to view the Song in a similar light.[92] Others have countered this approach,

---

90. Reinforcing the mystery of the Song are its fourteen hapax legomena, and many more rare and difficult to explain words and word forms. See Driver, *Deuteronomy*, 348.

91. Cf. Fisch, *Poetry with a Purpose*, 56; Rappel, *The Song of Moses*, 12.

92. Cf. Christopher Wright, *Deuteronomy*, 297–8, esp. 40, 66–7. Wright understands the Song of Moshe to be a covenantal lawsuit with hymnic themes; Herbert B. Huffman, "The Covenantal Lawsuit in the Prophets," *JBL* 78 (1959), 285–95; W.L. Moran, "Some Reflections on the Song of Moses," *Biblica* 43 (1962), 317–27; Anthony Phillips, *Deuteronomy*, 209; J.A. Thompson, *Deuteronomy*, 296–7; Mayes, *Deuteronomy*, 380 1; Wiebe, "The Song of Moses," 119–63; Patrick D. Miller, *Deuteronomy* (IS; Louisville: John Knox Press 1990), 226; Cairns, *Deuteronomy*, 278–9; Merrill, *Deuteronomy*, 407–9; Clements, *Deuteronomy*, 526.

citing the Song's failure to mention the covenant, and its presentation of Israel's relationship with God as a father-son relationship, as opposed to that of suzerain and vassal.[93] Furthermore, it should be noted that key terminology and theology associated with covenants are conspicuously absent from the Song.[94] Moreover, whereas biblical covenant theology demands strict adherence to the tenets of the covenant, the Song is paradoxically clear that God's relationship with Israel endures irrespective of breach of covenant. Such a one-sided approach bears little resemblance to the lawsuits (i.e., covenants) of the ancient Near East, which were uncompromising about the vassal's obligations.[95] Nicholson argues persuasively that the lawsuit approach to the Song exaggerates similarities to lawsuit texts of the ancient Near East while ignoring significant differences.[96] It is worthwhile for us to consider the following excerpt in which Nicholson highlights the critical differences between the Song and ancient Near Eastern lawsuits:

> Vassals did not as a rule "love" those who conquered and dominated them, and the very language of intimate and familial relationships employed in the treaties reflects, not the reality of

---

93. Tigay, *Deuteronomy,* 509–11. Tigay further argues that heaven and earth offer no testimony in the Song, nor do they act as God's agents in enforcing the covenant.

94. Cf. Wilhelm Gesenius, *A Hebrew and English Lexicon of the Old Testament: Including the Biblical Chaldee* (trans. Edward Robinson; Boston: Crocker and Brewster, 1849) 159a. Gesenius lists the verbs associated with the concept of the covenant in the Bible. While the word עזוב does appear in the Song, it is part of a hendiadys connecting it to עזוב, which fundamentally alters its meaning. The phrase 'עצור ועזוב' does not connote the abandonment of covenant. Cf. P.P. Saydon, "The Meaning of the Expression 'עצור ועזוב'," *VT* 2 (1952), 371–374.

95. According to Lundbom "the most serious problem with the Wright *rib* thesis is that we have yet to come up with any real example of the 'lawsuit' genre." Cf. Lundbom, *Deuteronomy,* 854.

96. E.W. Nicholson, "Covenant in a Century of study Since Wellhausen," pages 54–69 in *Crisis and Perspectives: Studies in Ancient Near Eastern Polytheism, Biblical Theology, Palestinian Archeology and Intertestamental Literature: Papers Read at the Joint British-Dutch Old testament Conference, Held at Cambridge, U.K.* (vol 24 of OTS; Johannes C. de Moore ed.; Leiden: Brill, 1986), 62–3.

the relationships, but the politically, strategically and economi-
cally motivated endeavor of suzerains to maintain with the least
amount of trouble possible the subservience of subject states.
To tell Israelites that Y-ahweh "loves" them in the same way as
Ashurbanipal or Nebuchadrezzar "loves" his vassals, including
Israel, and that they are to "love" Y-ahweh as vassals "love" their
suzerains would surely have been a bizarre depiction of Y-ahweh's
love for His people and of the love with which they were called
upon to respond to him. The use in Deuteronomy and related
texts of such imagery as the "father-son" relationship, the command to "love" Y-ahweh, "to know" Y-ahweh and so forth, need
not be seen as borrowing from treaty texts. Rather it is more
plausibly explained as the result of borrowing on the part of
both treaty scribes and Biblical authors from a common and
self-evident source: the familiar settings of everyday life.... The
search for a model that will explain how the covenant functioned
in the religious and social life of ancient Israel here over-reaches
itself.[97]

Mendenhall put it well when he commented: "The poem has nothing
to do with the 'divine assembly', 'covenant renewal', 'covenant lawsuit'
(whatever that may be), cultic confession and praise and a host of other
academic clichés that have been misused in order to escape the historic
reality."[98]

Alternative directions in understanding the essence of the Song have
included categorizing it as liturgy,[99] relating it to wisdom literature,[100]

---

97. Ibid, 63.
98. G.E. Mendenhall, "Samuel's Broken Rib: Deuteronomy 32," in *A Song of
    Power and the Power of Song; Essays on the Book of Deuteronomy* (ed. Duane
    L. Christensen; Winona Lake: Eisenbrauns, 1993), 169–80, 172–7.
99. Cf. Bentzen, *Introduction to the Old Testament,* 164; Moshe David Cassuto,
    Biblical and Oriental Studies: Bible and Ancient Orient Texts (2 vols.; Jerusalem:
    Magnes Press 1975), 1:44; Aubrey R. Johnson, *The Cultic Prophet and Israel's
    Psalmody* (Cardiff: Univ. of Whales Press 1979), 150–65. Johnson believes that
    The Song of Moshe was meant to be performed; Matthew Thiessen, "The
    Form and Function of the Song of Moses," *JBL* 123 (2004), 401–24.
100. Smith, *Deuteronomy,* 342; S.R. Driver, *Deuteronomy,* 345; Levy, *The Song of*

or assuming it to be a hybrid of forms.[101] In the interest of ascertaining the precise function of the Song, I will begin with a reflection on the Song's opening statement, in which Moshe enigmatically "proclaims of the name of the Lord":

כִּי שֵׁם ה', אֶקְרָא: הָבוּ גֹדֶל, לֵא-לֹהֵינוּ.

I will proclaim the name of the LORD. O, praise the greatness of our God! (Deut. 32:3)

Beyond the naming of God as the subject, what does the seemingly innocuous phrase "proclaiming the name of God" add? This particular formulation first appears in Genesis, in the days of Enosh (Gen. 4:26), although its implications there remain unclear.[102] We encounter the phrase again in the days of Avraham and Yitzchak, who erected altars while "proclaiming the name of the Lord." There too the precise indication of the phrase is shrouded in mystery.[103] The term is once again invoked in Moshe's dialogue with God following the sin of the golden

---

Moses, 39. Levy asserts that The Song of Moshe has an uncommon function as a 'final teaching'; Von Rad, *Deuteronomy*, 200; Boston, "the Wisdom Influence," 198–202; Steven Weitzman, "A Lesson from the Dying," 377–98. Weitzman contends that The Song of Moshe is both a teaching as well as an indictment; Berry, *Wisdom and Poetry*, 209; Fokkelman, *Major Poems*, 59,143; Alphonso Groenewald, "Is. 1:2–3, Ethics and wisdom: Is. 1:2–3 and the Song of Moses: Is Isaiah a Prophet Like Moses?" *HTS* 67, 1 (2011), 1–6.

101. Wright, *Deuteronomy*, 297–8. Wright assumes the Song of Moshe to be a didactic lawsuit; Nigosian, "The Song of Moses," 5–22. Nigosian understands the Song to be a covenantal lawsuit inverted to a salvation oracle; Britt, *Rewriting Moses*, 144, 163. Britt maintains that The Song of Moshe is a didactic song with a liturgical origin; Tigay, *Deuteronomy*, 509–10. Tigay argues against the suggestion that the Song conforms to a *rib* structure. He understands the Song as serving a primarily functional purpose, bearing a similarity to didactic psalms and prophecies, which contain features of different genres.

102. Onkelos and Rashi assume the word החל to stem from חלל or "mundane," indicating the beginning of profanity or possibly idolatry. Rashbam and Ibn Ezra understands the word החל to stem from תחלה or "beginning," which would suggest that prayer began in the days of Enosh.

103. Gen. 12:8, 13:4, 21:33, 26:25. Onkelos, Rashi, and Ibn Ezra on Gen. 12:8 explain the phrase to refer to prayer. Nachmanides ad loc. suggests the phrase to mean teaching others about God.

calf. There the text provides more information that will help shed light on the implications of the phrase.

> Then the LORD came down in the cloud and stood there with him and proclaimed his name, the LORD. And he passed in front of Moshe, proclaiming, "The LORD, the LORD, the compassionate and gracious God, slow to anger, abounding in love and faithfulness, maintaining love to thousands, and forgiving wickedness, rebellion and sin. Yet He does not leave the guilty unpunished; He punishes the children and their children for the sin of the parents to the third and fourth generation." (Ex. 34: 5–7)

God's essential attributes are depicted in Exodus as embodying both compassion as well as justice. God's attributes of kindness, compassion, and graciousness, expressed specifically through the clause רחום וחנון ארך אפים, is echoed verbatim in Psalm 145:

> The LORD is gracious and compassionate, slow to anger and rich in love (Ps. 145:8).

Psalm 145 contains a dedication to God as king in its opening verse and is essentially an exposition on God's monarchic attributes as delineated in Exodus 34. The word מלך, "king," which opens the psalm is repeated five times within the text (Ps. 145:1, 11, 12, 13). Psalm 145, like the Song, also features calling out in the name of God:

> The LORD is near to all who call on Him, to all who call on Him in truth. (Ps. 145:18)

The phrase "calling out the name of God" in the Psalm expresses the idea of God as monarch together with an explanation of His monarchic attributes. In the Song as well, the phrase is immediately followed by God's attributes which are declared to be above reproach:

> He is the Rock, His works are perfect, and all His ways are just. A faithful God who does no wrong, upright and just is He (Deut. 32:4).

The implications of the phrase "proclaiming the name of God" are more far reaching than merely naming God as the subject of the poem.

Rashi refers to the *Mechilta*, which cites our verse as the source for the responsive declaration, ברוך שם כבוד מלכותו לעולם ועד, "May the name of His honored dominion be forever blessed," which was uttered upon hearing God's name within the Temple.[104] This declaration is also recited silently following the recitation of the *Shema*, the formal declaration of God's sovereignty קבלת עול מלכות שמים, (Mishnah, *Berachot* 2:2). This supports the fundamental role of the Song as a declaration of God's eternal monarchy.

Constellation of Monarchic Themes in the Song

1. EXEMPLAR OF JUSTICE

One of the primary roles of the king in the ancient world was his role as judge and exemplar of justice (Cf. 1 Kings 3:9, 16–28; Ps. 72). In the Song, God is introduced as the paradigm of pure righteousness:

> He is the Rock, His works are perfect, and all His ways are just. A faithful God who does no wrong, upright and just is He (Deut. 32:4).

The Song sharply contrasts God's justice with the corruption of men in a critique on the prevailing beliefs of the ancient Near East, in which the king was held up as paragon and source of justice.[105]

2. PROTECTOR

The Song makes repeated use of the epithet צור, rock/source of protection, when referencing God.[106] This is especially significant given the fact that the word צור appears nowhere else in the Torah as a reference to God.[107] One of the primary implications of the epithet צור is

---

104. Cf. Rashi, Deut. 32:3; *Mechilta DeRabbi Yismael, Bo, Parsha DePischa*, 16.

105. In the prologue and epilogue of the code of Hammurabi, King Hammurabi is presented as the exemplar of justice. Cf. Martha T. Roth, *Law Collections from Mesopotamia and Asia Minor Vol. IV* (ed. Piotr Michalowski; Atlanta: Scholars Press, 1995), 80–81, 133.

106. The Song refers to God as צור five times, Deut. 32:4, 15, 18, 31, 37.

107. The word צור is found numerous times in the Bible in reference to God, especially in Psalms and Yeshayahu.

protection.[108] Chief among the functions of the king in the ancient world was of course the protection of their subjects.[109] In the Song, God is the ultimate champion of the meek, exemplified by His decision to vindicate Israel specifically due to their wretched state, ואפס עצור ועזוב.[110]

3. NOBLE WARRIOR

In the ancient world, one of the primary roles of the king was that of noble warrior.[111] In the Song, God raises His weapon and pledges to take vengeance upon His adversaries:

> When I sharpen My flashing sword and my hand grasps it in judgment, I will take vengeance on My adversaries and repay those who hate Me. I will make My arrows drunk with blood, while My sword devours flesh: the blood of the slain and the captives, the heads of the enemy leaders (Deut. 32: 41–42).

4. PROVISIONER OF LAND ALLOTMENTS

One of the foremost functions of ancient Near Eastern kings was the granting of land allotments. To that end there was a complex system of regulations concerned with the management of land allotted by Hittite kings, which ensured that the king would continue to receive the mandatory services commensurate with the land allotment, regardless of change in ownership.[112] The description of God allotting land to the nations in general, and to Israel in particular, in the opening verses of the Song, points most specifically to God within the role of divine monarch:

---

108. Fabry, "צור," TDOT XII: 311–321.

109. The Code of Hammurabi, by way of example, declares Hammurabi to be protector of the land. Cf. *The Code of Hammurabi* (WS Open Library, 2018), 73.

110. Deut. 32:36. Cf. Ibn Ezra ad loc. Cf. P.P. Saydon, "The Meaning of the Expression 'עצור ועזוב'," VT 2 (1952), 371–374.

111. Cf. Sa-Moon Kang, *Divine War in the Old Testament and in the Ancient Near East* (Berlin: Walter de Gruyter, 2011).

112. Mario Liverani, *The Ancient Near East: History, Society and Economy* (Abingdon: Routledge, 2013), 264.

When the Most High gave the nations their inheritance, when He divided all mankind, He set up boundaries for the peoples according to the number of the sons of Israel. For the LORD's portion is His people, Yaakov His allotted inheritance (Deut. 32:8–9).

5. PROCLAMATIONS OF MONARCHIC ASCENSION

The ascension of a new monarch to the throne was traditionally accompanied by proclamations of "long live the king." This ancient practice may be observed with the anointment of King Saul:[113]

Samuel said to all the people, "Do you see the man the LORD has chosen? There is no one like him among all the people." Then the people shouted, "Long live the king!" (1 Sam. 10:24)

In like fashion, the Song declares God to be firmly and eternally ensconced upon the divine throne:

I lift my hand to heaven and solemnly swear: surely I live forever (Deut. 32:40).[114]

6. GENTLE RAIN UPON DELICATE VEGETATION;
A METAPHOR FOR MONARCHIC WISDOM

In the Bible, the motif of gentle rainfall that quenches the thirst of delicate plant life is a metaphor associated with the sagacious words of a wise king. This may be observed in King David's last words, in King Solomon's enthronement Psalm, and in the Solomonic aphorisms of Proverbs:

The inspired utterance of David son of Jesse, the utterance of the man exalted by the Most High, the man anointed by the God of Yaakov, the hero of Israel's songs: "The spirit of the LORD spoke through me; His word was on my tongue. The God of Israel spoke, the Rock of Israel said to me: 'When one rules over people in righteousness, when he rules in the fear of God, he is like the light of morning at sunrise on a cloudless morning, like the brightness after rain that brings grass from the earth'" (2 Sam. 23:1–4).

---

113. Cf. 2 Sam. 16:16, 1 Kings 1:25, 1 Kings 1:34, 2 Kings 11:12, 2 Chron. 23:11.
114. The translation here deviates from the NIV.

May he (Solomon) be like rain falling on a mown field, like showers watering the earth (Ps. 72:6).

A king's rage is like the roar of a lion, but his favor is like dew on the grass (Prov. 19:12).

In the LORD's hand the king's heart is a stream of water that He channels toward all who please Him (Prov. 21:1).

When a king's face brightens, it means life; his favor is like a rain cloud in spring (Prov. 16:15).

In like manner, the Song opens with a metaphor of the life-giving qualities of its dew like words upon thirsty vegetation:

Let my teaching fall like rain and my words descend like dew, like showers on new grass, like abundant rain on tender plants (Deut. 32:2).

Whereas Moshe, rather than God, appears to be the speaker here, the dew analogy, placed within the Song's introduction to God's ways of righteousness, creates a fitting setting for God's enthronement.[115]

7. THE ROYAL TREASURY

Among the various fundamental monarchic institutions is the royal treasury. Linda Manzanilla discusses the various storage mechanisms used in ancient Near Eastern royal treasuries:

Unique to the Near East is a set of independent control mechanisms, seals and seal-impressed clay locks on doors and containers. As the use of these control mechanisms change over time, they develop into a bureaucratic tool to account for – that is, audit – these movements.[116]

---

115. Cf. Saadia Gaon's introduction to his commentary on Psalms in which he argues that God himself, as opposed to Moshe, is the speaker throughout the Song.
116. Linda R. Manzanilla, *Storage in Ancient Complex Societies* (ed. Linda R. Manzanilla, Mitchell Rothman; Abingdon: Routledge, 2016), 14.

God refers to His treasury in the Song:

> Have I not kept this in reserve, כמס, and sealed it in My vaults,
> באוצרתי? (Deut. 32:34)

The words כמס is a hapax. Its appearance here parallel to אוצר, "treasure," suggests the idea of a vault. This is further supported by its Akkadian cognate *kamāsu* meaning "to collect or deposit."[117] The word אוצר in the Bible is only used within the context of either God's treasury or royal treasuries. It is interesting to note that the reference in our verse to a "seal," חתם, matches what we know about the way in which royal vaults of the ancient Near East were constructed and managed. The description here of God's sealed treasury contributes to the Song's monarchic texture.

8. DIVINITY

Whereas to a greater or lesser extent the institution of the monarchy in practically all civilizations has been considered a sacred office, the degree of monarchic deification in the ancient Near East varied from civilization to civilization.[118] Mesopotamian kings were charged with maintaining harmonious relations between the gods and humankind, although they themselves were not universally worshipped as divine beings.[119] This, however, was notably not the case in ancient Egypt, where Pharaoh was not mortal but a God. As Frankfort explains:

> This was the fundamental concept of Egyptian kingship, that
> Pharaoh was of divine essence, a god incarnate; and this view can
> be traced back as far as texts and symbols take us. It is wrong to
> speak of a deification of Pharaoh. His divinity was not proclaimed
> at a certain moment, in a manner comparable to the *consecratio*

---

117. *HALOT*, "כמס," 481.

118. Evans-Pritchard, *Social Anthropology and other Essays* (New York: The Free Press, 1962), 210.

119. Henri Frankfort, *Kingship and the Gods: A Study of Ancient Near Eastern Religion as the Integration of Society and Nature* (Chicago: University of Chicago Press, 1948), 6.

of the dead emperor by the Roman senate. His coronation was not an apotheosis but an epiphany.[120]

The Song emphatically and unequivocally declares God to be the only divinity:

> See now that I Myself am He! There is no god besides Me ... (Deut. 32:39).

9. ROYAL PARDON

One of the most fundamental powers of ancient Near Eastern monarchs was the power of royal pardon in capital cases. Whereas the law specified the cases which were deemed to be capital offenses, it was solely the king's prerogative whether to implement the punishment proscribed by the law.[121] Moshe Greenberg points out that in biblical law it was otherwise:[122]

> Here would seem to be another indication of the literalness with which the doctrine of the divine authorship of the law was held in Israel. Only the author of the law has the power to waive it; in Mesopotamia he is the king, in Israel, no man.

In the discussion earlier on the Song's analogy between Israel and other archetypes of sin, and most specifically within the analogy to Sodom and Gomorrah, the paradox of Israel's unrepentant exoneration was raised. The special status afforded Israel in the Song sharply contrasts with God's approach to other individuals and societies who were judged in accordance with their actions and held fully accountable. In the

---

120. Ibid, 5.

121. Hittite Laws 187, 188, 198, 199. In laws 187, 188 and 199 the Hittite king is given the prerogative to either execute or pardon a person who committed bestiality. Law 198 deals with the case of a husband who wishes to spare his adulterous wife. The law stipulates that it is ultimately the king's decision whether to exercise a royal pardon. Cf. Laws of Eshnunna 48, which states that capital cases are only for the king.

122. Moshe Greenberg, "Some Postulates of Biblical Criminal Law," in *Essential Papers on Israel and the Ancient near East* (ed. Frederick E. Greenspahn; New York, London: New York Univ. Press, 1991), 333–352, 338.

Song's conclusion, an impenitent Israel is inexplicably bound to God, despite their treachery. What mechanism of Divine justice might explain the anomaly of God's unmitigated love for Israel? Understanding the Song as a declamation of God's enthronement explicates this glaring inconsistency. The power to pardon Israel resides exclusively with God, the Divine King. Royal pardon is the single most palpable expression of monarchic loftiness and grace. Israel's perplexing exoneration at the Song's conclusion is an expression of and a testimony to God's absolute and eternal sovereignty.

Conclusion

While the Song is an exultation of God's monarchic ascension, it also inexorably links Israel to God throughout history. Israel's connection to God in the Song is filial; God is their Father, and they are His children (Deut. 32:5, 6, 18–20). In a similar manner to family members inheriting each other, God claims Israel as His portion and inheritance (Deut. 32:9). The unbreakable bond between God and Israel elevates Israel and places them within the immutable role of God's eternal faithful servants. This adds perspective to the Song's concluding verse describing Israel's restoration, in which they once again take their place as God's steadfast servants:

Rejoice, you nations, with His people, for He will avenge the blood of His servants; He will take vengeance on His enemies and make atonement for His land and people (Deut. 32:43).

Summary of The Songs of the Torah

Acceptance of the Kingdom of God, קבלת עול מלכות שמים

Whereas substantial portions of the Torah are written in poetic language and style, only three distinct units are explicitly referred to by the Torah itself as שירה, song. These poems – the Song of the Sea, the Song of the Well, and the Song of Moshe – together advance a core theological tenet, namely: Israel's acceptance of and commitment to God as king. The Song of the Sea celebrates the defeat of Pharaoh and the establishment of the earthly manifestation of God's realm. The Song of the Well, in its astounding brevity, resonates with the principal themes of the Song of the Sea. It too attaches itself to the idea of God as warrior as it focuses the lens on Israel's role as the object of God's compassion and munificence, which had been formally articulated only at the tail end of the Song of the Sea. This idea becomes the singular thrust of the Song of the Well. The Song of Moshe, which concludes the Torah, is an amalgam of both core ideas. It reflects upon God's sovereignty as it meditates upon Israel's irrevocable bond with God throughout history.

Despite their similar agendas, there are critical differences between the Songs of the Sea and the Well on the one hand, and the Song of Moshe on the other. Unlike the Song of the Sea and the Song of the Well which concentrate on a single "watershed" moment in the establishment of the kingdom of God, the Song of Moshe explores God's dominion throughout history, from the dawn of time and into the distant future. Furthermore, whereas the Songs of the Sea and the Well pay homage to God as king, the Song of Moshe explores the parameters of that allegiance. The Song of the Sea opens with Israel's initial acceptance of the dominion of God, as a nation:

> And when the Israelites saw the mighty hand of the LORD displayed against the Egyptians, the people feared the LORD and put their trust in Him and in Moshe His servant (Ex. 14:31).

The Song of Moshe, on the other hand, is an articulation of the consequences of the rejection of God and His Torah. It is within this framework that the Song of Moshe's reflection on the iniquities of Adam, the generation of the Flood, Sodom and Gomorrah, Yehudah and Tamar, and the sin of the Golden Calf become most directly relevant. These biblical narratives establish the paradigm for man's covenantal relationship with God. One cannot suitably extrapolate the parameters of any relationship by focusing on its successes. Mapping out the absolute contours of the Divine covenant necessitates a painstaking examination of its limits. This offers perspective on the question of why so many seminal events are glaringly absent from the historical overview presented in the Song of Moshe, such as the exodus from Egypt, the revelation at Sinai, and the dedication of the Tabernacle. These celebratory highlights from Israel's past offer scant information on the parameters of God's covenantal relationship with Israel throughout history.

The Song's use of the negative formulations לא בניו, "not His children," and לא עם, "not a nation," (Deut. 32:5, 21), raises the specter of Israel's rejection.[123] The Elephantine papyri, a collection of ancient Jewish manuscripts dating from the 5th century BCE, contain a comment that may contribute to our understanding of these difficult passages. They cite an ancient marriage formula היא אנתי ואני בעלה, "she is my wife and I am her husband." This suggests that the reverse construct in Hosea 2:4, כי היא לא אשתי ואנכי לא אשה, "she is not My wife and I am not her husband," served as the traditional divorce formula.[124] We may apply this understanding to the distinctive negative formulations in the Song noted above. Israel's willingness to accept the potentially devastating

---

123. This is based on the reading that takes Israel as the referent in these verses.
124. Cf. John Adney Emerton, *Congress Volume: Vienna, 1980, Volume 32 of Supplements to Vetus Testament* (Leiden: Brill, 1981), 122.

consequences stipulated in this agreement is an accurate measure of
their unconditional dedication and love. The reciprocal devotion between God and Israel expressed in the first two songs of the Torah is
finalized by Israel's acceptance of consequences in the third. This very
idea is reflected at the conclusion of the Song of Songs, with Shulamit's
declaration that her love and commitment is sufficiently strong enough
to withstand trials of fire and water.

> Place me like a seal over your heart, like a seal on your arm; for
> love is as strong as death, its jealousy unyielding as the grave. It
> burns like blazing fire, like a mighty flame. Many waters cannot
> quench love; rivers cannot sweep it away. If one were to give all
> the wealth of one's house for love, it would be utterly scorned
> (Song 8:6–7).

In Rabbinic parlance the halachic obligation of formally acknowl-
edging God's dominion is referred to as the "acceptance of the yoke of
heaven," קבלת עול מלכות שמים. The Sages ordained the recitation of the
Shema, שמע ישראל ה' א-להינו ה' אחד, "Hear O Israel, the Lord is our God,
the Lord is one," as the prescribed declamation of this doxa (Berachot
2:2). The Midrash boldly states, "If you are My witnesses then I am God.
But if you are not My witnesses, then I am not God," intimating that
faith in God requires more than nonverbal contemplation.[1] Bearing
witness to God's dominion demands an active, vocal declaration of
faith. It is noteworthy that a prose text was chosen for this purpose.
Whereas the daily recitation of the Shema is the designated statement of
faith and affirmation of commitment, the songs of the Torah are lyrical
responses to God's clear and present intervention throughout Israel's
unfolding history. These responsive songs reinforce the principle that
the apprehension of God's intercession in the events of the natural world
ought to inspire His praise (BT Berachot 54b). Indeed, this very idea is
formally articulated in the introductory verses of the Song of Moshe.[2]

---

1. *Midrash Tehillim* 123:2, ed. Buber.
2. The role of song as the natural response to the experience of God's involvement in the natural world is also a primary subject in the book of Psalms. Cf.
   Ps. 107, 65, 148, 150.

כִּי שֵׁם ה' אֶקְרָא הָבוּ גֹדֶל לֵא-לֹהֵינוּ:

For I will proclaim the name of the LORD; ascribe greatness to
our God! (Deut. 32:3)

Rashi notes that the Sages understood this verse to be the source
for the halachic obligation to affirm God's sovereignty, fulfilled when
declaiming: "Blessed be the name of His honorable realm forever," ברוך
שם כבוד מלכותו לעולם ועד (Rashi, Deut. 32:3). This declamation, once
recited in the Temple upon hearing the utterance of God's name, is
also the traditional response to the *Shema*, the prescribed statement for
accepting the yoke of heaven.[3] Understanding the Song of Moshe as a
celebration of Israel's acceptance of the yoke of heaven notwithstanding
all of its prospective pitfalls and caveats, explains its placement at the
summation of the Torah.

The synchronic analysis of the three songs of the Torah presented
here casts them as a loosely connected set. When examined together, the
songs of the Torah express Israel's acceptance of the kingdom of God
in response to His punctuated intervention in the affairs of mankind
throughout history. The varied paradigms of events eliciting divine
intercession offered by the three Torah songs range from the mundane
to the unusual, suggesting the possibility of physical deliverance as well
as spiritual salvation. The Song of the Sea presents a moment of rescue
from acute existential crisis, the Song of the Well articulates the steadfast
provisioning of day-to-day needs, and the Song of Moshe offers the
possibility and the promise of atonement from sin. The Torah's three
songs harmoniously convey God's unwavering commitment to Israel,
and Israel's reciprocal devotion to God their king. The responsive quality
which these three songs share underscores their fundamental role as
articulations of Israel's unconditional love for God, in demonstration
of their unmitigated acceptance of the yoke of heaven.

---

3.   BT *Pesachim* 56a, BT *Yoma* 35b, *Devarim Rabbah* (Leiberman), *Ve'etchanan*.

Torah Blessings

Torah Blessings

In addition to the three core poems of the Torah, the Torah contains a large corpus of blessing written in elevated poetic style. Like the songs of the Torah, the Torah's blessings will also be shown to function as a loosely connected set promoting a common theological agenda.

The Torah's opening verses commence with the theme of blessing. God imbues His creation with blessing (Gen. 1:22, 28, 2:3). The deluge in the days of Noah is followed with re-creation and blessing (Gen. 9:1). Noah in turn blesses (and curses) his children (Gen. 9:25–27). The theme of blessing is further developed in the stories recounting the lives of the patriarchs.[1] These poetic verses appear embedded in the prose narration of events. I have chosen to examine the larger poetic units, the Blessings of Yaakov, Bilam, and Moshe, which stand unmistakably apart from the surrounding material. The clear break which these extended blessing units make from their prose backdrops underscores their role as distinct poetic interludes. Following the threads which both distinguish and unite these blessings leads towards an appreciation for the way in which the blessings of the Torah converge with its songs in the establishment and dissemination of core Torah theology.

---

1. Gen. 12: 2–3, 22:17–18, 24:60, 26:3–5, 27:27–29, 39–40, 28:3–4, 13–15, 32:29, 35:9–12.

The Blessings of Yaakov

This chapter reinforces the structural unity of the tribal blessings of Gen. 49 by identifying the blessings' unified theme. Anomalies inherent in the blessings are also addressed, such as the curious fact that only some of the tribes are compared to animals; the question of what Yaakov's intentions were in electing both Yehudah and Yosef to the role of leader; the incongruousness of Binyamin's comparison to a ravenous wolf, given his highly passive character in the book of Genesis; and the enigmatic interruption of the blessings with a brief and seemingly unrelated prayer beseeching God for salvation. Yaakov's Blessings emerge as the foundation for future Israelite leadership through the dual institutions of the monarchy and the priesthood.

בראשית פרק מט:א–כז

וַיִּקְרָא יַעֲקֹב אֶל־בָּנָיו וַיֹּאמֶר הֵאָסְפוּ וְאַגִּידָה לָכֶם אֵת אֲשֶׁר־יִקְרָא אֶתְכֶם בְּאַחֲרִית הַיָּמִים: הִקָּבְצוּ וְשִׁמְעוּ בְּנֵי יַעֲקֹב וְשִׁמְעוּ אֶל־יִשְׂרָאֵל אֲבִיכֶם: רְאוּבֵן בְּכֹרִי אַתָּה כֹּחִי וְרֵאשִׁית אוֹנִי יֶתֶר שְׂאֵת וְיֶתֶר עָז: פַּחַז כַּמַּיִם אַל־תּוֹתַר כִּי עָלִיתָ מִשְׁכְּבֵי אָבִיךָ אָז חִלַּלְתָּ יְצוּעִי עָלָה: שִׁמְעוֹן וְלֵוִי אַחִים כְּלֵי חָמָס מְכֵרֹתֵיהֶם: בְּסֹדָם אַל־תָּבֹא נַפְשִׁי בִּקְהָלָם אַל־תֵּחַד כְּבֹדִי כִּי בְאַפָּם הָרְגוּ אִישׁ וּבִרְצֹנָם עִקְּרוּ־שׁוֹר: אָרוּר אַפָּם כִּי עָז וְעֶבְרָתָם כִּי קָשָׁתָה אֲחַלְּקֵם בְּיַעֲקֹב וַאֲפִיצֵם בְּיִשְׂרָאֵל: יְהוּדָה אַתָּה יוֹדוּךָ אַחֶיךָ יָדְךָ בְּעֹרֶף אֹיְבֶיךָ יִשְׁתַּחֲווּ לְךָ בְּנֵי אָבִיךָ: גּוּר אַרְיֵה יְהוּדָה מִטֶּרֶף בְּנִי עָלִיתָ כָּרַע רָבַץ כְּאַרְיֵה וּכְלָבִיא מִי יְקִימֶנּוּ: לֹא־יָסוּר שֵׁבֶט מִיהוּדָה וּמְחֹקֵק מִבֵּין רַגְלָיו עַד כִּי־יָבֹא שִׁילֹה וְלוֹ יִקְּהַת עַמִּים: אֹסְרִי לַגֶּפֶן עִירֹה וְלַשֹּׂרֵקָה בְּנִי אֲתֹנוֹ כִּבֵּס בַּיַּיִן לְבֻשׁוֹ וּבְדַם־עֲנָבִים סוּתוֹ: חַכְלִילִי עֵינַיִם מִיָּיִן וּלְבֶן־שִׁנַּיִם מֵחָלָב: זְבוּלֻן לְחוֹף יַמִּים יִשְׁכֹּן וְהוּא לְחוֹף אֳנִיֹּת וְיַרְכָתוֹ

111

עַל־צִידֹן: יִשָּׂשכָר חֲמֹר גָּרֶם רֹבֵץ בֵּין הַמִּשְׁפְּתָיִם: וַיַּרְא מְנֻחָה כִּי טוֹב וְאֶת־הָאָרֶץ
כִּי נָעֵמָה וַיֵּט שִׁכְמוֹ לִסְבֹּל וַיְהִי לְמַס־עֹבֵד: דָּן יָדִין עַמּוֹ כְּאַחַד שִׁבְטֵי יִשְׂרָאֵל:
יְהִי־דָן נָחָשׁ עֲלֵי־דֶרֶךְ שְׁפִיפֹן עֲלֵי־אֹרַח הַנֹּשֵׁךְ עִקְּבֵי־סוּס וַיִּפֹּל רֹכְבוֹ אָחוֹר:
לִישׁוּעָתְךָ קִוִּיתִי יְהוָֹה: גָּד גְּדוּד יְגוּדֶנּוּ וְהוּא יָגֻד עָקֵב: מֵאָשֵׁר שְׁמֵנָה לַחְמוֹ
וְהוּא יִתֵּן מַעֲדַנֵּי־מֶלֶךְ: נַפְתָּלִי אַיָּלָה שְׁלֻחָה הַנֹּתֵן אִמְרֵי־שָׁפֶר: בֵּן פֹּרָת יוֹסֵף
בֵּן פֹּרָת עֲלֵי־עָיִן בָּנוֹת צָעֲדָה עֲלֵי־שׁוּר: וַיְמָרֲרֻהוּ וָרֹבּוּ וַיִּשְׂטְמֻהוּ בַּעֲלֵי חִצִּים:
וַתֵּשֶׁב בְּאֵיתָן קַשְׁתּוֹ וַיָּפֹזּוּ זְרֹעֵי יָדָיו מִידֵי אֲבִיר יַעֲקֹב מִשָּׁם רֹעֶה אֶבֶן יִשְׂרָאֵל:
מֵאֵל אָבִיךָ וְיַעְזְרֶךָּ וְאֵת שַׁדַּי וִיבָרֲכֶךָּ בִּרְכֹת שָׁמַיִם מֵעָל בִּרְכֹת תְּהוֹם רֹבֶצֶת
תָּחַת בִּרְכֹת שָׁדַיִם וָרָחַם: בִּרְכֹת אָבִיךָ גָּבְרוּ עַל־בִּרְכֹת הוֹרַי עַד־תַּאֲוַת גִּבְעֹת
עוֹלָם תִּהְיֶיןָ לְרֹאשׁ יוֹסֵף וּלְקָדְקֹד נְזִיר אֶחָיו: בִּנְיָמִין זְאֵב יִטְרָף בַּבֹּקֶר יֹאכַל
עַד וְלָעֶרֶב יְחַלֵּק שָׁלָל:

Genesis 49:1–27

Then Yaakov called for his sons and said: "Gather around so I can tell you what will happen to you in days to come. "Assemble and listen, sons of Yaakov; listen to your father Israel. "Reuven, you are my firstborn, my might, the first sign of my strength, excelling in honor, excelling in power. Turbulent as the waters, you will no longer excel, for you went up onto your father's bed, onto my couch and defiled it. "Shimon and Levi are brothers – their swords are weapons of violence. Let me not enter their council, let me not join their assembly, for they have killed men in their anger and hamstrung oxen as they pleased. Cursed be their anger, so fierce, and their fury, so cruel! I will scatter them in Yaakov and disperse them in Israel. "Yehudah, your brothers will praise you; your hand will be on the neck of your enemies; your father's sons will bow down to you. You are a lion's cub, Yehudah; you return from the prey, my son. Like a lion he crouches and lies down, like a lioness – who dares to rouse him? The scepter will not depart from Yehudah, nor the ruler's staff from between his feet, until he to whom it belongs shall come and the obedience of the nations shall be his. He will tether his donkey to a vine, his colt to the choicest branch; he will wash his garments in wine, his robes in the blood of grapes. His eyes will be darker than wine, his teeth whiter than milk. "Zevulun will live by the seashore and become a haven for ships; his border will extend toward Sidon. "Yissachar is a rawboned donkey lying down among the sheep pens. When he sees how good is his resting place and how pleasant is his land, he will bend his shoulder to the burden and submit to forced labor. "Dan will provide justice for his people as one of the tribes of Israel. Dan will be a snake by the roadside, a viper along the path, that bites the horse's heels so that its rider tumbles backward. "I look for your deliverance, LORD. "Gad will be attacked by a band of raiders, but he will attack them at their heels. "Asher's food will be rich; he will provide delicacies fit for a king. "Naphtali is a doe set free that bears beautiful fawns. "Yosef is a fruitful vine, a fruitful vine near a spring, whose branches climb over a wall. With bitterness archers attacked him; they shot at him with hostility. But his bow remained steady, his strong arms stayed limber, because of the hand of the Mighty One of Yaakov, because of the Shepherd, the Rock of Israel, because of your father's God, who helps you, because of the Almighty, who blesses you with blessings of the skies above, blessings of the deep springs below, blessings of the breast and womb. Your father's blessings are greater than the blessings of the ancient mountains, than the bounty of the age-old hills. Let all these rest on the head of Yosef, on the brow of the prince among his brothers. "Binyamin is a ravenous wolf; in the morning he devours the prey, in the evening he divides the plunder." All these are the twelve tribes of Israel, and this is what their father said to them when he blessed them, giving each the blessing appropriate to him.

Patriarchal Blessings?

The apparent inconsistencies in Yaakov's Blessings in Gen. 49 have posed challenges for the interpreters of the text in their attempts at classifying it.[1] To begin with, although most of the tribes receive a blessing, Reuven,

---

1. An earlier version of this chapter appears in Geula Twersky, "Genesis 49: The Foundation of Israelite Monarchy and Priesthood," *JSOT*, 43.3 (2019), 317–333.

Shimon, and Levi, are recipients of what may be best described as a malediction.[2] A further difficulty in understanding the blessings, aside from the obvious problems inherent in translating the chapter's numerous hapax legomena and obscure word forms, is the lack of temporal cohesion between the blessings; whereas some of the tribal blessings recount past events, others are set in the future. These issues led some scholars, such as Peters and Heck, to the erroneous conclusion that Gen. 49 should not be viewed as blessings but rather as a compilation of tribal sayings.[3] Sarna counters that approach to Gen. 49 as an anthology of tribal sayings, by arguing that it is constructed in a cohesive chiastic format, "in a descending order of seniority," with the sons of the concubines in the center of the chiasmus. He addresses the difficulties involved in ascribing a genre to the chapter by proposing that the unit be understood not as a collection of blessings, but as a final testament.[4]

Commentators who view Gen. 49 as either a collection of blessings or a final testament don't propose that the blessings share a common literary theme.[5] In my analysis of Yaakov's Blessings, I demonstrate

---

2. Note the word ארור, "cursed," in the address to Shimon and Levi in Gen. 49:7; Pehlke addresses the negative tenor of Yaakov's messages to Reuven, Shimon, and Levi. He observes that blessings and curses are often found side by side in the biblical text. Cf. H. Pehlke, *An Exegetical and Theological Study of Genesis 49:1–28* (Th.D., Dallas Theological Seminary, 1985), 59–60.

3. Cf. J.P. Peters, "Jacob's Blessings," *JBL* 6 (1886), 99–116, esp. 113; J.D. Heck, "A History of Interpretation of Genesis 49 and Deuteronomy 33," *BS* 147 (1990), 16–31, esp. 17.

4. Nahum Sarna, *The JPS Torah Commentary: Genesis* (Philadelphia: JPS, 1989), 331. Wenham also maintains that the blessings of Gen. 49 are linked both to each other and to the wider literary context of Genesis. All of the blessings featuring Yaakov as the speaker, comment on relations between the brothers, and focus on the major actors in the Yosef and Yaakov narratives. See Gordon J. Wenham, *Genesis 1–15* (WBC 2; Waco: Word, 1994), 469–470. De Hoop adds that the blessings' general orientation toward the future contraindicates the approach to Gen. 49 as tribal sayings. See Raymond De Hoop, *Genesis 49 in its Literary and Historical Context* (Leiden, Boston: Brill, 1999), 625.

5. Eric Burrows, in *The Oracles of Jacob and Balaam* (London: Burns Oates and Washbourne, 1939), posits that each of the blessings contain a combination of onomastic and/or astral motifs, based on the Babylonian zodiac; cf. C.J.

the structural unity of the tribal blessings in Gen. 49 by identifying the blessings' unified theme. Other anomalies inherent in the blessings are also addressed, such as the curious fact that only some of the tribes are compared to animals; the question of what Yaakov's intentions were in electing both Yehudah and Yosef to the role of leader; the incongruousness of Binyamin's comparison to a ravenous wolf, in light of his highly passive character in the book of Genesis; and the enigmatic interruption of the blessings with a brief prayer (Gen. 49:18). We will begin with an examination of Yaakov's distinctive use of animal metaphors to represent the tribes.

Animal Metaphors

Gen. 49 portrays Yehudah as a lion (v. 9), Yissachar as a donkey (v. 14), Dan as a snake (v. 17), Naphtali as a deer (v. 21), and Binyamin as a wolf (v. 27).[6] At first glance, these animals appear to be a motley group, lacking in significant shared characteristics.[7] However, a closer look at the collection reveals the shared military role that these animals possess.[8]

Ball, *The Book of Genesis* (Sacred Books of the Old Testament, P. Haupt, ed; Johns Hopkins: Baltimore, London, 1896), 114ff. Ball demonstrates that the zodiac system and all of its perceived parallels to the tribal blessings could not possibly have been known before the Persian period; cf. H. Zimmern, "Der Jakobssegen und der Tierkreis," *Zeitschrift fur Asyriologie* 7 (1892), 161–172; cf. F.M. Cross and D.N. Freedman, *Studies in Ancient Yahwistic Poetry* (Baltimore: Johns Hopkins Press, 1950), 55, where it is further countered that no direct correlation exists between the two corpuses.

6.   It may perhaps be possible to infer a comparison to a bull in Yosef's blessing, Gen. 49:6, especially when keeping in mind the comparison between the two in Deut. 33:17, however this is uncertain. Cf. Yehuda Keel, *Genesis* (Daat Mikra vol. 3; Jerusalem: Mosad Harav Kook, 2003), 290, (Heb.); cf. Peters, "Jacob's Blessing", 111 and B. Vawter, "The Canaanite Background of Genesis 49," CBQ 17 (1955), 1–17, esp. 8, who adopt the 'bull' definition. While it is inconclusive if "bull" is the referent of שׁור, its clear military role in Moshe's blessings, Deut. 33:17, is certainly interesting considering the military orientation of the other animals.

7.   Cf. Burrows, *The Oracles,* who understands the animals in the blessing as Babylonian zodiac motifs.

8.   It has been suggested by some that the very difficult term בן פּרת from

THE LION

Yehudah's portrayal as a lion connotes more than just his future role as monarch. Like Bilam's description of Israel in his blessing, the sleeping lion in Yehudah's blessing conveys his latent power, which dare not be roused.

> Like a lion they crouch and lie down, like a lioness – who dares to rouse them? (Num. 24:9)

The image of the lion was a formidable power symbol in the ancient Near East.[9] Strawn writes, "It is in fact exactly the power and threat inherent in leonine image and metaphor that makes possible visions of the 'peaceable kingdom,' familiar from the Hebrew Bible."[10] The depiction of Yehudah in Gen. 49 as a lion in repose conveys his role in providing a potent military deterrence.

Yosef's blessing in Gen. 49:22 refers not to a plant but to an animal; that the word פרת is the feminine form of פרא or wild ass, cf. Vawter, "The Canaanite Background," 7. This reading was adopted by E.A. Speiser, *Genesis* (New York: Doubleday, 1981), 368; S. Gevirtz, "Of Patriarchs and Puns: Joseph at the Fountain, Jacob at the Ford," 38–39, and Sarna, *Genesis*, 344. De Hoop, however, argues that since פרת is feminine, it is most likely that it is not an adjective modifying בן, son. He concludes that "a fruit bearing bough" seems to be the most correct translation. Cf. De Hoop, *Genesis 49*, 182. Onkelos translates פורת as a grape vine, and Ibn Ezra understands it to mean a fruit-bearing tree. Keel draws attention to Ps. 80, which equates Yosef with a fruitful grape vine (*Genesis*, 322). Especially in light of Moshe's blessing to Yosef in Deut. 33:13–17, which opens with numerous references to an abundance of fruit, and Yaakov's blessing of fecundity to Yosef's children in Gen. 48:16, the traditional definition which equates פרת with flora as opposed to fauna, is preferable.

9. Numerous depictions of Ba'al riding a lion point to the lion as an ANE symbol of power. Cf. Izak Cornelius, *The Iconography of the Canaanite Gods Reshef and Ba'al: Late Bronze and Iron Age Periods* (Gottingen: Vandenhoeck & Ruprecht, 1994), 196–197, esp. 362.

10. Brent A. Strawn, *What is Stronger than a Lion? Leonine Image and Metaphor in the Hebrew Bible and the Ancient Near East* (Vol. 212 Orbis Biblicus et Orientalis; Fribourg: Academic Press, 2005), 228.

THE DONKEY

The comparison to the donkey in Yissachar's blessing brings to mind the lion from the blessing to Yehudah, as the donkey, like the lion, is squatting in repose, רובץ. Yissachar's donkey is also described as גרם, which is generally understood to mean of great bone size and strength, although the word also connotes a bone-chewing fierceness.[11] The donkey is depicted as lying between the משפתים, a rare word often translated as "saddle-baskets," based on its similarity to the Ugaritic *mtpdm* and the Arabic *maṯafid*.[12] However, others explain it as referring to sheep pens, based on the word's only other appearance, Jud. 5:16, in which Devorah ridicules Reuven for remaining in the pastures, heeding shepherds' calls instead of the clarion call to war. The context in Judges strongly suggests the word to mean "sheepfolds."[13] The donkey representing Yissachar in Gen. 49, which rests between sheepfolds, is an herbivore of immense strength. It serves as a dual symbol of terrifying power on one hand, and peace and prosperity on the other. This orientation to the donkey in Yaakov's Blessings fits well within the ancient Near East conception of donkeys, which were often depicted as a mount for the warrior headed for war, and seen as symbols of power, prestige, and military might.[14] This approach also matches the Bible's orientation to the donkey as both a symbol of peace as well as an animal closely associated with war.[15]

---

11. *HALOT*, 'גרם,' CD-ROM ed. p. 203; Bilam's blessing uses the same lexical term to describe Israel devouring the bones of their enemies, in Num. 24:8; cf. also Zeph. 3:3.

12. *HALOT*, 'משפתים,' 652; *BDB*, 'שפת,' 1052a.

13. Moshe Weinfeld, *Genesis*, (Olam Hatanach 1; Jerusalem: Revivim, 1982), p. 250, (Heb.); Ibn Ezra derives משפתים from the root שפת, explaining it to mean army encampments. Cf. Ibn Ezra and Kimchi on Isa. 26:12; Eissfeldt advocates for this definition based on archaeological findings from Transjordan. Cf. Otto Eissfeldt, "Gabelhurden im Ostjordanland," *Forschungen und Fortschrittep* 25 (1949), 8–10; idem, "Noch einmal: Gabelhurden im Ostjordanland," *Forschungen und Fortschrittep* 28 (1954), 54–56.

14. Michael Mullins, *The Gospel of Luke: A Commentary* (New York: Columbia Press, 2010), 429.

15. In der Smitten, "חמור," *TDOT* 4: 465- 470, esp. 468–469. "In war asses carried supplies and equipment in the baggage train (2 K. 7:7) and also served as mounts for soldiers (Isa. 21:7)."

Understanding the donkey from Yissachar's blessing as incorporating both the symbols of military power and of the prosperity resulting from peaceful coexistence, explicates the implied link to Yehudah's blessing, through the word רובץ, "squatting." The donkey from Zechariah's prophecy is also understood to be a symbol of humility, peace, and royalty.[16]

> Rejoice greatly, Daughter Zion! Shout, Daughter Jerusalem! See, your king comes to you, righteous and victorious, lowly and riding on a donkey, on a colt, the foal of a donkey. (Zech. 9:9)

The central role of the donkey in Israel's early monarchy,[17] and its prominent place in the prophecies heralding the Messiah in Zechariah, may be assumed to be based on the affinities between the blessings of Yissachar and Yehudah.[18]

THE SNAKE

In Dan's blessing a snake ambushes a war-horse and chariot, intimating Dan's future military prowess.

> Dan will be a snake by the roadside, a viper along the path, that bites the horse's heels so that its rider tumbles backward (Gen. 49:17).

Snakes and horses in a combative role are again linked together in Yirmiyahu; this time however, they are ironically poised against Dan:

> The snorting of his horses is heard from Dan; at the sound of the neighing of his strong ones the whole land trembles; for they are come, and have devoured the land and all that is in it, the city and those that dwell therein. For, behold, I will send serpents, basilisks, among you, which will not be charmed; and they shall bite you, says the Lord. (Jer. 8:16–17)

---

16. Clay Alan Ham, *Minor Prophets Vol. II: Nahum*-Malachi (Joplin: College Press, 2006), 332.
17. Sam. 9:3ff. 1 Kg. 1:33, 38.
18. Ham, *Minor Prophets*, 469.

Snake images in the Levant often were depicted in combat.[19] In a number of images they appear together with lions. Amos describes another terrifying attack of snakes and lions on the day of the Lord.

> Woe to you who long for the day of the LORD! Why do you long for the day of the LORD? That day will be darkness, not light. It will be as though a man fled from a lion only to meet a bear, as though he entered his house and rested his hand on the wall only to have a snake bite him (Amos 5:18–19).

The correlation between snakes and lions is also made evident by the appearance in Psalms of the word שחל, "lion," in a hendiadys together with the word פתן, "viper," and then again with the coupling of כפיר, "lion," and תנין, "snake." The word שחל may connote a composite of both creatures.[20]

> You will tread on the lion, שחל, and the cobra, פתן; you will trample the great lion, כפיר, and the serpent, תנין (Ps. 91:13).

Dan's appearance as a lion in Moshe's blessing and as a serpent in Yaakov's blessing is especially interesting in light of the military association between these two animals.

> About Dan he said: "Dan is a lion's cub, springing out of Bashan" (Deut. 33:22).

Gevirtz notes that the word בשן, which appears in Moshe's blessing to Dan, in which Dan is compared to a lion cub, intimates the word פתן, serpent.[21] The military association of the snake in Yaakov's blessing to Dan is reinforced by the presence of the lion image close by in his blessing to Yehudah. Whereas Yehudah's blessing conveys passive strength, Dan's blessing expresses offensive might.

---

19. Anselm C. Hagedorn and Andrew Mein *Aspects of Amos: Exegesis and Interpretation* (Edinburgh: A&C Black, 2010), 97.

20. Botterweck, "ארי," *TDOT* 1:374–388, esp. 377.

21. S. Gevirtz, "Adumbrations of Dan in Jacob's Blessing on Judah," *ZAW* 93 (1981), 21–37, esp. 30.

THE DEER

Yaakov's blessing to Naphtali has challenged biblical interpreters, who struggled to relate the second half of the verse speaking of "goodly words," אמרי שפר, with the first half of the verse describing a fleet footed deer, אילה שלוחה.[22]

The Septuagint renders the verse as a plant bearing beautiful produce.[23] This interpretation is based on reading the word אילה, as a tree, אלה, which sends out, שלוחה,[24] its fruit laden branches, אמרי שפר, derived from the rare meaning of אמר as "branch."[25] When the word אילה is interpreted as an animal as opposed to a plant, then the term אמרי שפר is assumed to be either pleasant words,[26] or horned fawns.[27] This reading is supported by the Aramaic *immera* meaning "lamb," the Akkadian cognate *immeru*, and the Ugaritic *imr*, meaning "sheep."[28] Gevirtz understands the word שלוחה, generally translated as "sent," to mean in this case "calved, or given birth to," based on its similar usage in Job.[29]

Naphtali's military association is reinforced by the text describing his birth, where his name signifies wrestling, and by the commendation he receives in the Song of Deborah for his performance on the battlefield.[30]

---

22. Gerhard von Rad comments that "The saying about Naphtali can scarcely be interpreted by us anymore," *Genesis, Revised Edition: A Commentary* (OTL; Louisville: Westminster John Knox Press, 1973), 427.

23. John William Wevers, *Notes on the Greek Text of Genesis*, (Septuagint and Cognate Studies Series 35; Atlanta: Scholars Press, 1993), 831.

24. Cf. Ps. 80:12 and Ezek. 17:6, 7, where the word שלח has this very connotation.

25. *HALOT*, 'אמיר,' 63. See also Isa. 17:9.

26. Cf. Prov. 22:21, which supports this reading.

27. *HALOT*, 'שפר,' 1635.

28. Cf. Stanley Gevirtz, "Naphtali in the Blessing of Jacob," *JBL* 103.4 (1984), 513–521. Gevirtz finds further support for this reading of אמרי שפר from the Akkadian *immir supüri* meaning "sheep of the fold," 516.

29. Ibid, 519. Cf. Job 21:10–11, 39:1–3. Gevirtz further explains that נתן, to give, may be used in the sense of 'giving birth' as in Isa 9:5, "a child is born (יולד) to us, a son is given (נתן) to us," cf. 520.

30. The Song of Devorah is assumed to correlate closely with Yaakov's blessings. Cf. Adele Berlin, Marc Zvi Brettler, Michael A. Fishbane, *The Jewish Study Bible* (JPS; Oxford: Oxford Univ. Press, 2004), 96; Moshe Weinfeld, "The

Then Rachel said, "I have wrestled mightily with my sister, and I have won." So she named him Naphtali (Gen. 30:8).

The people of Zebulun risked their very lives; so did Naphtali on the terraced fields (Jud. 5:18).

The roots אמר and שפר in אמרי שפר, used here to describe the actions of deer, occur together only once more in the Bible, and that appearance is in Job, also in a military context. The word combination is used there in a description of the sound of battle trumpets:

At the blast of the trumpet (שפר) it snorts (יאמר), "Aha!" It catches the scent of battle from afar, the shout of commanders and the battle cry (Job 39:25).

The deer's military orientation in the Bible is reinforced by Samuel's comparison of the light-footed warrior Asahel to a deer, and by King David's description of his own military performance as that of a swift hind.

The three sons of Zeruiah were there: Joab, Abishai, and Asahel. Now Asahel was as fleet-footed as a wild gazelle (2 Sam. 2:18).

He makes my feet like the feet of a deer; he causes me to stand on the heights (2 Sam 22:34).

Testimony to the deer's military role in the ancient Near East may be observed in Resheph, the God of battle, whose trademark cap sported deer horns.[31] Furthermore, it has been suggested that a Phoenician-Luwian text which attributes the epithet *sprm* to Resheph, understood by some to be referring to צפרים, birds, may also be understood as describing deer, as in שופר, horn, or possibly to the hart, as in עפר.[32]

Davidic Empire: Realization of the Promise to the Patriarchs," pages 87–92 in *Eretz Israel* 24 (Jerusalem Exploration Society, 1993). In the Song of Deborah, Jud. 5:18, Naphtali is described gallivanting upon mountaintops, the natural habitat of deer.

31. Mulder, "רשׁף," *TDOT* 16:10–16.

32. Cf. Maria J. Lopez-Grande, "Winged Reshep: Egyptian Iconographic Evidence," *Egyptology at the Dawn of the Twenty-first Century: History Religion:*

Polysemy is one of the hallmarks of biblical poetry. Peters comments that "on the whole, the best example of a sustained playing upon words which I have observed in the Old Testament is the so-called Blessing of Yaakov."[33] While Naphtali's blessing in Genesis appears to be military oriented, that is not to the exclusion of the alternative suggestions, which propose that the blessing refers to either bountiful fruits or ewe-bearing fawns. The inherent tension between the different renderings of the verse may explain the lack of gender agreement between the feminine word אילה, "doe," and the masculine, הנותן, "to give." Whereas the word הנותן presupposes that the deer is a stag, which complements the battlefield orientation of the verse, the feminine אילה connotes the bearing of offspring. These renderings will be reassessed later, in the analysis of the overarching theme of the Blessings.

THE WOLF

Binyamin's description as a wolf lying in wait ready to attack its unsuspecting prey indicates that Binyamin will overcome his enemies militarily.[34]

> Binyamin is a ravenous wolf; in the morning he devours the prey,
> in the evening he divides the plunder (Gen. 49:27).

The military indication of the wolf may be observed again in Habakkuk, where the horses of the Chaldean army are compared to wolves (Hab. 1:6, 8).

> I am raising up the Babylonians, that ruthless and impetuous
> people, who sweep across the whole earth to seize dwellings not

---

Proceedings of the Eighth International Congress of Egyptologists (ed. Zahi Abass Hawass; 3 vols; Cairo: American University in Cairo Press, 2000), 2: 389–395, esp. 392; R. Donner, "רשף," *HALOT* 1297–1298 esp. 1297. Cf. Manfred Cassirer, "A Scarab with an Early Representation of Resheph," *The Journal of Egyptian Archaeology* 45 (1959), 6–7, who brings evidence of a winged Resheph on an Egyptian scarab.

33. Peters, "Gen. 49," 99; cf. also Gary A. Rendsburg, "Double Polysemy in Genesis 49:6 and Job 3:6," *CBQ* 44.1 (1982), 48–51.

34. Binyamin is depicted as a warlike tribe in the story of the concubine in Jud. 19–20 when twice Binyamin alone waged war and defeated all the other tribes.

their own. They are a feared and dreaded people; they are a law to themselves and promote their own honor. Their horses are swifter than leopards, fiercer than wolves at dusk. Their cavalry gallops headlong; their horsemen come from afar. They fly like an eagle swooping to devour (Hab. 1:6–8).

In the Bible, when the lion is cast as a symbol of power, as it is in Yaakov's blessing, the wolf often appears close by. Zephaniah and Yechezkel linked images of lions and wolves in their reprimand of the officials of Jerusalem who abused the power invested in them.

Woe to her who is rebellious and defiled, the oppressing city! She listens to no voice; she accepts no correction. She does not trust in the LORD; she does not draw near to her God. Her officials within her are roaring lions; her judges are evening wolves that leave nothing till the morning. Her prophets are fickle, treacherous men; her priests profane what is holy; they do violence to the law (Zeph. 3:1–4).

And the word of the LORD came to me: "Son of man, say to her, You are a land that is not cleansed or rained upon in the day of indignation. The conspiracy of her prophets in her midst is like a roaring lion tearing the prey; they have devoured human lives; they have taken treasure and precious things; they have made many widows in her midst. Her priests have done violence to my law and have profaned my holy things. They have made no distinction between the holy and the common, neither have they taught the difference between the unclean and the clean, and they have disregarded my Sabbaths, so that I am profaned among them. Her princes in her midst are like wolves tearing the prey, shedding blood, destroying lives to get dishonest gain (Ezek. 22:23–27).

Yeshayahu prophesied about a future time when lions and wolves would no longer sow terror.

The wolf shall dwell with the lamb, and the leopard shall lie down with the young goat, and the calf and the lion and the fattened

calf together; and a little child shall lead them. The cow and the
bear shall graze; their young shall lie down together; and the
lion shall eat straw like the ox. The nursing child shall play over
the hole of the cobra, and the weaned child shall put his hand
on the adder's den. They shall not hurt or destroy in all My holy
mountain; for the earth shall be full of the knowledge of the LORD
as the waters cover the sea (Isa. 11:6–9).

The wolf and the lion also experience a change of character in the
ancient Sumerian cosmological myth of Enki and Ninhursag, in the
paradise of Dilmun, where "the lion kills not, the wolf snatches not the
lamb...."[35]

The shared military orientation of the animal metaphors in Yaakov's
Blessings points to their interconnected role and to the likelihood of a
shared literary theme between the blessings. Yaakov's remarks to Shimon
and Levi alluding to the massacre at Shechem provide the first clue in
the quest for the blessings' common theme.

The Massacre at Shechem

The consensus among classical and modern interpreters of the text is
that Yaakov's rebuke of Shimon and Levi refers back to their role in the
massacre at Shechem in Gen. 34.[36] The appearance of the hapax מכרתיהם
in these verses provides a strong thematic link to the massacre.[37] The
word מכרתיהם likely derives from the verb כרת, "to circumcise," rendering
מכרת as meaning "circumcision blade."[38] This interpretation is well

---

35. S.N. Kramer, *Enki and Ninhursag* (BASOR Sup. 1, New Haven: American
Schools of Oriental Research, 1945), 11, lines 13–17.

36. Cf. De Hoop, *Gen. 49*, 99 nt. 104; cf. also Rashi and Ibn Ezra on Gen. 49:5.

37. A comprehensive table charting the history of interpretation of the word
מכרתיהם is provided by Aaron J. Koller in *The Semantic Field of Cutting Tools
in Biblical Hebrew: The Interface of Philological, Semantic, and Archaeological
Evidence* (CBQ monograph series 49; Washington, D.C.: The Catholic Biblical
Association of America, 2012), 249.

38. Mitchell Dahood, "MKRTYHM, in Genesis 49, 5," CBQ 23 (1961), 54–56; cf. M.
Cohen, "*mekerotehem* (Genese XLIX 5)", VT 31 (1981), 472–482, esp. 474–475,
for examples of words which have a 'מ' pre-formative added, which is often
used to form names of instruments, without affecting the consonants.

substantiated by the context which strongly suggests an instrument of violence.[39] Koller discusses the specific use of this rare word connoting a scalpel in the blessing of Shimon and Levi:[40]

> In condemning Shimon and Levi, Yaakov uses a rare word that captures three themes of their act simultaneously: they replaced circumcision and covenant with cutting, all *krt*.

Interpreting the diatribe to Shimon and Levi against the backdrop of the slaughter at Shechem is complicated by the fact that our verse speaks of an individual, איש and a bull, שור; however, the singular term איש may also be understood as a having a plural connotation. (Singular forms in the Bible are sometimes used for referencing a larger group. For example איש in Gen. 32:7 references an army of men). Kimchi quotes Yaakov ben Elazar who explains the bull to be synonymous with "prince," who in this case was quite literally חמור, which also means "donkey." The bull's use in Ugaritic texts to connote a prince confirms this interpretation.[41] The correlation between the donkey and the bull is further reinforced by their appearance as a pair throughout the Bible.[42] Allusions in Shimon and Levi's "blessing" to חמור, the prince of Shechem, and to the public circumcision turned massacre which transpired there, are reinforced by the repetition of the same key elements in the subsequent blessings of the rest of the sons of Leah: Yehudah, Zevulun, and Yissachar.

To review, the three essential themes from the massacre perpetrated by Shimon and Levi, and which reverberate in the subsequent blessings to the sons of Leah, include שכם the name of both the city and its prince (as well as meaning the upper portion of the back); חמור, the father of שכם (in addition to meaning a donkey); and circumcision, which was perverted by Shimon and Levi as a ruse for carnage. I will now examine

39. Cf. C. Westermann, *Genesis. 3. Teilband: Genesis 37–50* (BKAT, 1/3, Neukirchen-Vluyn: Neukirchener Verlag, 1982), 37–50, 255.

40. Aaron J. Koller, *The Semantic Field of Cutting Tools in Biblical Hebrew*, p. 247.

41. B. Vawter, "The Canaanite Background of Genesis 49," CBQ 17 (1955), p. 1–17, esp. 4; P.D. Miller, "Animal Names as Designations in Ugaritic and Hebrew," *Ugarit Forschungen* 2 (1970), 177–186, esp. 178–179, 185.

42. Cf. Deut. 22:11; Gen. 32:6, (32:5 English); Isa. 1:3, 32:20.

the blessing cluster of the rest of Leah's sons, Yehudah, Zevulun, and Yissachar, as a cohesive unit.

The Monarchic Blessings

The blessings to Yehudah and Yissachar both highlight the role of the donkey:

> He will tether his donkey to a vine, his colt to the choicest branch; he will wash his garments in wine, his robes in the blood of grapes (Gen. 49:11).

> Yissachar is a rawboned donkey lying down among the sheep pens (Gen. 49:14).

Yissachar's blessing also features the word שכם, "shoulder."

> When he sees how good is his resting place and how pleasant is his land, he will bend his shoulder to the burden and submit to forced labor (Gen. 49:15).

Yehudah's blessing oddly refers to his future progeny as issuing "from between his feet," meaning his loins; the anatomical place of the circumcision:[43]

> The scepter will not depart from Yehudah, nor the ruler's staff from between his feet, until he to whom it belongs shall come and the obedience of the nations shall be his (Gen. 49:10).

The blessing of Zevulun, which immediately follows Yehudah's blessing, features the word ירך, "inner thigh," in a description of Zevulun's coastal territory.[44]

> Zebulun will live by the seashore and become a haven for ships; his border will extend toward Sidon (Gen. 49:13).

---

43. The term בין רגליו, between his loins, an expression connoting the area of the genitals, is attested to by the expression's only two other appearances in the Bible. Cf. Deut. 28:57 and Jud. 5:27. The awkwardness of the expression is probably what led to its emendation in the Samaritan text as דגליו 'his standards or banners'. Cf. De Hoop, *Genesis 49*, 140, nt. 340.

44. *HALOT*, "ירך," 439.

The term יָרֵךְ is a common metaphor for the "spur" of a mountain,[45] and the land strip along the coast does have the appearance of a thigh.[46] Nonetheless, its usage in Zevulun's blessing, sandwiched between Yehudah and Yissachar's blessings which reference both שכם and חמור, and its close proximity to Yehudah's blessing which also contains an unmistakable reference to his loins, suggests that the hint to Zevulun's groin is not accidental.

The linking of verses to each other through the repetition of a common word or phrase is a hallmark of biblical poetry.[47] This phenomenon may be observed throughout Yaakov's Blessings in the following cases: The word עַז, "strength," repeats consecutively in Reuven's, Shimon's, and Levi's blessings/condemnations (Gen. 49:3, 7); the word עָקֵב, "heel," repeats successively in Dan and Gad's blessings (Gen. 49:17, 19); and the verb נָתַן, "to give," repeats in Asher and Naphtali's blessings (Gen. 49:20, 21). Given the multiple instances of lexical repetition in Yaakov's Blessings, the appearance of a term connoting the loins in the blessing to Zevulun, immediately following Yehudah's blessing containing a synonymous expression, may be assumed to be a deliberate allusion to the groin and to circumcision.

The blessings beginning with Shimon and Levi, and concluding with Yissachar, allude to three fundamental leitmotifs associated with the massacre at Shechem: שכם, חמור, and the ברית, circumcision. While Yaakov lays the blame for the massacre on Shimon and Levi, the tribes of Yehudah, Zevulun, and Yissachar did not participate in the carnage. They are rewarded here for transcending the desire for revenge and refraining from perversion of the covenant. Yehudah merits a position of leadership while Yissachar and Zevulun are charged with sharing the responsibility of underwriting the expenses of the future Judean monarchy; as insinuated by their blessings' collective focus on trade and wealth, as well as the direct reference in Yissachar's blessing to the

---

45. De Hoop, *Genesis 49*, 150.

46. Keel, *Genesis*, 304.

47. Cf. Adele Berlin, "On the Interpretation of Psalm 133," pages 141–147 in Elaine Follis, *Directions in Biblical Hebrew Poetry* (Edinburgh: A&C Black, 1987); Amos Hakham, *Psalms* (Daat Mikra 2; Jerusalem: Mosad Harav Kook, 1981), 438, (Heb.).

payment of tribute.[48] The close connection between Zevulun's and Yissachar's blessings is reinforced by Moshe's linkage of the two in his blessings.

> And of Zevulun he said, "Rejoice, Zevulun, in your going out, and Yissachar, in your tents" (Deut. 33:18).

The election of Yehudah to the monarchy, and the supportive role played by Zevulun and Yissachar appears to be contradicted by the subsequent designation of Yosef as נזיר אחיו, prince of his brothers (Gen. 49:26).

> Your father's blessings are greater than the blessings of the ancient mountains, than the bounty of the age-old hills. Let all these rest on the head of Yosef, on the brow of the prince among his brothers (Gen. 49:26).

I will begin my investigation into this inconsistency with an examination of the priestly role conferred upon Yosef in his blessing.

Yosef the Prince/Priest

In addition to being referred to as a נזיר, "prince," the sheer length of the blessing to Yosef (v. 22–26), indicates that Yosef's blessing is parallel to Yehudah's (v. 8–12); both receive a "lion's share" of the blessings.[49] Some

---

48. Some scholars assume Issachar's blessing to be describing his subjugation to the Canaanites. Cf. M. Noth, *The History of Israel* (New York: Harper, 1958), 78–79; Skinner, *Genesis* (ICC; Edinburgh: T & T Clark, 2nd ed, 1930), 526; S.I. Feigin, "*Hamor Garim*, Castrated Ass," *JNES* 5 (1946), 230–233; Heck argues that the blessing to Issachar describes his hard-working character, not his enslavement. Cf. Joel Heck, "Issachar: Slave or Freeman? (Gen. 49: 14–15)," *JETS* 29.4 (1986), 385–396.

49. Cf. Karin Schopflin, "Jakob Segnet Seinen Sohn: Genesis 49:1–28 im Kontext von Josefs- und Vatergeschichte," *ZAW* 115 (2003), 501–523. Schopflin believes that the tension between the election of Yehudah and Yosef in Gen. 49 are vestiges of older versions of the story in which either Yosef or Yehudah was elected; cf. also de Hoop, *Genesis 49*, 568–581, who argues that the original text included only Yosef's blessing. Sparks argues that the close relationship between the tribal lists in Gen. 49 and Deut. 33 indicates otherwise. Cf. Kent

have suggested that given the fundamental definition of the word נזיר as "withdrawn from normal usage or singled out",[50] then Yosef's description as נזיר אחיו is a reflection of the brothers' attempt to dispose of him.[51] This interpretation isn't compelling – as both our verse, and Moshe's blessing to Yosef – twice reference the top of Yosef's head, ראש, and קדקד, relating directly to Yosef's role as a crowned prince.[52]

> Let all these rest on the head of Yosef, on the brow of the prince among his brothers (Deut. 33:16).

The Akkadian cognate *qaqqadu* meaning "crown," lends further support to the insinuation of election as opposed to rejection.[53] Yosef's leadership role is expressed through service and divine blessing, in what has been referred to as "a hint of kingship."[54] The book of Chronicles corroborates the dual leadership roles that Yaakov confirms on Yehudah and Yosef.[55] The blurring of the roles of the king and the priest was a common phenomenon in the ancient world, and may be observed in Genesis' recounting of Avraham's meeting with Melchizedek, king of Salem and priest to El-Elyon (Gen. 14:18).

The term נזיר connotes an affinity with the spiritual function of the priesthood, made evident through the many restrictions which they share.[56] While the Bible never uses the term נזר in the description of

---

Sparks, "Genesis 49 and the Tribal List Tradition in Ancient Israel," ZAW 115.3 (2003), 327–347, esp. 335.

50. G. Mayer, TDOT "נזר," 9: 306- 311, esp. 307; J. Kuhlewein, "'נזיר' *nazir*, Geweihter," THAT, Bd. II, 50–53, esp. 50.

51. De Hoop, *Genesis 49*, 217.

52. HALOT, "נזר," p. 684; Moshe adds the imagery of horns which represent the two princes Ephraim and Menashe in Deut. 33:17.

53. *The Assyrian Dictionary of the Oriental Institute of the University of Chicago* (CAD), 13: 100–106.

54. Cf. Kristin Swenson, "Crowned with Blessings: The Riches of Double-Meaning in Gen. 49, 26b," ZAW 120 (2008), 423.

55. Cf. 1 Chron. 5:1–2; cf. P.J. Williams, "The LXX of 1 Chronicles 5:1–2 as an Exposition of Genesis 48–49," *Tyndale Bulletin* 49 (1998), 369–371. Williams proposes that the LXX in Chron. 5:1-2 was influenced by Gen. 49.

56. Cf. Mayer, "נזר", p. 309; Also, the diadem of the high priest in the Bible is called a נזר, cf. Ex. 29:6.

kings, it is used five times in the Pentateuch to describe aspects of the priesthood.[57]

Yosef and the Mountain-Temple

One of the most fundamental architectural symbols in the ancient world and in the Bible was the "mountain-temple," which was integrally connected to the institution of the priesthood, and whose primary context was the temple. The theme of the "mountain-temple" is elaborated upon in Yeshayahu's utopian vision of God's holy mountain.[58]

> In the last days the mountain of the LORD's temple will be established as the highest of the mountains; it will be exalted above the hills, and all nations will stream to it. Many peoples will come and say, "Come, let us go up to the mountain of the LORD, to the temple of the God of Yaakov. He will teach us his ways, so that we may walk in his paths. The law will go out from Zion, the word of the LORD from Jerusalem (Isa. 2:2–3).

The "mountain-temple" motif plays a significant role in Yaakov's blessing to Yosef, which references גבעת עולם alongside Yosef's appellation as נזיר.

> Your father's blessings are greater than the blessings of the ancient mountains, than the bounty of the age-old hills, גבעת עולם (Gen. 49:26).

The phrase גבעת עולם, commonly rendered "age-old hills,"[59] recurs in Moshe's blessing to the tribe of Yosef in Deuteronomy, and again in Habakkuk's theophany (Hab. 3:6). In Genesis, Avraham refers to God as א-ל עולם, thereby linking the deity with עולם (Gen. 21:33). The word עולם by itself may be used as an appellation of the deity, even when not

---

57. Cf. Ex. 29:6; 39:30; Lev. 8:9; 21:12; 22:2.
58. Barker discusses the significance of this theme in the Bible. Cf. Margaret Barker, "Isaiah," pages 489–542, esp. 499 in *Eerdmans Commentary on the Bible* (James Dunn and John W. Rogerson eds.; Grand Rapids: Eerdmans, 2003).
59. Cf. JPS trans. Gen. 49:26.

associated with א‑ל.[60] The phrase זרועות עולם may then be understood
to be referring to the arms of God.[61] The Talmud supports the approach
to עולם as a divine epithet.[62] This understanding of the term גבעת עולם
associates God's holy mountain, or mountain temple, with Yosef.

Support for the term גבעת עולם as "the mountain of God" may be
gleaned from its reappearance in Moshe's blessing to Yosef, where it
appears positioned parallel to הררי קדם.

> And for the tops of the ancient mountains, and for the precious
> things of the everlasting hills, גבעות עולם (Deut. 33:15).

While the most straightforward, geographical understanding of הררי
קדם is the Bashan mountain range located to the north-east of Yosef's
land allotment,[63] it is significant that the Bashan mountain range is
referred to elsewhere as הר הא‑להים, mountain of God (Ps. 68:16). The
correlation between גבעת עולם and הררי קדם / הר הא‑להים, lends further
support to the understanding of גבעת עולם as the mountain of God.

In addition to the geographical connotations of the word קדם, it
also has several theological focal points. קדם is noted for its primeval
undertones, and Eden-esque nuances.[64] It appears as a locational marker
for the Garden of Eden (Gen. 2:8), and for the gates east of Eden where
the cherubim were placed (Gen. 3:24). The word קדם also plays a fundamental role in temple-related texts. It repeatedly appears in instructions
regarding the Tabernacle, and is mentioned frequently in relationship

60. A. Van Den Branden, "Les Dieux des Patriarches," *Bibbia e Oriente* 162 (1990),
27–53, esp. 36.

61. Cf. Deut. 33:27; A. De Pury does not consider Olam to be a divine name, as
it does not appear in the pantheons of the ancient Near East. This reason
is not sufficient to discount the suggestion of Olam as a divine epithet. Cf.
A. De Pury, "El-Olam," pages 288- 290, esp. 389 in *Dictionary of Deities and
Demons in the Bible* (K. Van Der Toorn, B. Becking and P. Van Der Horst
eds.; Leiden, Boston, Koln: Brill, 1999).

62. Cf. BT *Hagigah* 12b, where the Sages attribute storms to the hands of God
based on the words ומתחת זרעת עולם in our verse.

63. Yehuda Keel, *Genesis* (Daat Mikra vol. 3; Jerusalem, Mosad Harav Kook,
2003), 329 (Heb.).

64. *HALOT* "קדם," 1070.

to the Temple service.[65] Yechezkel's vision of the Temple in Jerusalem highlights the word קדם, from the easterly wind which transported God's glory away from Jerusalem, to the eastern gate of the Temple through which Yechezkel enters the Temple and approaches the holy of holies.[66] Bilam's association with הררי קדם contributes to the term's theophanic tenor (Num. 23:7). God Himself is linked with קדם in the appellation א־להי קדם (Deut. 33:27), and by the psalmist's description of God's abode in קדם (Ps. 55:20, 68:34). The juxtapositioning of the terms קדם and עולם in Moshe's blessing to Yosef further supports the "divine mountain temple" understanding of the phrase גבעת עולם, contributing to the priestly texture of Yaakov's blessing to Yosef.[67]

Priestly Undertones in the Life of Yosef

Undertones of Yosef's election to a priestly station are not exclusive to the blessings of Yaakov and Moshe. Numerous undercurrents may be observed throughout the Yosef narratives associating him with the priesthood. To begin with, Yaakov provides Yosef with a כתנת, a full body tunic,[68] which is also among the primary vestments of the Temple priests.[69] When the brothers later disrobe Yosef, the word ויפשיטו, "shed," is used (Gen. 37:23). The verb פשט occurs throughout the Bible in connection with the transfer of office.[70] For example, God orders Moshe to strip Aharon of his vestments, הפשט, (*p-sh-t, hiphil*), before his death and to put them on his oldest son, Elazar (Num. 20:26). The rest of the occurrences of the verb פשט in the Torah describe either the removal of

---

65. Kronholm, "קדם," *TDOT* 12: 505- 511, esp. 508.

66. Kronholm, "קדים," *TDOT* 12: 501–505, esp. 502.

67. It is relevant that whereas God's name is not mentioned in any of the other tribal blessings, it appears several times in Yosef's blessing; Gen. 49:25, vs. 24 may also be understood as twice referring to God. (God's name in v. 18, following Dan's blessing is considered by the classical interpreters of the text to be a prayerful interruption, while Bible critics generally view it as a gloss. Cf. Keel, *Genesis*, 314 and De Hoop, *Genesis 49*, 169.)

68. The כתנת appears five times in the Yosef story. Cf. Gen. 37:3, 23, 31, 32, and 33.

69. The Sages link Yosef's coat with the priestly vestments in BT *Zevachim* 88b, *Midrash Rabbah Gen.* 37:3, and BT *Arachin* 16a.

70. Schmoldt, 'פשט,' *TDOT* 12, 129–133, esp. 130.

the hide from sacrificial offerings or the shedding of priestly vestments, further bolstering the connection between Yosef and the priesthood (Cf. Lev. 1:6, 6:4, and 16:23).

Another key theme in the Yosef story is his role as interpreter of dreams. The role of priests in interpreting dreams in ancient Egypt is recorded in hieroglyphic inscriptions.[71] Diviners in the ancient world were typically priests. Similarly, the Urim and the Thummim worn by the High Priest in the Temple had a divining function. Yosef himself asserts in a fascinating disclosure, that it should be presumed that a man of his elevated stature in Egypt would practice divination.[72] Yosef's declaration that he is a God-fearing man adds weight to the presumption of his priestly station (Gen. 42:18). Yosef's entrance into the Egyptian priestly class through his marriage to Osnat, the daughter of the high priest of On, further raises the speculation of his priestly status (Gen. 41:50). Additionally, the term עומד לפני, "standing before," used to describe Yosef's administrative function in the royal court, points to his priestly role.

> Yosef was thirty years old when he entered the service of Pharaoh, בעמדו לפני פרעה, king of Egypt. And Yosef went out from the presence of Pharaoh and went through all the land of Egypt (Gen. 41:46).

This presumably commonplace expression is in fact a technical term often associated with the ministrations of the Levites who were chosen to "stand before" the Lord (Deut. 10:8; 18:5, 7).[73] Yosef's priestly role may also be detected in the text's recounting of the feast which Yosef prepared for his brothers. Yosef instructed the head of his household to prepare meat for the banquet, וטבח טבח (Gen. 43:16). The basic

---

71. Pat Remler, *Egyptian Mythology, A to Z* (New York: Infobase Pub., 2010), 53–55 esp. 54; James R Lewis, Evelyn Dorothy Oliver, "Egypt, Ancient" pages 76–78 in *The Dream Encyclopedia* (Detroit: Visible Ink Press, 2009).

72. Gen. 44:15. While the silver chalice episode was a ruse, Yosef's declaration that divination by a man of his station should have been presumed remains significant.

73. David Baron, *The Visions and Prophecies of Zechariah: "The Prophet of Hope and of Glory"* (Eugene: Wipf and Stock), 87.

meaning of טבח is "slaughter"; however it too is a technical term closely related to the ritual slaughter of sacrificial animals.[74] Furthermore, the word מִשְׂאֵת, meaning "tribute or present," which is used to describe the portions allotted to the brothers at the feast (Gen. 43:34), harbors strong sacrificial connotations.[75] The constellation of terms harboring priestly undertones permeating the story of Yosef support the assumption of a priestly tenor in Yosef's blessings.

Yosef's Priestly Legacy

The memory of an erstwhile priestly legacy within the tribe of Ephraim, Yosef's son, is chronicled throughout the biblical record. Yehoshua, a member of the tribe of Ephraim, established an altar on Mount Ebal, in the territory of Ephraim (Josh. 8:30–35). In the end of the book of Joshua, we read of a temple dedicated to God, established in Yehoshua's hometown of Shechem, probably by Yehoshua himself (Josh. 24:25–26). The Tabernacle, the official center of Israelite worship, was first erected in Shilo, in the hill country of the tribe of Ephraim (Jud. 21:19). Micah, also from the tribe of Ephraim, established a cultic center in his home (Jud. 17). The ambiguity of the text regarding Shmuel's lineage from both the tribes of Ephraim and Levi (1 Sam. 1:1–2; 1 Chron. 6:33–38), his priestly ephod (1 Sam. 2:18), and officiation over sacrificial offerings (1 Sam. 7:9; 10:8), contribute to the suggestion of Ephraim's priestly legacy. Yeravam, from the tribe of Ephraim (1 Kings 11:26), founder of the Northern Kingdom, established himself as high priest, officiating over the Bethel altar (1 Kings 13:1). His re-establishment of the cult of the calves, innovated by Aharon the High Priest, and his sons names, Nadav and Aviya, which are unmistakably patterned after Aharon the high priest's sons' names Nadav and Avihu, contribute to the notion of an ancient tradition of priesthood in Ephraim.

In his blessings to Yehudah and Yosef, Yaakov appears to have split the roles of king and priest, conferring royalty upon Yehudah and

---

74. Hamp, TDOT "טבח," 5: 283–287, esp. 283. Cf. the following in which the word טבח is used in the context of sacrificial offerings: 1 Sam. 9:23, Isa. 34:6.

75. HALOT, "מִשְׂאֵת," 640. Cf. the following in which the word מִשְׂאֵת is used in the context of priestly offerings: Ezek. 20:40, 2 Chron. 24:6.

priesthood upon Yosef.[76] The Rabbinic understanding that before the priestly role was conferred upon the Levites, it was considered to be part of the birthright of the firstborn, supports this assumption (Mishnah, Zevachim, 14:4). Yosef's acquisition of the birthright, and his twofold land allotment, lend further weight to this understanding (Gen. 48:22; Deut. 33:17; 1 Chron. 5:1–2). The Sages allude to Yaakov's confirmation of Yosef as high priest in a series of homilies linking the priestly tunic given to Adam in the Garden of Eden to the one given to Yosef by Yaakov.[77] The blessings of Asher and Naphtali which lead into Yosef's blessing will be shown to lend further support to the notion of Yosef as priest.

Asher and Naphtali, Bearers of Tribute

Asher is described as providing מעדני מלך, royal delicacies.

Asher's food shall be rich, שמנה לחמו, and he shall yield royal delicacies, מעדני מלך (Gen. 49:20).

That the "fat bread," שמנה לחמו described in Asher's blessing refers specifically to olive oil may be inferred from Moshe's blessing to Asher which makes explicit mention of olive oil.

About Asher he said: "Most blessed of sons is Asher; let him be favored by his brothers, and let him bathe his feet in oil. (Deut. 33:24).

The Bible confirms that olive oil was used as a form of payment of taxation in the ancient world (Hos. 12:2). The verb נתן, "to give," which is repeated for both Asher and Naphtali, insinuates a connection between the two blessings.

Asher's food shall be rich, and he shall yield, יתן, royal delicacies. Naphtali is a doe set free, שלוחה, that bears, הנתן, beautiful fawns (Gen. 49:20–21).

---

76. The parameters of the priesthood were later redefined by Moshe, who conferred the role upon members of the tribe of Levi.

77. *Midrash Tanchuma* (Buber) *Toldot* 12 s.v. *veyiten lecha Elohim*; Genesis Rabbati *Vayehi*, s.v. *vaani natati elu begadim*, 231; Midrash manuscript brought in *Torah Shleima* on Gen. 37:3, par. 50, s.v. *kutonet passim*.

It was mentioned above that in addition to referring to a swift footed doe, Naphtali's blessing also connotes fruit producing trees and ewe bearing fawns. Fruit and ewes are commodities which were also associated with taxation and tithing. The repetition of the verb נתן in both Asher and Naphtali's blessings suggests that like Asher's olive oil, Naphtali's fruit and fawns are also intended for tribute. This interpretation is reinforced by the appearance of the word שלוחה in Naphtali's blessing in vs. 21. שלוחה is a word closely associated with offerings.[78] The word שלוחה appears only twice more in the Bible; one of those instances within the context of the offering which Yaakov presents to Esav.

> Then you shall say, "They belong to your servant Yaakov. They are a present sent, שלוחה, to my lord Esav. And moreover, he is behind us" (Gen. 32:19).

The positioning of Asher and Naphtali's blessings before Yosef's implies that the beneficiary of their offering is Yosef. While this alone does not prove conclusively that Yosef is to be viewed as a priestly figure, a re-examination of Naphtali's blessing will provide further evidence in support of Yosef's blessing conferring upon him the role of priest.

Naphtali, Herald of Theophany

Naphtali's depiction as a swift-footed doe brings to mind biblical texts featuring the appearance of God, coupled with the deer trope. King David's valedictory song depicts a theophany in which he appears as a deer (Ps. 18:34).

> In my distress I called upon the LORD; to my God I cried for help. From His temple He heard my voice, and my cry to Him reached His ears. Then the earth reeled and rocked; the foundations also of the mountains trembled and quaked, because He was angry.... He made my feet like the feet of a deer and set me secure on the heights. (Ps. 18:7, 8, 34)

Hinds in the throes of calving, which is one of the possible readings of Naphtali's blessing discussed earlier, is a variation on the deer trope

---

78. The verb נתן is used to describe the giving of tithes in Gen. 14:20.

noted above. The theme of the calving hind conveys the notion of fear and trembling before God:[79]

> The voice of the LORD makes the hinds to calve,[80] and strips the forests bare; and in His temple all say: 'Glory'" (Psalm 29:9).

Naphtali's appearance as a calving hind, heralding splendor הנתן אמרי שפר, supports the supposition that Yosef's blessing, which immediately follows, elects him to a position of religious significance. An examination of the final blessing, that of Binyamin, confirms that the blessing cluster beginning with Asher and extending through Binyamin, casts Yosef in a priestly role.

Wolves and Temples

Binyamin's analogy to a ravenous wolf in a relentless state of devouring its prey seems at odds with his exceedingly passive character in the book of Genesis, where he is consistently portrayed in need of protection.[81] In Deuteronomy, Moshe describes Binyamin as the beneficiary of divine shelter. This description would appear to relate to the more familiar passive image of Binyamin in Genesis. The imagery of Binyamin – the otherwise passive figure – as a voracious wolf, in Yaakov's blessing, is unexpected:

> Of Binyamin he said, "The beloved of the LORD dwells in safety. The High God surrounds him all day long, and dwells between his shoulders" (Deut. 33:12).

In my analysis of Yaakov's blessing to Binyamin, I begin with an examination of the connotations of the word טרף, prey, and then consider the role of animals of prey vis-à-vis the Temple and its altar.

The word טרף is generally used to mean "prey," although it can also refer to nourishment, or provisions.[82] In Malachi, its use connotes

---

79. Cf. also Job 39:1–4, for another example of the theophanic trope of the calving hind.

80. HALOT, "חיל," 310.

81. Gen. 42:4; 43:29; 44:20–23.

82. Wagner, TDOT "טרף," 5:350–357, esp. 353. Cf. Prov. 31:15 and Ps. 111:15.

tithes (Mal. 3:10). Psalm 76 compares God's theophany at His Temple on Mount Zion to the awesome majesty of the northern mountains rich with animals of prey, הררי טרף:

Glorious are You, more majestic than the mountains full of prey, מהררי טרף (Ps. 76:5).

The implication of this analogy is that the mountain of God's Temple in Jerusalem is also to be considered a הר טרף, a mountain of prey. The word טרף may connote either the predatory animal or its prey.[83] The enormous number of animals which were consumed as sacrificial offerings in the Temple service justifies the application of the term הררי טרף as both predator and prey. In other words, the Temple and its sacrificial altar are the "predator" implied by the phrase בנימין זאב יטרוף, Binyamin is a wolf of prey.[84]

The association between the Temple Mount and animals of prey is reinforced by Psalm's descriptions of the location of God's Temple in Jerusalem in the northern heights, home to predators such as lions (Song 4:8), even though the Temple was not located in the north (Ps. 48:1–3). This designation of the Temple in the north is generally understood to be a reflection of a Ugaritic mythology, which placed the abode of the gods in the far north. The Psalmist calls Mount Zion, צפון, to declare that "Zion is the *real* Mount Zaphon where the *true* supreme God dwells."[85]

Animals of Prey and the Altar

The notion of the Temple altar and Jerusalem, by extension, as a "predator," is alluded to in Yechezkel, who refers to the altar as האריאל, literally, "the lion of God," although it is also understood by many to mean an altar hearth.[86]

---

83. *HALOT,* "טרף," 380.

84. The Midrash associates Binyamin's blessing with the sacrificial offerings in the Temple. Cf. *Genesis Rabbah* 99:3.

85. Richard J. Clifford, *The Cosmic Mountain in Canaan and the Old Testament,* (Eugene: Wipf & Stock, 2010), 143.

86. Cf. *HALOT,* "אריאל," 87; The appearance of the term Ariel in the Mesha inscription is difficult to translate; By extension, Isa. 29:1 refers to the entire vicinity of Jerusalem as אריאל.

And the altar hearth, וההראל, four cubits; and from the altar hearth, ומהאריאל projecting upward, four horns. The altar hearth, והאריאל shall be square, twelve cubits long by twelve broad (Ezek. 43:15–16).

Munger argues that the appearance of the word אריאל in 2 Samuel, in which the mighty warrior Benaiah is credited with smiting two אֲרִאֵל מוֹאָב, Moabite 'Ariels,' suggests that the translation of אריאל is indeed 'lion of God' (although here referring to the Moabite warriors).[87]

And Benaiah the son of Yehoyada was a valiant man of Kabzeel, a doer of great deeds. He struck down two ariels of Moab, אראל מואב. He also went down and struck down a lion in a pit on a day when snow had fallen (2 Sam. 23:20).

The leonine theme in both halves of the verse supports this reading. The two definitions of אריאל; altar hearth, and lion-god, may be understood as having merged together in Yechezkel, as the Temple altar consumed burnt-offerings as a lion does its prey.[88]

It should be noted that whereas predatory animals were considered to be ritually impure and unfit for sacrificial offering, it is specifically the altar, not the offerings, which is being referenced by the word אריאל. Furthermore, leonine images played a central role in the temple décor.[89] The Sages used lion and wolf imagery to describe the Temple and its sacrificial altar. The Mishnah describes the architectural plan of the Temple as a leonine (M. *Middot* 4:7), and the Babylonian Talmud uses the word לוקוס, wolf,[90] as an epithet for the altar (BT *Sukkah* 56b).

---

87. S. Munger, *Dictionary of Deities and Demons in the Bible* "Ariel," 88–89, esp. 89.
88. Cf. W. Rosenau "Harel und Ha-Ariel; Ezechiel 43:15–16," *Monatsschrift für Geschichte und Wissenschaft des Judentums, Jahrg* 65 (1921), 350–356; The classical commentators interpreted the word אריאל as the temple altar. Cf. Targum Johnathan, Rashi and Kimchi on Isa. 29:1.
89. Kings 7:27–29 describes the ten movable stands of bronze which stood in the outer courtyard, and their decorative lion reliefs. Additionally, Ezek. 41:17–20 describes the cherubim which appeared in relief along the temple's inner walls with leonine faces.
90. *Jastrow* "לוקוס," 701a.

The Bible generally portrays the wolf as a greedy, nocturnal animal (Ezek. 22:27, Zeph. 3:3). The wolf appearing in Binyamin's blessing, however, is depicted as benevolent, and as active throughout the morning as well as the evening.

> Binyamin is a ravenous wolf; in the morning he devours the prey,
> in the evening he divides the plunder. (Gen. 49:27)

The behavioral shift that the wolf undergoes in Yaakov's blessing to Binyamin matches the character reversal associated with the wolf in Yeshayahu; where the wolf undergoes a radical social change and lies together with the lamb 'upon God's holy mountain' (Isa. 65:25). Understanding the ravenous wolf from Binyamin's blessing as a representation of the Temple altar upon God's holy mountain explains why Targum Onkelos interpreted Binyamin's blessing as referring to the Temple.[91] The sacrificial service upon the altar was one of the primary functions of the Temple. This also explicates the relevance of Moshe's blessing to Binyamin, which describes God's presence in a constant state of hovering above Binyamin:

> Of Binyamin he said, "The beloved of the LORD dwells in safety. The High God surrounds him all day long, and dwells between his shoulders." (Deut. 32: 12)

The Priestly Blessings

The blessing cluster of Asher, Naphtali, Yosef, and Binyamin may be understood as the priestly cluster. These blessings function together as a unit; Asher and Naphtali herald and pay tribute to Yosef the priest, who serves God in the holy Temple, located within the tribal boundaries of Binyamin. The priestly blessing constellation appears opposite the monarchic blessing cluster, (Yehudah, Zevulun, and Yissachar), thereby balancing the two institutions.

The blessings to the tribes of Dan and Gad residing between the monarchic and the priestly blessing clusters are linked together themat-

---

91. Targum, Gen. 49: 27; The Sages interpreted Binyamin's blessing as referring to the Temple altar. Cf. *Midrash Aggadah Gen. 49:27.*

ically through their shared military offensive role. They are also linked lexically through the striking repetition in both blessings of the unusual word עֵקֶב, heel:

> Dan shall judge his people as one of the tribes of Israel. Dan shall be a serpent in the way, a viper by the path, that bites the horse's heels, עִקְבֵי סוּס, so that his rider falls backward. I wait for your salvation, O LORD. "Raiders shall raid Gad, but he shall raid at their heels, עָקֵב" (Gen. 49:16–19).

Yaakov charged Dan and Gad with providing both the monarchic and priestly institutions with military protection. The supplication which appears between their blessings is neither a part of the blessing to Dan, as many have assumed,[92] nor is it a gloss.[93] Yaakov's prayer, located at the center of the two blessing clusters, is an appeal to God for the success and wellbeing of the Israelite monarchic and priestly establishments.[94] The prayer for divine success and salvation is the very fulcrum around which the two blessing clusters revolve.[95]

Conclusion

The military orientation of the animal metaphors in Yaakov's Blessings suggests that the tribal blessings themselves also harbor a mutual function, and a cohesive literary theme. Yaakov's blessings innovate the division in the responsibilities and privileges traditionally associated

---

92. Cf. Rashi, Rashbam, Ibn Ezra, Bechor Shor, Nachmanides and Hizkuni on Gen. 49:18.
93. Cf. R. de Hoop, "Genesis 49 Revisited; The Poetic structure of Jacob's Testament and the Ancient Versions," pages 1–32, esp. 7 in *Unit Delimitation in Biblical Hebrew and Northwest Semitic Literature* (ed. Marjo Korpel and Joseph Oesch; Assen: Uitgeverij Van Gorcum, 2003); Waschke, *TDOT*, "קוה," p. 564–573, esp. 566.
94. The Midrash also interprets Yaakov's prayer as referring to all the tribes of Israel. Cf. *Shemot Rabbah* 30:24; *Aggadah Bereishit*, Buber ed., 62, s.v. *lamah tomar*.
95. Seebass also maintains that Yaakov's prayer in Gen. 49:18 relates to all the tribes. Cf. Horst Seebass, *Genesis* (3 vols.; Neukirchen-Vluyn: Neukirchener, 2000), 3:177–178.

with the patriarchal birthright. Reuven's impropriety with his father's concubine, and Shimon and Levi's barbarism at Shechem, constituted a de facto abdication of their claim to the birthright. This afforded Yaakov the opportunity to redefine the parameters of the birthright which was formerly a zero-sum game. Yaakov's Blessings to his sons constitute a reformation of the patriarchal birthright, in which the leadership role was separated into two major subdivisions: the monarchic and the priestly. Yehudah's blessing which installed him as monarch, supported politically and financially by Zevulun and Yissachar, sons of Leah, represents the cluster of monarchic blessing. Yosef's blessing electing him to the role of priest, heralded and sustained by the tribes of Asher, Naphtali, and Binyamin, represent the priestly blessing cluster. The blessings to the tribes of Dan and Gad, which appear between these two blessing clusters, charge them with the protection of both institutions. The brief prayer wedged between the blessings of Dan and Gad is the pivot around which the two blessing constellations revolve. Yaakov's Blessings emerge as a unified vision of the establishment of two separate pillars of leadership – the monarchic and the priestly – supported by the tribes of Israel and sustained by God.

The approach to the three main songs of the Torah as a tripartite expression of Israel's acceptance of the yoke of Heaven, קבלת עול מלכות שמים advanced above, is reinforced and complemented by the Blessings of Yaakov. In his tribal blessings, Yaakov addresses the kingdom of God, albeit with a shift in focus. Yaakov's Blessings establish the dual institutions of Israelite leadership, the monarchy and the priesthood. These establishments are charged with promoting allegiance to the kingdom of God and dedication to its precepts. Yaakov's prayer for heavenly salvation at the epicenter of the tribal blessings points to the kingdom of God as the fulcrum of the two synergistic realms of Israelite leadership. Yaakov's blessings emerge as an exposition on Israel's fundamental mission as a nation of priests, ממלכת כהנים, charged with supporting the kingdom of God.

Bilam's Prophecies

In this chapter, Bilam's three blessings are examined and demonstrated to work together forming a single, interconnected blessing. The relevance of Bilam's final oracle, which differs from the first three orations in style as well as content, is shown to be directly relevant to the three blessings which precede it, as it connects Bilam's orations to the body of biblical blessings developed throughout the Torah. The Blessings of Bilam draw upon imagery from Yaakov's blessings as they move the idea of Israelite leadership forward, suggesting a synthesis between the kingdoms of Israel and God.

1. במדבר כג:ז–י

וַיִּשָּׂא מְשָׁלוֹ וַיֹּאמַר מִן־אֲרָם יַנְחֵנִי בָלָק מֶלֶךְ־מוֹאָב מֵהַרְרֵי־קֶדֶם לְכָה אָרָה־לִּי יַעֲקֹב וּלְכָה זֹעֲמָה יִשְׂרָאֵל: מָה אֶקֹּב לֹא קַבֹּה אֵל וּמָה אֶזְעֹם לֹא זָעַם יְקֹוָק: כִּי־מֵרֹאשׁ צֻרִים אֶרְאֶנּוּ וּמִגְּבָעוֹת אֲשׁוּרֶנּוּ הֶן־עָם לְבָדָד יִשְׁכֹּן וּבַגּוֹיִם לֹא יִתְחַשָּׁב: מִי מָנָה עֲפַר יַעֲקֹב וּמִסְפָּר אֶת־רֹבַע יִשְׂרָאֵל תָּמֹת נַפְשִׁי מוֹת יְשָׁרִים וּתְהִי אַחֲרִיתִי כָּמֹהוּ:

Numbers 23:7–10

Then Bilam spoke his message: "Balak brought me from Aram, the king of Moav from the eastern mountains. 'Come,' he said, 'curse Yaakov for me; come, denounce Israel.' How can I curse those whom God has not cursed? How can I denounce those whom the LORD has not denounced? From the rocky peaks I see them, from the heights I view them. I see a people who live apart and do not consider themselves one of the nations. Who can count the dust of Yaakov or number even a fourth of Israel? Let me die the death of the righteous, and may my final end be like theirs!"

2. במדבר כג:יח-כד

וַיִּשָּׂא מְשָׁלוֹ וַיֹּאמַר קוּם בָּלָק וּשְׁמָע הַאֲזִינָה עָדַי בְּנוֹ צִפֹּר: לֹא אִישׁ אֵל וִיכַזֵּב וּבֶן־אָדָם וְיִתְנֶחָם הַהוּא אָמַר וְלֹא יַעֲשֶׂה וְדִבֶּר וְלֹא יְקִימֶנָּה: הִנֵּה בָרֵךְ לָקָחְתִּי וּבֵרֵךְ וְלֹא אֲשִׁיבֶנָּה: לֹא־הִבִּיט אָוֶן בְּיַעֲקֹב וְלֹא־רָאָה עָמָל בְּיִשְׂרָאֵל יְקֹוָק אֱלֹהָיו עִמּוֹ וּתְרוּעַת מֶלֶךְ בּוֹ: אֵל מוֹצִיאָם מִמִּצְרָיִם כְּתוֹעֲפֹת רְאֵם לוֹ: כִּי לֹא־נַחַשׁ בְּיַעֲקֹב וְלֹא־קֶסֶם בְּיִשְׂרָאֵל כָּעֵת יֵאָמֵר לְיַעֲקֹב וּלְיִשְׂרָאֵל מַה־פָּעַל אֵל: הֶן־עָם כְּלָבִיא יָקוּם וְכַאֲרִי יִתְנַשָּׂא לֹא יִשְׁכַּב עַד־יֹאכַל טֶרֶף וְדַם־חֲלָלִים יִשְׁתֶּה:

Numbers 23:18–24

Then he spoke his message: "Arise, Balak, and listen; hear me, son of Zippor. God is not human, that He should lie, not a human being, that He should change his mind. Does He speak and then not act? Does He promise and not fulfill? I have received a command to bless; He has blessed, and I cannot change it. "No misfortune is seen in Yaakov, no misery observed in Israel. The LORD their God is with them; the shout of the King is among them. God brought them out of Egypt; they have the strength of a wild ox. There is no divination against Yaakov, no evil omens against Israel. It will now be said of Yaakov and of Israel, 'See what God has done!' The people rise like a lioness; they rouse themselves like a lion that does not rest till it devours its prey and drinks the blood of its victims."

3. במדבר פרק כד:ג-ז

וַיִּשָּׂא מְשָׁלוֹ וַיֹּאמַר נְאֻם בִּלְעָם בְּנוֹ בְעֹר וּנְאֻם הַגֶּבֶר שְׁתֻם הָעָיִן: נְאֻם שֹׁמֵעַ אִמְרֵי־אֵל אֲשֶׁר מַחֲזֵה שַׁדַּי יֶחֱזֶה נֹפֵל וּגְלוּי עֵינָיִם: מַה־טֹּבוּ אֹהָלֶיךָ יַעֲקֹב מִשְׁכְּנֹתֶיךָ יִשְׂרָאֵל: כִּנְחָלִים נִטָּיוּ כְּגַנֹּת עֲלֵי נָהָר כַּאֲהָלִים נָטַע יְקֹוָק כַּאֲרָזִים עֲלֵי־מָיִם: יִזַּל־מַיִם מִדָּלְיָו וְזַרְעוֹ בְּמַיִם רַבִּים וְיָרֹם מֵאֲגַג מַלְכּוֹ וְתִנַּשֵּׂא מַלְכֻתוֹ: אֵל מוֹצִיאוֹ מִמִּצְרַיִם כְּתוֹעֲפֹת רְאֵם לוֹ יֹאכַל גּוֹיִם צָרָיו וְעַצְמֹתֵיהֶם יְגָרֵם וְחִצָּיו יִמְחָץ: כָּרַע שָׁכַב כַּאֲרִי וּכְלָבִיא מִי יְקִימֶנּוּ מְבָרֲכֶיךָ בָרוּךְ וְאֹרְרֶיךָ אָרוּר:

Numbers 24:3–10

And he spoke his message: "The prophecy of Bilam son of Beor, the prophecy of one whose eye sees clearly, the prophecy of one who hears the words of God, who sees a vision from the Almighty, who falls prostrate, and whose eyes are opened: "How beautiful are your tents, Yaakov, your dwelling places, Israel! "Like valleys they spread out, like gardens beside a river, like aloes planted by the LORD, like cedars beside the waters. Water will flow from their buckets; their seed will have abundant water. "Their king will be greater than Agag; their kingdom will be exalted. "God brought them out of Egypt; they have the strength of a wild ox. They devour hostile nations and break their bones in pieces; with their arrows they pierce them. Like a lion they crouch and lie down, like a lioness – who dares to rouse them? "May those who bless you be blessed and those who curse you be cursed!"

4. במדבר פרק כד:טו-כה

וַיִּשָּׂא מְשָׁלוֹ וַיֹּאמַר נְאֻם בִּלְעָם בְּנוֹ בְעֹר וּנְאֻם הַגֶּבֶר שְׁתֻם הָעָיִן: נְאֻם שֹׁמֵעַ אִמְרֵי־אֵל וְיֹדֵעַ דַּעַת עֶלְיוֹן מַחֲזֵה שַׁדַּי יֶחֱזֶה נֹפֵל וּגְלוּי עֵינָיִם: אֶרְאֶנּוּ וְלֹא עַתָּה אֲשׁוּרֶנּוּ וְלֹא קָרוֹב דָּרַךְ כּוֹכָב מִיַּעֲקֹב וְקָם שֵׁבֶט מִיִּשְׂרָאֵל וּמָחַץ פַּאֲתֵי מוֹאָב וְקַרְקַר כָּל־בְּנֵי־שֵׁת: וְהָיָה אֱדוֹם יְרֵשָׁה וְהָיָה יְרֵשָׁה שֵׂעִיר אֹיְבָיו וְיִשְׂרָאֵל עֹשֶׂה חָיִל: וְיֵרְדְּ מִיַּעֲקֹב וְהֶאֱבִיד שָׂרִיד מֵעִיר: וַיַּרְא אֶת־עֲמָלֵק וַיִּשָּׂא מְשָׁלוֹ וַיֹּאמַר רֵאשִׁית גּוֹיִם עֲמָלֵק וְאַחֲרִיתוֹ עֲדֵי אֹבֵד: וַיַּרְא אֶת־הַקֵּינִי וַיִּשָּׂא מְשָׁלוֹ וַיֹּאמַר אֵיתָן מוֹשָׁבֶךָ וְשִׂים בַּסֶּלַע קִנֶּךָ: כִּי אִם־יִהְיֶה לְבָעֵר קָיִן עַד־מָה אַשּׁוּר תִּשְׁבֶּךָ: וַיִּשָּׂא מְשָׁלוֹ וַיֹּאמַר אוֹי מִי יִחְיֶה מִשֻּׂמוֹ אֵל: וְצִים מִיַּד כִּתִּים וְעִנּוּ אַשּׁוּר וְעִנּוּ־עֵבֶר וְגַם־הוּא עֲדֵי אֹבֵד: וַיָּקָם בִּלְעָם וַיֵּלֶךְ וַיָּשָׁב לִמְקֹמוֹ וְגַם־בָּלָק הָלַךְ לְדַרְכּוֹ:

Numbers 24:15–25

Then he spoke his message: "The prophecy of Bilam son of Beor, the prophecy of one whose eye sees clearly, the prophecy of one who hears the words of God, who has knowledge from the Most High, who sees a vision from the Almighty, who falls prostrate, and whose eyes are opened: "I see Him, but not now; I behold Him, but not near. A star will come out of Yaakov; a scepter will rise out of Israel. He will crush the foreheads of Moab, the skulls of all the people of Sheth. Edom will be conquered; Seir, his enemy, will be conquered, but Israel will grow strong. A ruler will come out of Yaakov and destroy the survivors of the city." Then Bilam saw Amalek and spoke his message: "Amalek was first among the nations, but their end will be utter destruction." Then he saw the Kenites and spoke his message: "Your dwelling place is secure, your nest is set in a rock; yet you Kenites will be destroyed when Ashur takes you captive." Then he spoke his message: "Alas! Who can live when God does this? Ships will come from the shores of Cyprus; they will subdue Ashur and Eber, but they too will come to ruin." Then Bilam got up and returned home, and Balak went his own way.

Introduction

The Sages referred to the Torah narratives which contain the story and Blessings of Bilam as פרשת בלעם, the Bilam portion (BT *Bava Batra* 14b). In scholarly parlance, this material is referred to as the "Balaam pericope." It is a most colorful, entertaining, story, with its sorcerer for hire, menacing angel, and even a talking donkey. The narrative climaxes with Bilam reluctantly showering Israel with three blessings, which are topped off by an apocalyptic, end of days oracle. I will present an examination of Bilam's three blessings and demonstrate how they together form a single, interconnected blessing. The relevance of Bilam's final oracle, which differs from the first three orations in style as well as content, will be shown to be directly relevant to the three blessings which precede it, as it connects Bilam's orations to the body of biblical blessings developed throughout the Torah.

A Unified Text

The first indication of the cohesive nature of Bilam's three blessings may be detected with the lampooning of Bilam in ch. 22. There, Bilam is thrice confronted by a menacing angel whom his donkey apprehends perfectly well, while Bilam, the renowned seer, somehow fails to see. Commentators take note of how Bilam's ensnarement in ch. 22, in which he finds himself caught three times between his donkey and the divine angel, foreshadows the three blessings of ch. 23–24, in which Bilam once again finds that he is powerless to go against the will of God.[1]

While the three-part ensnarement of Bilam in ch. 22 suggests that Bilam's three failed attempts to curse Israel in ch. 23 are loosely inter-

---

1. Cf. James s. Ackerman, "Numbers," in Robert Alter and Frank Kermode (eds.), *The Literary Guide to the Bible* (Cambridge: Harvard University Press, 1987), 78–91, (86); G.J. Wenham, *Numbers* (TOTC; Leicester: Inter-Varsity Press, 1981), 171; Amos Frisch, "The Story of Balaam's She-ass (Numbers 22:21–35): A New Literary Insight, " *Hebrew Studies* 56 (2015), 103–113, (111); Clinton Moyer, "Who is the Prophet, and Who the Ass? Role-Reversing Interludes and the Unity of the Balaam Narrative (Numbers 22–24)," *JSOT* 37.2 (2012), 167–183. Moshe Garsiel, *The First Book of Samuel: A Literary Study of Comparative Structures, Analogies and Parallels* (Ramat-Gan: Revivim, 1st English ed., 1983), 122–133; R.W.L.; R.W.L. Moberly, "On Learning to be a True Prophet: The Story of Balaam and his Ass," in *New Heaven and New Earth Prophecy and the Millennium: Essays in Honour of Anthony Gelston* (ed. P.J. Harland and C.T.R. Hayward; SVT 77; Leiden: Brill, 1999), 1–17; Rene Vuilleumier, "Bileam Zwischen Bibel und Deir Alla," *Theologische Zeitschrift* 52 (1996), 150–163. Vuilleumier supports a single tradition in which Bilam goes from being good to bad to reprehensible. These scholars oppose taking a diachronic approach which views the donkey episode as a later interpolation intended to serve as an anti-prophetic satire aimed at undermining the notion of Bilam as a pagan prophet. Cf. Alexander Rofé, *The Book of Balaam: Numbers 22:2–24:25* (JBS, 1: Jerusalem: Simor, 1979 [Hebrew]), 53–57; Jacob Milgrom, *The JPS Torah Commentary: Numbers* (Philadelphia: Jewish Publication Society, 1990), 468–69; Baruch A. Levine, *Numbers 21–36: A New Translation with Introduction and Commentary* (AB, 4A: New York: Doubleday, 2000), 155; David Marcus, *From Balaam to Jonah: Anti-prophetic Satire in the Hebrew Bible* (BJS, 301; Atlanta: Scholars Press, 1995), 29–41, (41); A. Kuenen, *Historisch-kritische Einleitung in die Bucher des Alten Testaments* (Leipzig: Schulze, 1887), 224; B. Baentsch, *Exodus-Leviticus-Numeri* (GHAT; Göttingen: Vandenhoeck & Ruprecht, 1903), 598–599; H. Rouillard, "L'anesse de Balaam," *RB* 87 (1980), 5–36; M.M. Kalisch, *Bible Studies* 1: *The Prophecies of Balaam* (London: Longmans, Green, 1877), 126–128. Kalisch disassociated the donkey episode from the surrounding material; Sigmund Mowinckel, "Der Ursprung der Bilamsage," *ZAW* 48 (1930), 233–271; Martin Noth, *Numbers: A Commentary* (trans. James D. Martin; OTL; London: SCM Press, 1968), 178. Mowinckel and Noth argue that the donkey episode predates the rest of the Bilam pericope.

related, the common themes and language shared by the outer framework of each of the orations provide additional evidence for the literary
cohesion of the blessings. All three of Bilam's attempts at cursing Israel
commence with the offering of seven bulls and rams (Num. 23:1–2, 14,
29), are introduced with the phrase וישא משלו,[2] feature Bilam referencing
himself (Num. 23:7, 18, 24:3), and contain a description of the particular
high place upon which Bilam stood as he fixed his gaze upon Israel (Num.
22:41, 23:14, 28). One of the primary themes shared between the outer
structure of the three blessings is the concept of seeing, which finds expression in a rich multiplicity of terms. In addition to the more common
verb for "seeing," ראה,[3] we also find the roots שור (23:9),[4] צופה (23:14),[5]
הבט (23:21),[6] השקיף (23:28),[7] and חזה (24:4),[8] as well as the phrases גלוי
עינים (24:4),[9] and שתם העין (24:3, 15), or open-eyed.[10]

Another central theme common to the blessings' outer structure
as well as their core message is the contrast between rising and falling.
The blessings' emphasis on this theme highlights the disparity between
Israel's indomitable strength and Bilam's impotence. All three blessings
open with the image of Bilam standing upon a tall mountain, and with
Israel situated in the valley below. The sacrifices which are offered prior
to the first two failed attempts to curse Israel are burnt offerings, עולה,
meaning "to rise up," with Balak being told to stand, התיצב, in close
proximity (Num. 23:3, 15). The oracles are consistently introduced
with the word וישא, deriving from the root נשא, meaning "to raise or lift"

---

2. Num. 23:7, 18, 24:3. The word משל in this context probably means wise saying,
or epigrammatic poetry. Cf. Koehler, L., Baumgartner, W., Richardson, M.E.J.,
& Stamm, J.J., "משל," The Hebrew and Aramaic lexicon of the Old Testament
(electronic ed., 648), (Leiden: E.J. Brill, 1994–2000).

3. Num. 22:41, 23: 3, 9, 13, 21, 24:1, 2, 17, 20.

4. HALOT, "שור," 1450; BDB, "שור," 1003b.

5. HALOT, "צפה," 1044; BDB, "צפה," 859a.

6. HALOT, "נבט," 661; BDB, "נבט," 613b.

7. HALOT, "שקף," 1645; BDB, "שקף," 1054b.

8. HALOT, "חזה," 301; BDB, "חזה," 302a.

9. HALOT, "גלה," 191; BDB, "גלה," 162b.

10. Cf. Onkelos, Pseudo-Johnathan, Rashi, Rashbam, and Ibn Ezra, Gen. 24:3.
Rashi suggests both open and closed as possible definitions, although he
bases the latter definition on a Rabbinic homily.

(Num. 23:7, 18; 24:3, 15), which is contrasted by Bilam lying fully prone and functionally incapacitated (Num. 24:4). Israel, on the other hand, is depicted by Bilam as a roused lion that refuses to lie down (Num. 23:24), and later again as a crouching lion ready to pounce (Num. 24:9).

Resonances Between the Latter Two Blessings

While the outer structure of all three blessings shares a variety of significant themes and motifs, the subject of the monarchy which resonates between the latter two blessings, represented by the mighty lion motif (Num. 23:24; 24:9), and the majestic ראם, re'em,[11] with its impressive תועפות, horns/antlers,[12] are all curiously absent from the first blessing. I will begin my inquiry into this apparent lacuna with an analysis of the way in which the monarchic theme resonates and is developed between the final two blessings. An appreciation for the correlation between the monarchic theme in the latter two blessings intensifies the problem of its absence from the first. Bilam declares in the second blessing:

> No misfortune is seen in Yaakov, no misery observed in Israel. The LORD their God is with them; the shout of the King is among them (Num. 23:21).

The commentators tend to agree that the king in our verse is God himself.[13] This reading is based on the parallelism between the latter two sections of the verse: "the majesty of the King is among them" and

---

11. The identity of the re'em is uncertain. Suggestions range from unicorn, wild bull, or buffalo, to white antelope. Cf. HALOT, "ראם," 1163; Feliks maintains that in ancient times there were two different traditions which identified the re'em in its various spellings as either a wild ox or the Oryx. Cf. Yehuda Feliks, *Nature and Man in the Bible* (London, Jerusalem, New York: Soncino, 1981), 263.

12. The word תועפות is probably related to the Arabic *yf'*, meaning "towering high." This understanding works well with the word's appearance in Ps. 95:4, where it relates to tall mountains, Job 22:25, where it refers to large sums of money, and Ben Sira 45:7 where it connotes magnificent splendor. Cf. HALOT, "תועפות," 1705; BDB, "יעף," 419a. Rashi relates the word to the root עוף, meaning "to fly," as the antlers of the re'em go straight up, representing strength.

13. Onkelos, Nachmanides, Hizkuni and Ibn Ezra on our verse agree that the referent is God, the Divine monarch who dwells among Israel.

"The LORD their God is with them." Gray comments that "the shout of triumph and welcome with which the people were wont to greet their divine king is heard in Israel. The parallel and the continuation of the reference to God in v. 22 are in favor of thus understanding *the king* to be Yahweh."[14] The theme of divine royalty in vs. 21 is immediately followed by the metaphor of the majestic *re'em* in vs. 22, which continues the suggestion of God as the referent. The monarchic theme is again coupled together with the ראם in the third blessing, where its description is repeated verbatim:

> Their king will be greater than Agag; their kingdom will be exalted. God brought them out of Egypt; having the horns/antlers of a *re'em*, א־ל מוציאו ממצרים כתועפת ראם לו (Num. 24:7–8).

The striking word for word repetition of the description of the majestic ראם in the third blessing suggests that just as God is understood to be the divine monarch in the second blessing, so too is God the implied monarch in the third blessing. This notion however seems to be internally contradicted with a description of God planting Israel like a well irrigated garden from which the Israelite monarchy will emanate (Num. 24:5–7). This progression implies a coregency between God and Israel. In this way the third blessing intensifies the monarchic theme as it develops and expands between the second and third blessings.

Thematic Intensification Between the Second and Third Blessings

Themes from the second blessing become intensified in the third. The lion metaphor from the second blessing is developed further with its reappearance in the third blessing. Whereas the lion in the second blessing is poised and ready to pounce upon its prey (Num. 23:24), the third blessing describes the lion after the hunt, fully satiated:

---

14. G.B. Gray *A Critical and Exegetical Commentary on Numbers* (ICC; Edinburgh: T & T Clark, 1903), 353. Albright agrees that the king in our verse refers to God, although he rejects the association of the word תרועה with the root רוע, meaning "to cry out or shout," see HALOT, "רוע," 1206; BDB, "רוע," 929b. He relates it instead to the root ירע, meaning to cause to fear, which also implies royalty and majesty. See HALOT, "ירע," 440; BDB, "ירע," 438b.

Crouched and lying down, like a lion, who dares to rouse them?
(Num. 24:9)

The theme of the *re'em* is also developed between the second and
third blessings. While the second blessing focuses exclusively on the
majestic appearance of the *re'em*, the third blessing adds the elements of
victory and ferocity, wherein the *re'em* smashes the enemy, יִמְחַץ,[15] and
gnaws at their bones, גֶרֶם (24:8).[16]

Another theme which is intensified between the two blessings is
the futility of using sorcery against Israel. The second blessing states
emphatically that all forms of sorcery directed against Israel are destined
to fail:

There is no divination against Yaakov, no evil omens against Israel
(Num. 23:23).

The third blessing takes this axiom a step further, warning that those
who dare to curse Israel shall themselves be cursed:

...those who bless you be blessed and those who curse you be
cursed! (Num. 24:9)

Intensification between the second and third blessings may also be
detected in Israel's shifting role from the object of the blessing, to the
addressee of the blessing. Whereas Israel is spoken of in the first two
blessings, the nation is formally addressed in the third (Num. 24:5).
Also, whereas Bilam specifically addresses Balak in the first two oracles,
the third oracle contains no direct references to him. A fundamental
and dramatic shift takes place between the second and third blessing,
wherein Balak is rendered irrelevant, and Israel replaces him in the role
of Bilam's interlocutors.

Word repetition and theme chains linking consecutive poetic verses
are a hallmark of biblical poetry.[17] The presence of a chain linking major
topics and key words of the latter two blessings raises the expectation

---

15. *HALOT*, "מחץ," 571; *BDB*, "מחץ," 563.

16. *HALOT*, "גרם," 203; *BDB*, "גרם," 175a.

17. Adele Berlin, "On the Interpretation of Psalm 133," in Elaine Follis, *Directions
     in Biblical Hebrew Poetry* (Edinburgh: A&C Black, 1987), 141–147; Amos

that a similar chain ought to be present correlating the first two blessings. A comparison of the message of the first two blessings, however, fails to yield any obvious thematic or lexical link. While the first blessing praises Israel's fecundity and dwellings, the second blessing shifts gears, highlighting the monarchic theme. There is, however, a semantic and thematic link connecting the first blessing with the third, which points to the relevance of the first blessing to the latter two.

The Correlation Between the First and Third Blessings

The main thrust of the first blessing revolves around the root שכן, "dwelling."[18] Israel is described there as dwelling, ישכן, apart from the other nations. In the third blessing the theme of dwelling is developed further, with Israel being praised for the utopian magnificence of their dwellings, משכנתיך, which are compared to an aromatic garden planted by God himself.

Another significant theme linking the first and third blessings relates to the enigmatic word רבע which appears in the first blessing, parallel to the word עפר, "dust" (Num. 23:10).[19] Some have suggested that the word רבע is related to the Akkadian word for "dust cloud," *tarbu'(t) u(m), turbu'/ttu*.[20] While this interpretation does seem appealing, as it neatly matches the dust metaphor from the parallel section of the verse, it is nonetheless doubtful, as it assumes the word to have lost an initial 't' sound. Onkelos translates רבע as a quarter; suggesting that even a quarter of the nation is too numerous to count.[21] Difficulties with this reading include the unusual vocalization, *rova* as opposed to *reva*,[22] and the awkward syntax of a modifier following the definite article. Furthermore, the idea of "quarter" is generally not associated with the biblical dust-offspring metaphor (Cf. Gen. 13:16, 28:14). Many

Hakham, *Psalms* (Daat Mikra 2; Jerusalem: Mosad Harav Kook, 1981), 438, (Heb.).

18. *HALOT*, "שכן," 1496; *BDB*, "שכן," 1014b.

19. *HALOT*, "עפר," 861; *BDB*, "עפר," 779b.

20. *HALOT*, "רבע," 1181; *BDB*, "רבע," 918a; Albright, "The Oracles of Balaam," 213.

21. The LXX suggests "clans," which derives from the notion of quarters, or family units. Cf. Albright, "The Oracles of Balaam," 213 nt. 28.

22. Cf. 1 Sam. 9:8 where the word *reva* is used to mean a "quarter."

of the classical commentators equate the word רבע with the emission of
זרע, seed or semen,[23] relating רבע to the act of copulation.[24] Following
this interpretation, the term רבע ישראל would refer to the seed of Yaakov.
This matches well with the first half of the verse, as it harkens back to
the Genesis metaphor comparing Yaakov's seed to dust (Cf. Gen. 28:14).
The preference of the seed/semen interpretation is strengthened by a
parallel concept in the third blessing. Bilam declares there, "Water shall
flow from their buckets; their seed (shall flow) in abundant water" (Num.
24:7). The image of human seed flowing in fluid, an apt description of
semen, corresponds seamlessly with the notion of רבע ישראל, Yaakov's
seed, in the first blessing.

The preference of the sexual connotation of the word רבע in our verse
also matches the general thrust of sexual undertones which pervade the
broader framework of the Bilam pericope. To begin with, Num. 31:16
explicitly identifies Bilam as having advised fornication. A number of
unusual words and phrases in the Bilam narrative contribute to its sexual
tenor. The text uses the uncommon ויקר – which stems from the root קרה,
meaning a "chance occurrence" – to describe Bilam's encounter with
God. The same root is also used by the Bible to refer to ritually unclean
nocturnal emissions.[25] The she-ass which lies, רבץ, beneath Bilam,[26] even
as he continues to ride, רכב (Num. 22:22, 30),[27] upon her, conjures a
provocative image. The she asses' choice of words, הסכנתי ההסכן, "have I
not been of service," noted for their suggestive undertone, raises the suspicion of deliberate wordplay.[28] Bilam's reaction, in response to the she-ass
that he struck her because she played a "dirty trick" on him, כי התעללת

---

23. Cf. Rashi, Rashbam and Ibn Ezra on Num. 23:10; cf. HALOT, "רבע," 1180.

24. HALOT, "זרע," 283; BDB, "זרע," 282a.

25. HALOT, "קרה," 1137; BDB, "קרה," 899b.

26. Cf. Num. 22:27; HALOT, "רבץ," 1181; BDB, "רבץ," 918a.

27. Cf. Barrick, Ringgren, "רכב," TDOT 18: 485- 491, (485). Akkadian also uses
    the verb in a sexual context. The sexual connotation of the word רכב may
    possibly be observed in Lev. 15:9. Ibn Ezra comments there, that the Karaites
    understood the word רכב, and hence the verse, to harbor a sexual undertone.
    Ibn Ezra's disagreement with the Karaite interpretation is likely polemical.

28. Num. 22:30. The word סכן means "to be of service," but it also carries a sexual
    undertone in several biblical texts. Cf. HALOT, "סכן," 755; BDB, "סכן," 698a;

בִּי,[29] adds another sexual innuendo to the growing list.[30] In addition, the conspicuous stress on the word רגל, used as both foot/leg, as well as פעם, meaning times but also foot,[31] within the short span of four verses, draws attention (Num. 22:25–28). The Bible, which uses euphemism instead of anatomically correct language for identifying sex organs, uses the "foot" as a synonym for genitalia.[32] Urine in the Bible is referred to as foot water,[33] pubic hair is called foot hair (Cf. Isa. 7:20), and the sex organ is termed *regel*, or "foot."[34] In the Bilam story, the donkey crushes Bilam's "foot," suggesting his genitalia.[35] Whereas the word רגל connotes either the foot, the lower portion of the leg beneath the knee, or the entire leg, it is never used to specify the anatomy of the upper leg or hips.[36] When the Bible uses the word רגל in a way which appears to be suggesting the thighs, it is intended to be understood euphemistically. In Genesis, Yaakov blesses Yehudah with children who shall issue from between his legs, מבין רגליו, intimating the reproductive organ (Gen. 49:10). Deuteronomy's

---

1 Kings 1:4, Ps. 139:3. It is interesting to note the appearance of both the words סכן and רבע in Ps. 139:3.

29. *HALOT*, "עלל," 834; *BDB*, "עלל," 760b.

30. The word עלל is used to describe the rape of the concubine of Giva in Jud. 19:25.

31. *HALOT*, "פעם," 952.

32. Stendebach, "רגל," *TDOT* 13:309–324, (315).

33. Cf. 2 Kings 18:27, Isa. 36:12.

34. Cf. Ezek. 16:25. This text uses רגל to connote female genitalia.

35. B.J. Embry links the Bilam episode to the story involving Moshe in Ex. 4:24–26, pointing to the use of the term *regel* in both places as genitals. Embry calls attention to the larger context of both as near-death scenarios and part of a formalized rite of passage. Cf. B.J. Embry, "The Endangerment of Moses: Towards a New Reading of Exodus 4: 24–26," *VT* 60 (2010), 177–196, (185–187).

36. The use of the word רגל to connote the lower leg to the exclusion of the thighs may be observed in the description of Goliath's armor: "On his legs, על רגליו, he wore bronze greaves, and a bronze javelin was slung on his back" (1 Sam. 17:6). The primary purpose of greaves is to shield the tibia, a bone located very close to the skin, from attack. The verse depicting Goliath's leg armor, על רגליו, describes protective gear worn upon the lower leg, not thighs. Cf. Jeffrey R. Zorn, "Reconsidering Goliath: An Iron Age I Philistine Chariot Warrior," *BASOR* 360 (2010), 1–22, (8).

admonitions warn of the ravages of war wherein mothers shall consume their own offspring, who were delivered "between the legs," בין רגלי (Deut. 28:57). The Song of Devorah strongly suggests a sexual encounter in its description of a crouching Sisera lying between Yael's legs, בין רגליה.[37] In the Bilam story, the she-ass does not step on Bilam's foot; rather, it crushes his רגל between its body and an adjacent wall (Num. 22:25). Bilam's position upon the donkey, with his legs straddling the sides of the donkey, suggests that it would have been Bilam's thigh, not his foot, which got crushed between the animal's body and the wall. The stress on the lexical term רגל to suggest the area of the thigh, in a story riddled with sexual humor, adds weight to the assumption of deliberate sexual undertones permeating the Bilam narrative.

We may add to the discussion Deuteronomy's injunction against a Moabite man or any man whose sex organs have been crushed or castrated, from marrying within Israel. This ban is immediately followed by references to Bilam and his thwarted attempt to curse Israel (Deut. 23:2–7). While the juxtapositioning of these two otherwise non-sequitur items in Deuteronomy doesn't prove what did or did not happen to Bilam, it does reinforce the suspicion of sexual undertones throughout the telling and retelling of the Bilam story. The Sages, in their sensitivity to the collective weight of the many textual undercurrents in the Bilam narrative, painted Bilam as a practitioner of bestiality.[38]

The consistent pattern of sexual undertones throughout the Bilam pericope adds further support to the preference of the seed/semen definition of רבע over the other proposed suggestions. Whereas the rest of the sexual innuendoes in the story are related specifically to Bilam and are inherently disparaging in nature, the רבע inference relates specifically to Israel, and has a positive connotation. The Sages contend that Bilam's Blessings are to be understood as an inverse reflection of what he

---

37. Jud. 5:27; Cf. Susan Niditch, *Women in the Hebrew Bible: A Reader* (ed. Alice Bach; New York: Routledge, 1999), 305–316, (310–311). Niditch comments that "Double meanings of violent death and sexuality emerge in every line."

38. Cf. Midrash Aggadah, ed. Buber: Num. 22:30; Pseudo-Johnathan, Num. 22:30; It is interesting to note that every reference to Bilam in New Testament literature connects him to sexual impropriety. Cf. Carolyn Sharp, *Irony and Meaning in the Hebrew Bible* (Bloomington: Indiana Univ. Press, 2008), 135.

intended to say (Cf. BT *Sanhedrin* 105b). Instead of cursing Israel with a reduction in their numbers, Bilam unwittingly blessed their fertility.[39] Further references to Israel's fertility may be detected as well in Bilam's final oracle in which he declares ישראל עשה חיל or "Israel will grow strong" (Num. 24:18). The term עשה חיל has a military connotation as well as a sexual one.[40] In the book of Ruth, the phrase ועשה חיל appears at the crux of a fertility blessing (Ru. 4:11). The allusions to Israel's fecundity which permeate the Bilam orations are inextricably linked to the pattern of sexual undertones which bring together the entire Bilam pericope; from the satirical donkey episode and the stress on Bilam's "foot," to the fertility focus of the blessings, and to the story's postscript which names Bilam as mastermind of the orgies linked to the Baal Peor affair. The theme of sexuality is an unmistakably essential component of the larger Bilam story demanding our attention.

One of the most fundamental Torah values is *kedushah*, holiness. Sexual misconduct throughout the Torah is consistently portrayed as an act of defilement, and an obstacle to the attainment of holiness. The unmistakably disparaging sexual jibes aimed at Bilam cast him as a charlatan and a fundamentally polluted character, wholly unfit for contact with the sacred. Bilam professed to be in possession of divine knowledge and in control of its power, yet he was quickly outdone both physically and prophetically by a lowly she-ass. His base character is clearly attested to by the text when he is singled out as the chief architect of the Baal Peor affair, which was rooted in seduction (Num. 31:16). Bilam's eagerness to amass a personal fortune in exchange for occult services, exposes Bilam as an oracular prostitute (Num. 22:18, 24:13). The satirization of Bilam through a string of comical sexual innuendoes foreshadows his ultimate downfall after the Baal Peor episode, as it sharply contrasts the inversely proportionate description of Israel's fertility. The presentation of Bilam and Israel as polar opposites is achieved in this way.

---

39. Merneptah Stele's declaration that "Israel is laid waste; his seed is not" provides us with an authentic and contemporary glimpse of what Bilam probably had in mind. Cf. inscription in I. Provan, V. Long, T. Longman, *A Biblical History of Israel* (Louisville: Westminster John Knox, 2003), 169.

40. Cf. H. Eising, "חיל," *TDOT* IV: 348–355; H. Kosmala, "גבר," *TDOT* II: 373–374.

Identifying a Unifying Pattern in Bilam's Blessings

Identifying the presence of a clear linguistic and thematic correlation between the first and third blessings through the recurrence of the term שכן and the central theme of Yaakov's seed, points to the presence of a larger pattern, which may be represented in the following way: A, B, A+B, in which A represents the first blessing, B represents the second blessing, and A+B represents the fusion of the third. On a thematic level the pattern may be written out in the following way:

A	B	A+B
(Num. 23:7–10)	(Num. 23:18–24)	(Num. 24:3–9)
dwellings and fecundity	divine monarchy	dwellings and fecundity + divine monarchy

The A, B, A+B pattern functioning here may also be observed operating as a poetic device elsewhere in the Bible. I will present a few examples of this pattern in other poetic texts.

The Song of Songs opens with the A, B, A+B pattern:

A	B	A+B
(Song 1:2)	(Song 1:3)	(Song 1: 4)
"Let him kiss me with the kisses of his mouth – for your love is more delightful than wine, דדיך מיין."	"Pleasing is the fragrance of your perfumes; your name is like perfume poured out. No wonder the young women love you, עלמות אהבוך."	"Take me away with you – let us hurry! Let the king bring me into his chambers. We rejoice and delight in you; the upright will praise your love more than wine, דדיך מיין מישרים אהבוך."

Note how each of the first two verses concludes with a short phrase which then join together and form the concluding phrase of the third verse.[41]

---

41. The use of the word מישרים in the place of עלמות in vs. 4 essentially refers to

The Song of Songs' conclusion, like its opening, is built upon the A, B, A+B pattern.

The fact that this pattern emerges from both the introduction and the conclusion of the same book makes the possibility that this configuration is random extremely remote.

A	B	A+B
(Song 8:8)	(Song 8:9)	(Song 8:10)
We have a little sister, and her breasts שדיים, are not yet grown. What shall we do for our sister on the day she is spoken for?	If she is a wall, חומה, we will build towers of silver on her. If she is a door, we will enclose her with panels of cedar.	I am a wall, חומה, and my breasts, שדיים, are like towers. Thus I have become in his eyes like one bringing contentment.

In vs. 8 the Shulamite is accused of having under-developed breasts, vs. 9 compares the Shulamite to a wall, and vs. 10 combines the images of the wall with breasts.

A similar thematic phenomenon may be observed in the priestly blessing, which the Masoretic Text divides into three separate and distinct units:

A	B	A+B
(Num. 6:24)	(Num. 6:25)	(Num. 6:26)
"The LORD bless you and keep you."	"The LORD make His face shine on you and be gracious to you."	"The Lord turn His face toward you and give you peace."
יברכך ה' וישמרך:	יאר ה' פניו אליך ויחנך:	ישא ה' פניו אליך וישם לך שלום:
God's protection	God's face shines in graciousness	God's face + God's protection

---

the same idea. מישרים, or the upright who would praise, are parallel to the young women or עלמות from vs. 3. Cf. *HALOT*, "מישרים," 578; *BDB*, "מישר," 449b.

Psalm 67 is divided into three distinct units through the use of a chorus which repeats in verses 3 and 5: "May the peoples praise You, God; may all the peoples praise You."

The three sections that emerge follow the A, B, A+B pattern:

A (Ps. 67:1–2)	B (Ps. 67:4)	A+B (Ps. 67:6–7)
May God be gracious to us and bless us and make His face shine on us, so that Your ways may be known on earth, Your salvation among all nations.	May the nations be glad and sing for joy, for You rule the peoples with equity and guide the nations of the earth.	The land yields its harvest; God, our God, blesses us. May God bless us still, so that all the ends of the earth will fear him.
God's blessing	Nations will recognize God	God's Blessing + Nations will recognize God

The presence of the A, B, A+B pattern linking Bilam's three blessings demonstrates their unified message heralding the Israelite monarchy.

The Relevance of the Fourth Oracle

While the outer structure of Bilam's fourth oracle is a verbatim repetition of the introduction to the third blessing (with the additional phrase יודע דעת עליון, privy to knowledge known to God Almighty), its content appears to be at variance with Bilam's earlier orations. The subject shifts from Israel to the nations, many of whom seem to have no direct relevance to the Israel-Moab conflict, and for whom the message is apocalyptic. Complicating the matter is the obscure language of the fourth oracle, and the lack of agreement among interpreters of the text concerning the identity of several of the nations which it addresses. The role of the foreign nations is particularly strange in view of vs. 14, in which Bilam warns Moab concerning what Israel has in store specifically for *them* (Moab) in the future.[42] In my discussion of the relevance of the

---

42. Cf. Gray, *Numbers*, 373. Gray is of the opinion that the oracles addressed to

fourth oracle to the material preceding it, I will restrict my comments to those things about which we may be reasonably certain.

In broad strokes, the fourth oracle predicts the future downfall of several nations which include Moab, Esav, Amalek, Assyria, and the Kittim,[43] with Israel ultimately dominating all of the descendants of Seth, or mankind.[44] The notion of Israel's dominion is derived from the verb וירד, stemming from רדה, meaning "to rule," with the associated meaning of oppression.[45] The suggestion in the scholarship that the reference to Seth in vs. 17 denotes the ancient Transjordan nomadic *Shutu* tribe attested to in ancient Egyptian execration texts is extremely doubtful.[46] To begin with, the *Shutu* tribe is not mentioned anywhere in the Bible. While it is true that the nomadic tribes of Amalek and Keini are mentioned in the oracle, these tribes were well known for the significant role that they played in Israel's history. Furthermore, the placement of Seth parallel to Moab, in the second half of the poetic verse, ought to move the intensity of the message forward, by referencing an

---

each of the different nations here, and which are introduced with the word וירא, and he saw, are to be understood as separate oracles. However, the redaction of the oracles directed at individual nations into a single text is clearly meant to relate their messages to the larger context.

43. The identity of the Kittim are discussed by R. Goossens, "Les Kittim du Commentaire d'Habacuc," *NC* (1952) 137–170; by Otto Eissfeldt, *The Old Testament: An Introduction* (trans. P.R. Ackroyd; New York: Harper & Row, 1965), 419–420; and by Hanan Eshel, "The Kittim in the *War Scroll 1*, and in Pesharim," in *Historical Perspectives: From the Hasmoneans to Bar Kokhba in Light of the Dead Sea Scrolls: Proceedings of the Fourth International Symposium of the Orion Center for the Study of the Dead Sea Scrolls and Associated Literature, 27–31 January, 1999* (Leiden: Brill, 2001), 29–44; Albright eliminates Kittim altogether and amends the text to read מירכת-ים, "the farthest reaches of the sea." Cf. Albright, "The Oracles of Balaam," 222–223, nt. 111.

44. Chron. 1:1 Consists solely of three names, Adam, Seth and Enosh; names which are used by the Bible to connote all of mankind.

45. *HALOT*, "רדה," 1190; *BDB*, "רדה," 921b; Albright points out that the word דרך in vs. 17 may be related to the Ugaritic word *darkatu*, meaning "rule, dominion." Cf. Albright, "The Oracles of Balaam," 219.

46. Cf. A.H. Sayce, "Ur of the Chaldees," *ExpTim* 13 (1901–1902), 64–66; Albright, "The Oracles of Balaam," 220, nt. 89.

enemy even more formidable, not less so. Additionally, the reference to קין, Kayin, in vs. 22 creates a deliberate echo to Seth and Kayin from Genesis.[47] Yirmiyahu's reformulation of our verse using the word שאון (Jer. 48:45),[48] "uproarious multitudes," in place of "all the descendants of Seth," indicates that Num. 24:17 was traditionally interpreted as connoting the masses, not an obscure tribe.[49]

A brief thematic review of Bilam's four orations yields the following:

- Oracle 1: Israel dwelling in security: Israel is depicted as a nation set apart from the rest, quantitatively as well as qualitatively.

- Oracle 2: Israel and the monarchy: With God, the divine monarch, dwelling in their midst, Israel is analogous to a mighty lion ready to pounce and devour its prey.

- Oracle 3: Israel victorious over its enemies: The serenity and fecundity which characterize Israel's lodging, likened to a divinely planted garden, generate the necessary conditions for the ascent and victory of its king.

- Oracle 4: Israel dominating the nations: Israel is destined to defeat its enemies and dominate all the descendants of Seth, or all mankind.

Evaluating the oracles of Bilam synchronically shows them to work together in a unified polemic against each of Balak's original contentions. Whereas Balak likened Israel to a bovine horde, suggesting disorganization and lack of leadership, Bilam's first and third blessings negate this misconception (Num. 22:4). Together, these two blessings develop the theme of Israel's encampment, likened to an intricately well-planned garden, planted and maintained by God Himself. The monarchic theme

---

47. Resonances between קין and the קיני tribe from the previous verse are no doubt intentional, although that fact does not detract from the verse's clear and direct reference to Kayin.

48. *HALOT*, "שאון," 1370; BDB, "שאון," 981a.

49. Cf. Jer. 48:45. While it could possibly be argued that the verse in Yirmiyahu is a misreading of the verse in Numbers, the appearance of the word שאון once again coupled with Moab in Amos 2:2 suggests that the word's appearance in Yirmiyahu was also not accidental.

which links the second and third blessings, wherein God the divine monarch elevates Israel to the role of sovereign and affirms Israel's possession of independent leadership. The analogy of the majestic lion and ראם in these blessings further negates Israel's bovine portrayal as it mocks Balak for his faulty assessment. Finally, Balak's expressed desire to defeat Israel in battle is thwarted in Bilam's final oracle which portends Israel's ultimate dominion over Moab and all their enemies (Num. 22:6).

Bilam's Orations and Yaakov's Blessing to Yehudah

The essential themes and language which form the crux of the Bilam orations and much of the surrounding narrative are strikingly resonant with the core themes and terms found in Yaakov's blessing to Yehudah. An analysis of Yehudah's blessing and an exploration of its relevance to the Bilam material is in order. In considering the multiple correspondences between the Bilam and Yehudah material it is relevant to take into account the similarities between the surrounding contexts. Both texts contain words of admonition, although their general thrust is one of blessing.[50] Both texts also project the fulfillment of their prophecy in the distant future; אחרית הימים, the end of days (Cf. Gen. 49:1, Num. 23:10; 24:14, 20).

Yaakov's Blessing to Yehudah

Yehudah, your brothers shall praise you; your hand will be on the nape of your foes; your father's sons will bow down to you. You are a lion's whelp, Yehudah; you have grown on prey, my son. Like a lion he crouches and lies down, like a lioness – who dares to rouse him? The scepter shall not depart from Yehudah, nor the ruler's staff from between his feet, so that tribute shall come to him, and the obedience of the nations shall be his. He tethers his donkey to a vine, his colt to the choicest branch; he will wash his garments in wine, his robes in the blood of grapes.

---

50. Bilam admonishes Moab together with other nations in the fourth oracle, and Yaakov's address in Gen. 49 commences with admonishments directed at Reuven, Shimon, and Levi.

His eyes are darker than wine, his teeth are whiter than milk.
(Gen. 49:8–12)

Yaakov's blessing to Yehudah opens with a description of his battle
victories and monarchic ascension. The themes of victory, security and
monarchy which are conveyed in Yehudah's blessing match the core
themes of Bilam's three blessings. The near verbatim repetition in Bilam's
third prophecy of the crouching lion that dare not be roused, clearly
evokes Yaakov's blessing, and provides further basis for the assumption
of a correlation between the two:[51]

כרע רבץ כאריה וכלביא מי יקימנו (Gen. 49:9)

כרע שכב כארי וכלביא מי יקימנו (Num. 24:9)

Yehudah's blessing proceeds with the promise of dynastic continuity,
symbolized by the royal staff, שבט, between his feet, מבין רגליו.[52] The
evocative terminology "between his feet" coupled with the theme of
dynastic continuity and the notion of human seed, matches key imagery
from Bilam's Blessings.[53] The staff metaphor שבט also appears in Bilam's

---

51. Cf. Martin Rosel, *Jakob Bileam, und der Messias: Messianische Erwartungen in
Gen 49 und Num* (Leuven: Leuven Univ. Press, 2006), 151–175. Rosel finds it
likely that Greek translators understood both texts to refer to eschatological
rulers. Whereas the figure in Genesis is specified as issuing from the tribe of
Yehudah, the Bilam oracles do not specify a pedigree.

52. Richard Steiner maintains that the word עד in Yehudah's blessing is deliberately ambiguous, and can mean "ever, forever, until-and then no more,
until-and after." He assigns the word עד to the end of the preceding clause
ומחוקק בין רגליו, as opposed to before the clause כי יבא שילה. Cf. Richard
Steiner, "Four Inner-Biblical Interpretations of Genesis 49:10: On the Lexical
and Syntactic Ambiguities of עד as Reflected in the Prophecies of Nathan,
Ahijah, Ezekiel, and Zechariah, " *JBL* 132.1 (2013), 33–60.

53. Cf. Onkelos, Pseudo-Johnathan and Kimchi on Gen. 49:10, who understand
"from between his feet" to refer to Yehudah's seed. The theme of the continuity and integrity of Yehudah's clan's seed is central in the Yehudah Tamar
narrative of Gen. 38 and is probably hinted at here as well. The enigmatic
and polysemic word שילה may also suggest the role of Yehudah's son שלה in
that episode.

fourth oracle, where it again connotes monarchy.[54] Yehudah's blessing continues with a description of his dominion over the nations, and their obedience to him, ולו יקהת עמים.[55] Subservience to a dominant power, manifest through the payment of tribute, שי, may be hinted at in the word שילה, which is believed by many to be a combination of שי and לו, "tribute to him."[56] One of the central themes noted above in Bilam's fourth oracle is the subservience of the nations to Israel. The term חיל in Bilam's declaration וישראל עשה חיל connotes victory and power, as well as material wealth, resonating with Yehudah's blessing.[57]

While it might be argued that the themes of victory, domination,

---

54. Num. 24:17; The monarchic reference of the staff, שבט, in Yaakov's blessing is supported by the word's juxtapositioning with the word מחקק, ruler. Cf. HALOT "חקק," 348. The only other instance of the blending of these two terms, שבט and מחקק, is in the Song of Devorah, where the reference is again tribal leadership. Cf. Jud. 5:14.

55. The word יקהת in Gen. 49:10 is a construct form of יקהה, meaning "obedience." Cf. HALOT, "יקהה," 430; BDB, "יקהה," 429a; Prov. 30:17.

56. The lexeme שילה in Yaakov's blessing has troubled translators throughout the generations. An exhaustive list of possibilities is provided by Th. C. Vriezen, A.S. van der Woude in *De literatuur van Oud-Israel* (Wassenaar: Servire, 1973), 98–100. שילה has been interpreted as אשר לו, his progeny, cf. Onkelos Gen. 49:10. Alternatively, it has been interpreted as שי לו, tribute to him. Cf. William Moran, "Gen. 49,10 and its use in Ezek 21:32," *Biblica* 39.4 (1958), 405–425, (412–414); Richard Steiner, "Poetic Forms in the Masoretic Vocalization and Three Difficult Phrases in Jacob's Blessing: יתר שאת (Gen. 49:3), יצועי עלה (49:4), and יבא שילה (49:10)," *JBL* 129 (2010), 219–226; *Bereishit Rabbah* (ed. J. Theodor and Ch. Albeck; 1903–29; Jerusalem, 1965), 1219 lines 7–8. It has also been interpreted as the toponym, Shilo. Cf. Lindblom, "The Political Background of the Shilo Oracle," in *Congress Volume, Copenhagen 1953* (SVT, 1: Leiden, 1953), 78–87, 86; Serge Frolov, "Judah Comes to Shiloh: Genesis 49:10a, One More Time," *JBL* 131.3 (2012), 417–422. Some have suggested that שילה is a derivative of the Akkadian word for ruler, *silu*. Cf. Driver, "Some Hebrew Roots and Their Meanings," *JThS* 23 (1922), 69–73; William Moran, "Gen. 49: 10," argues against this. Another candidate for secondary meaning is שאילה, his requested one. The many plays on words in the story of Samuel's birth make this suggestion quite interesting. Cf. Ran Zadok, "On Five Biblical Names," *ZAW* 89 (1977), 266–268. Zadok argues that the name שילה itself derives from שאל, to ask or borrow.

57. HALOT, "חיל," 311; BDB, "חיל," 298b.

and monarchy, together with the symbol of the mighty lion, may be found in other biblical texts, the shared presence of other unique and significant features between these two texts points to their intended correlation. Bilam's quarrel with his she-ass, one of the Bible's most amusing stories, harbors several of these correlating features. The scene is set in a vineyard along a narrow footpath upon which Bilam is injured. Interestingly, Yaakov's blessing also features the unusual elements of a she-ass in a vineyard, followed by a description of Yehudah's clothing getting stained with blood; the blood of grapes, דם ענבים (Gen. 49:11). Yehudah's blessing concludes with the striking image of wine painted upon his eyes (Gen. 49:12).[58] In Bilam's latter two orations, he introduces himself as שתם העין (Num. 24:3, 15). The classical commentators tend to agree, based on the surrounding context which stresses a variety of words connoting clarity of vision, that the hapax שתם means "open," rendering the expression שתם העין as "open eyed."[59] The commentators draw upon the Aramaic word שתם, meaning "to open," which is attested to in the Talmud.[60] To be precise, the word שתם in its most common context means "to bore a hole into a wine barrel."[61] Wine which is distilled

---

58. *HALOT*, "כחל," 469; BDB, "כחל," 471a.
59. Cf. Onkelos, Pseudo-Johnathan, Rashi, Rashbam, and Ibn Ezra, Gen. 24:3. Rashi suggests both open and closed as possible definitions, although he bases the "closed" definition on a Midrash. The Samaritan text reads סתום העין, "having closed eyes." Cf. *HALOT*, "שתם," 1670–1671. This is likely interpolative and does not reflect the general sense of the surrounding verse which lauds Bilam's prophetic abilities, not disabilities! Albright understands the word שתם to be a contraction of אשר תמה עין, "of perfect vision." Cf, Albright, "The Oracles of Balaam," 216 nt. 56. This definition is unlikely however, as it requires reassigning the letter *heh* in העין to the end of the previous word, תם.
60. Cf. BT *Avodah Zarah* 69a; Aramaic terminology at the heart of the Bilam orations is not at all surprising, especially in light of Bilam's origins from Aram, cf. Num. 23:7, and in light of the Aramaic dialect which characterizes the Bilam inscription at Deir Alla. Cf. P. Kyle McCarter, "The Dialect of the Deir Alla Texts," in Jacob Hoftijzer and Gerrit Van der Kooij (eds.), *The Balaam Text from Deir Alla Re-evaluated: Proceedings of the International Symposium Held at Leiden, 21–24 August 1989* (Leiden: Brill, 1991), 87–99.
61. Jastrow, *A Dictionary of the Targumim, the Talmud Babli and Yerushalmi, and the Midrashic Literature*, "שתם," 1639a.

from grapes, and wisdom which is distilled from knowledge, are often correlated in biblical wisdom literature.[62] The unique expression שתם העין may be a poetic means of expressing Bilam's direct access to divine knowledge which poured effortlessly from his mouth like wine from a freshly uncorked barrel. The implied association between eyes/vision and wine/wisdom in both Bilam's orations and Yehudah's blessing is especially interesting in light of the many motifs and lexical terms which these two texts share.

Bilam's first three orations focus on the themes of the Israelite monarchy and military supremacy, negating any Moabite attempt to thwart Israel's unique standing as a nation apart from the rest. These three oracles are structured upon the A, B, A+B pattern, forming a tight unified set.

Another important pattern at work in the Bilam material is referred to as the $x/x+1$ ascending number pattern.[63] This pattern contains succeeding numbers that are clearly defined as a set, and which are topped off by one more marking the climax. A good example of the $x/x+1$ pattern is in the two opening chapters of Amos where the peaking of successive numbers is the central motif:

> For three sins of Damascus, even for four, I will not relent. Because she threshed Gilead with sledges having iron teeth (1:3)...For three sins of Gaza, even for four, I will not relent. Because she took captive whole communities and sold them to Edom (1:6)...For three sins of Tyre, even for four, I will not relent. Because she sold whole communities of captives to Edom, disregarding a treaty of brotherhood (1:9)...For three

---

62. Cf. Prov. 9:2, 5; Sir. 31:27; 40:20; Dommershausen, "יין," *TDOT* 6: 59–64, (64). Arnold Wieder, "Ben Sira and the Praises of Wine," *The Jewish Quarterly Review* 61.2 (1970), 155–166. While Ben Sira is not part of the biblical canon it does enjoy a semi-canonical status and is quoted from frequently in the Talmud.

63. Cf. Wolfgang M.W. Roth, "The Numerical Sequence $x/x+1$ in the Old Testament," *VT* 12.3 (1962), 300–311, (303); Y. Zakovitch, על שלושה...ועל ארבעה: הדגם הספרותי שלשה-ארבעה במקרא (For three...and for four: The Pattern for the numbers three and four in the Bible: Jerusalem: Makor, 1979), I: 108–109.

sins of Edom, even for four, I will not relent. Because he pursued his brother with a sword and slaughtered the women of the land, because his anger raged continually, and his fury flamed unchecked (1:11)...For three sins of Ammon, even for four, I will not relent. Because he ripped open the pregnant women of Gilead in order to extend his borders (1:13)...For three sins of Moab, even for four, I will not relent. Because he burned to ashes the bones of Edom's king (2:1)...For three sins of Yehudah, even for four, I will not relent. Because they have rejected the law of the Lord and have not kept his decrees, because they have been led astray by false gods, the gods their ancestors followed (2:4)...For three sins of Israel, even for four, I will not relent. They sell the innocent for silver, and the needy for a pair of sandals (2:6)....

The $x/x+1$ pattern seen in Amos is predicated on the idea of three which establishes a pattern, and a fourth which tops it off. This is referred to as "the topped off triad."[64] Bilam's final oracle completes the successive number pattern, and serves as the climax of all three preceding oracles, peaking at the top of the $x/x+1$ ascending number pattern, in a topped off triad, which features Israel's ultimate supremacy not only over Moab, but over all its enemies.[65] The overall poetic structure of the Bilam pericope reflects its core message: The Divine monarchy represented by the Israelite monarchy. Bilam's prophecies establish Israel's monarchic supremacy not only within its own internal tribal context, but within the wider international arena. This idea was first introduced in the Blessings of Yaakov, and is later reinforced and expanded upon in the Bilam orations.

---

64. Shemaryahu Talmon, "The 'Topped Triad': A Biblical Literary Convention and the 'Ascending Numerical' Pattern," *Maarav* 8 (1992), 181–198.
65. Moberly links the she–ass episode with the rest of the Bilam material, citing the three plus one pattern. Cf. Moberly, "On Learning to be a True Prophet," 14, nt. 31.

Conclusion

The common themes and language shared between the outer frameworks of each of Bilam's orations point to their literary cohesion. The presence of a chain linking major topics and key words between the latter two blessings, together with lexical and thematic consistency between Bilam's first and third blessings, points to the presence of an A, B, A+B pattern connecting all three. Sexual wordplay throughout the orations of Bilam further points to their unity and serves as a thematic link to the larger narrative. Whereas the outer structure of Bilam's fourth oracle closely matches the introduction to the third blessing, its content seems to be at variance with Bilam's earlier orations. The essential themes of Bilam's four orations point to Yaakov's blessing to Yehudah in Genesis 49 as the template of the Bilam narrative. Reverberations of significant themes and language between the Bilam and Genesis material corroborate their association. Bilam's final oracle serves as the climax of the topped off triad number pattern and emerges as an expansion upon the theme of the Israelite monarchy which originated with Yaakov's blessing to Yehudah.

The Blessings of Yaakov establish the dual institutions of Israelite leadership, monarchy and priesthood. Bilam's Blessings draw upon imagery from Yaakov's Blessings specifically relating to the idea of the Israelite monarchy. Bilam's orations move the idea of Israelite leadership forward by suggesting a synergistic correlation between the Israelite monarchy and the kingdom of God. The absence of any reference to the institution of the Israelite priesthood in Bilam's Blessings will be addressed in the chapter on the Blessings of Moshe. The Blessings of Bilam have been shown, like the Blessings of Yaakov, to relate directly to the fundamental theological tenet of קבלת עול מלכות שמים, acceptance of the yoke of heaven.

The Blessings of Moshe

This chapter opens with a discussion on the hymnal framework that encases the Blessings of Moshe. The survey and exposition on the tribal blessings which follow demonstrate their structural unity. When viewed holistically, the Blessings of Moshe are shown to form a composite picture of a human being. In addition to featuring body parts, the figure that emerges is adorned with the priestly vestments. The Blessings of Moshe conjure images of the priesthood, an institution originally intended to include the entire nation of Israel. The structure of Moshe's Blessings, together with their content, are shown to showcase the nation of Israel as a nation of priests, entrusted with the task of safeguarding the covenant.

דברים פרק לג:א–כט

וְזֹאת הַבְּרָכָה אֲשֶׁר בֵּרַךְ מֹשֶׁה אִישׁ הָאֱלֹהִים אֶת־בְּנֵי יִשְׂרָאֵל לִפְנֵי מוֹתוֹ: וַיֹּאמַר יְקֹוָק מִסִּינַי בָּא וְזָרַח מִשֵּׂעִיר לָמוֹ הוֹפִיעַ מֵהַר פָּארָן וְאָתָה מֵרִבְבֹת קֹדֶשׁ מִימִינוֹ אֵשׁ דָּת לָמוֹ: אַף חֹבֵב עַמִּים כָּל־קְדֹשָׁיו בְּיָדֶךָ וְהֵם תֻּכּוּ לְרַגְלֶךָ יִשָּׂא מִדַּבְּרֹתֶיךָ: תּוֹרָה צִוָּה־לָנוּ מֹשֶׁה מוֹרָשָׁה קְהִלַּת יַעֲקֹב: וַיְהִי בִישֻׁרוּן מֶלֶךְ בְּהִתְאַסֵּף רָאשֵׁי עָם יַחַד שִׁבְטֵי יִשְׂרָאֵל: יְחִי רְאוּבֵן וְאַל־יָמֹת וִיהִי מְתָיו מִסְפָּר: וְזֹאת לִיהוּדָה וַיֹּאמַר שְׁמַע יְקֹוָק קוֹל יְהוּדָה וְאֶל־עַמּוֹ תְּבִיאֶנּוּ יָדָיו רָב לוֹ וְעֵזֶר מִצָּרָיו תִּהְיֶה: וּלְלֵוִי אָמַר תֻּמֶּיךָ וְאוּרֶיךָ לְאִישׁ חֲסִידֶךָ אֲשֶׁר נִסִּיתוֹ בְּמַסָּה תְּרִיבֵהוּ עַל־מֵי מְרִיבָה: הָאֹמֵר לְאָבִיו וּלְאִמּוֹ לֹא רְאִיתִיו וְאֶת־אֶחָיו לֹא הִכִּיר וְאֶת־בָּנָיו לֹא יָדָע כִּי שָׁמְרוּ אִמְרָתֶךָ וּבְרִיתְךָ יִנְצֹרוּ: יוֹרוּ מִשְׁפָּטֶיךָ לְיַעֲקֹב וְתוֹרָתְךָ לְיִשְׂרָאֵל יָשִׂימוּ קְטוֹרָה בְּאַפֶּךָ וְכָלִיל עַל־מִזְבְּחֶךָ: בָּרֵךְ יְקֹוָק חֵילוֹ וּפֹעַל יָדָיו תִּרְצֶה מְחַץ מָתְנַיִם קָמָיו וּמְשַׂנְאָיו מִן־יְקוּמוּן: לְבִנְיָמִן אָמַר יְדִיד יְקֹוָק יִשְׁכֹּן לָבֶטַח עָלָיו חֹפֵף עָלָיו כָּל־הַיּוֹם וּבֵין כְּתֵפָיו שָׁכֵן: וּלְיוֹסֵף אָמַר מְבֹרֶכֶת יְקֹוָק אַרְצוֹ מִמֶּגֶד שָׁמַיִם מִטָּל וּמִתְּהוֹם רֹבֶצֶת תָּחַת: וּמִמֶּגֶד תְּבוּאֹת שָׁמֶשׁ וּמִמֶּגֶד גֶּרֶשׁ

יְרָחִים: וּמֵרֹאשׁ הַרְרֵי־קֶדֶם וּמִמֶּגֶד גִּבְעוֹת עוֹלָם: וּמִמֶּגֶד אֶרֶץ וּמְלֹאָהּ וּרְצוֹן
שֹׁכְנִי סְנֶה תָּבוֹאתָה לְרֹאשׁ יוֹסֵף וּלְקָדְקֹד נְזִיר אֶחָיו: בְּכוֹר שׁוֹרוֹ הָדָר לוֹ וְקַרְנֵי
רְאֵם קַרְנָיו בָּהֶם עַמִּים יְנַגַּח יַחְדָּו אַפְסֵי־אָרֶץ וְהֵם רִבְבוֹת אֶפְרַיִם וְהֵם אַלְפֵי
מְנַשֶּׁה: וְלִזְבוּלֻן אָמַר שְׂמַח זְבוּלֻן בְּצֵאתֶךָ וְיִשָּׂשכָר בְּאֹהָלֶיךָ: עַמִּים הַר־יִקְרָאוּ
שָׁם יִזְבְּחוּ זִבְחֵי־צֶדֶק כִּי שֶׁפַע יַמִּים יִינָקוּ וּשְׂפֻנֵי טְמוּנֵי חוֹל: וּלְגָד אָמַר בָּרוּךְ
מַרְחִיב גָּד כְּלָבִיא שָׁכֵן וְטָרַף זְרוֹעַ אַף־קָדְקֹד: וַיַּרְא רֵאשִׁית לוֹ כִּי־שָׁם חֶלְקַת
מְחֹקֵק סָפוּן וַיֵּתֵא רָאשֵׁי עָם צִדְקַת יְקֹוָק עָשָׂה וּמִשְׁפָּטָיו עִם־יִשְׂרָאֵל: וּלְדָן אָמַר
דָּן גּוּר אַרְיֵה יְזַנֵּק מִן־הַבָּשָׁן: וּלְנַפְתָּלִי אָמַר נַפְתָּלִי שְׂבַע רָצוֹן וּמָלֵא בִּרְכַּת
יְקֹוָק יָם וְדָרוֹם יְרָשָׁה: וּלְאָשֵׁר אָמַר בָּרוּךְ מִבָּנִים אָשֵׁר יְהִי רְצוּי אֶחָיו וְטֹבֵל
בַּשֶּׁמֶן רַגְלוֹ: בַּרְזֶל וּנְחֹשֶׁת מִנְעָלֶךָ וּכְיָמֶיךָ דָּבְאֶךָ: אֵין כָּאֵל יְשֻׁרוּן רֹכֵב שָׁמַיִם
בְּעֶזְרֶךָ וּבְגַאֲוָתוֹ שְׁחָקִים: מְעֹנָה אֱלֹהֵי קֶדֶם וּמִתַּחַת זְרֹעֹת עוֹלָם וַיְגָרֶשׁ מִפָּנֶיךָ
אוֹיֵב וַיֹּאמֶר הַשְׁמֵד: וַיִּשְׁכֹּן יִשְׂרָאֵל בֶּטַח בָּדָד עֵין יַעֲקֹב אֶל־אֶרֶץ דָּגָן וְתִירוֹשׁ
אַף־שָׁמָיו יַעַרְפוּ טָל: אַשְׁרֶיךָ יִשְׂרָאֵל מִי כָמוֹךָ עַם נוֹשַׁע בַּיקֹוָק מָגֵן עֶזְרֶךָ
וַאֲשֶׁר־חֶרֶב גַּאֲוָתֶךָ וְיִכָּחֲשׁוּ אֹיְבֶיךָ לָךְ וְאַתָּה עַל־בָּמוֹתֵימוֹ תִדְרֹךְ:

Deuteronomy 33:1–29

This is the blessing that Moshe the man of God pronounced on the Israelites before his death. He said: "The LORD came from Sinai and dawned over them from Seir; He shone forth from Mount Paran. He came with myriads of holy ones from the south, from His mountain slopes. Surely it is You who love the people; all the holy ones are in Your hand. At our feet they all bow down, and from You receive instruction, the law that Moshe gave us, the possession of the assembly of Yaakov. He was king over Yeshurun when the leaders of the people assembled, along with the tribes of Israel. "Let Reuven live and not die, nor his people be few." And this he said about Yehudah: "Hear, LORD, the cry of Yehudah; bring him to his people. With his own hands he defends his cause. O, be his help against his foes!" About Levi he said: "Your Thummim and Urim belong to your faithful servant. You tested him at Massah; you contended with him at the waters of Meribah. He said of his father and mother, 'I have no regard for them.' He did not recognize his brothers or acknowledge his own children, but he watched over Your word and guarded Your covenant. He teaches Your precepts to Yaakov and Your law to Israel. He offers incense before You and whole burnt offerings on Your altar. Bless all his skills, LORD, and be pleased with the work of his hands. Strike down those who rise against him, his foes till they rise no more." About Binyamin he said: "Let the beloved of the LORD rest secure in him, for he shields him all day long, and the one the LORD loves rests between his shoulders." About Yosef he said: "May the LORD bless his land with the precious dew from heaven above and with the deep waters that lie below; with the best the sun brings forth and the finest the moon can yield; with the choicest gifts of the ancient mountains and the fruitfulness of the everlasting hills; with the best gifts of the earth and its fullness and the favor of Him who dwelt in the burning bush. Let all these rest on the head of Yosef, on the brow of the prince among his brothers. In majesty he is like a firstborn bull; his horns are the horns of a wild ox. With them he will gore the nations, even those at the ends of the earth. Such are the ten thousands of Ephraim; such are the thousands of Menashe." About Zevulun he said: "Rejoice, Zevulun, in your going out, and you, Yissachar, in your tents. They will summon peoples to the mountain and there offer the sacrifices of the righteous; they will feast on the abundance of the seas, on the treasures hidden in the sand." About Gad he said: "Blessed is he who enlarges Gad's domain! Gad lives there like a lion, tearing at arm or head. He chose the best land for himself; the leader's portion was kept for him. When the heads of the people assembled, he carried out the LORD's righteous will, and his judgments concerning Israel." About Dan he said: "Dan is a lion's cub, springing out of Bashan." About Naphtali he said: "Naphtali is abounding with the favor of the LORD and is full of his blessing; he will inherit southward to the lake." About Asher he said: "Most blessed of sons is Asher; let him be favored by his brothers, and let him bathe his feet in oil. The bolts of your gates will be iron and bronze, and your strength will equal your days. "There is no one like the God of Yeshurun, who rides across the heavens to help you and on the clouds in His majesty. The eternal God is your refuge, and underneath are the everlasting arms. He will drive out your enemies before you, saying, 'Destroy them!' So Israel will live in safety; Yaakov will dwell secure in a land of grain and new wine, where the heavens drop dew. Blessed are you, Israel! Who is like you, a people saved by the LORD? He is your shield and helper and your glorious sword. Your enemies will cower before you, and you will tread on their heights."

The Hymnal Framework of Deut. 33[1]

Moshe's blessings to the tribes of Israel in Deut. 33 are introduced by four poetic verses recounting God's revelation at Sinai (Deut. 33:2–5). The relevance of the preamble to the blessings which follow is the subject of much debate. Rashi takes the approach that the blessings are essentially prayerful requests for the welfare of the tribes. As such, they are preceded by praises recounting the glory of God at the time of His revelation at Sinai. This approach is in line with the standard formula for prayer in which requests are preceded by praise, and followed by thanksgiving (Rashi, Deut. 33:2). Ibn Ezra suggests that the introductory verses of Deut. 33 and their fiery depiction of God's theophany is a prelude to God's continued fiery protection over all of the tribes within their homeland (Ibn Ezra, Deut. 33:2). Nachmanides proposes that Moshe's blessings are preceded by verses reviewing the giving of the law at Sinai in order to link the fulfillment of the blessings with adherence to the divine mandate (Nachmanides, Deut. 33:2).

Modern commentators have noted that the opening and closing verses of ch. 33 function as a unit, forming a hymnal framework around the blessings (vs. 2–5 and 26–29).[2]

---

1. An earlier version of this chapter appears in Geula Twersky, *Song of Riddles: Deciphering the Song of Songs* (Jerusalem: Gefen Pub., 2018), 201–213.

2. Some contend that these verses were originally an independent hymn into which the blessings were later inserted. Cf. A.D.H. Mayes, *Deuteronomy* (NCB 5; Grand Rapids: Eerdmans, 1979), 396; Ian Cairns, *Deuteronomy, Word and Presence; a Commentary* (ITC; Grand Rapids: Eerdmans Pub., 1992), 294; D.N. Freedman, "The Poetic Structure of the Framework of Deuteronomy 33," pages 85–107 in *Divine Commitment and Human Obligation, vol. 2: Poetry and Orthography* (ed. J. Huddlestun; Grand Rapids: Eerdmans, 1997). This conjecture is rooted in the seeming lack of cohesion between the tribal blessings and the outer framework. Other scholars have suggested that the hymn may have been composed for the purpose of fusing the references to individual tribes in the chapter into one cohesive story of the entire nation

Christensen points out that the two halves of the outer framework form a chiasmus:[3]

A. (v. 2) God comes to deliver His people.
    B. (v. 3–4) God protects and provides for His people.
        C. (v. 5) God is king over Yeshurun.
        C. (v. 26) There is no God like the God of Yeshurun.
    B. (v. 27–28) Israel is secured in and blessed by God.
A. (v. 29) Israel is delivered by God.

This hypothesis is weakened by the fact that whereas the concluding verse does describe Israel's deliverance from their enemies by God, vs. 2 does not. Rather, it recounts the giving of the law. While the giving of the law may indeed be a prerequisite for salvation, that does not necessarily make the two concepts synonymous. Nonetheless, the overall approach to the outer framework of the Blessings as forming of a chiasmus is well taken. An alternative approach to understanding the exact nature of the chiasm will be suggested following a survey of the tribal blessings.

The Tribal Blessings

Whereas we begin with the tribe of Reuven, it will soon become clear that Moshe's parting words to Reuven are not to be understood as a part of the formal tribal blessings.

REUVEN

Let Reuven live and not die, nor his people be few (Deut. 33:6).

While Moshe appears to commence the tribal blessing with Reuven, the text seems to indicate otherwise. Moshe's prayerful message that Reuven should not cease to exist does not bode well for the tribe's future. Moshe's words here do seem to correlate with the tribe's eventual disappearance from the historical record. The last time the Bible men-

---

of Israel. Cf. Richard D. Nelson, *Deuteronomy: A Commentary*, (Louisville: Presbyterian, 2004), 386. Duane Christensen, "Two Stanzas of a Hymn in Deuteronomy 33," *Biblica* 65 (1984), 382–389.

3.   Ibid, "Two Stanzas of a Hymn in Deuteronomy 33," 382–389.

tions Reuven is in the days of King Jehu (2 Kg. 10:32, 33), after which the tribe seems to vanish into oblivion. The Midrash comments on the repetition (33:1, 7) of the word 'וזאת' in the opening of Yehudah's blessing that Moshe's earlier words to Reuven are parenthetical, set apart from the body of the blessings.[4] A further indication that Moshe's words to Reuven are not to be regarded as part of the tribal blessings is that whereas all of the blessings are introduced in the following way; "to (name)," with Moshe addressing the tribe directly, this formula is conspicuously absent from Moshe's parting words to Reuven. Furthermore, whereas all the tribal blessings follow a fixed rubric in which they reference either a feature of human physiognomy or an analogy to an animal, Moshe's address to Reuven does not fit this pattern. This point will be elaborated upon in the coming discussion.

In addition to Reuven's apparent displacement from the blessings of Moshe, we also find the tribe of Shimon to have been overlooked by Moshe in his blessings. Whereas Reuven – who ostensibly does not receive a blessing – is addressed by Moshe, Shimon does not merit any mention at all. In the discussion on the blessings of Yaakov, the address to Shimon and Levi was explained as being closer to a curse than to a blessing. We will see that Moshe reframes the blessing to Levi in light of his reformed character. Shimon's role on the other hand does not merit Mosaic reinterpretation.

Understanding Moshe's words to Reuven as set apart from the rest of the tribal blessings is important for evaluating the chapter as a whole. When we begin with Yehudah, a pattern begins to emerge. To begin with, as noted above, each of the tribal blessings conveys a distinctly human or an animal-like description. In addition, we find that each of the blessings focuses upon either the theme of the inheritance of the land of Israel or the centrality of the divine law. The inherent duality between the land of Israel and Torah law is one of the primary focuses of the book of Deuteronomy, and is clearly formulated in the recitation of the *Shema* prayer:

---

4.   *Midrash Pitron Torah*, Deut. 33; 334.

So if you faithfully obey the commands I am giving you today –
to love the Lord your God and to serve Him with all your heart
and with all your soul – then I will send rain on your land in its
season, both autumn and spring rains, so that you may gather
in your grain, new wine and olive oil. I will provide grass in the
fields for your cattle, and you will eat and be satisfied. Be careful,
or you will be enticed to turn away and worship other gods and
bow down to them. Then the Lord's anger will burn against you,
and He will shut up the heavens so that it will not rain and the
ground will yield no produce, and you will soon perish from the
good land the Lord is giving you (Deut. 11:13–17).

The inseparable relationship between the Land of Israel and Torah
law, and their fundamental interdependence is again made abundantly
clear in the book of Joshua.

Be strong and courageous, because you will lead these people to
inherit the land I swore to their ancestors to give them. Be strong
and very courageous. Be careful to obey all the law My servant
Moshe gave you; do not turn from it to the right or to the left,
that you may be successful wherever you go. Keep this Book of
the Law always on your lips; meditate on it day and night, so that
you may be careful to do everything written in it. Then you will be
prosperous and successful. Have I not commanded you? Be strong
and courageous. Do not be afraid; do not be discouraged, for the
LORD your God will be with you wherever you go (Josh. 1:6–9).

The significance of our observations here regarding the human
being/animal images and the law/land motifs will be evaluated after a
presentation and evaluation of the individual blessings.

YEHUDAH

The blessing to Yehudah focuses on the role of Yehudah's hands in
battle:

And this he said about Yehudah: "Hear, LORD, the cry of Yehudah;
bring him to his people. With *his own hands* he defends his cause.
O, be his help against his foes! (Deut. 33:7)

Human/*animal-like description*	land/*law*
"With *his own hands* he defends his cause"	Yehudah's blessing implies his leadership role within the context of the battle for the land.

LEVI

Levi's blessing highlights his role in the dissemination of the Divine law. Like Yehudah's blessing, Levi's blessing also features hands. In addition, it describes the breastplate, אורים ותומים, which was worn upon the breast of the high priest. The blessing also praises Levi for his being a guardian of the ברית, the covenant. This may be understood as a general praise of Levi's faithful adherence to Torah law, and/or as a reference to the tribe's steadfast dedication to circumcision, the sign of the covenant or ברית.[5]

> About Levi he said: "Your Thummim and Urim belong to Your faithful servant. You tested him at Massah; You contended with him at the waters of Meribah. He said of his father and mother, "I have no regard for them." He did not recognize his brothers or acknowledge his own children, but he watched over Your word and guarded Your covenant. He teaches Your precepts to Yaakov and Your law to Israel. He offers incense before You and whole burnt offerings on Your altar. Bless all his skills, LORD, and be pleased with the work of his hands. Strike down those who rise against him, his foes till they rise no more (Deut. 33:8–11).

Human/*animal-like description*	land/**law**
In addition to the reference to his *hands*, Moshe refers to the *breastplate* and the *brit*. The image conjured by the blessing is that of the high priest.	"He teaches your precepts to Yaakov and your law to Israel."

---

5.   Gen. 17:11; Rashi comments on vs. 9 that Moshe was praising Levi's adherence to the laws of circumcision, even during the desert sojourn.

BINYAMIN

Moshe's blessing to Binyamin describes the divine protection which rests upon his shoulders, ostensibly protecting him in battle. Classic and modern commentators alike have generally interpreted Binyamin's blessing as meaning that God shall dwell in the Temple, which is so to speak, between his shoulders.[6]

About Binyamin he said: "Let the beloved of the LORD rest secure in him, for He shields him all day long, and the one the LORD rests between his shoulders (Deut. 33:12).

Human/*animal-like description*	**land**/*law*
"the LORD rests between his shoulders."	"He shields him all day long" implies protection in the battle for the Land.

YOSEF

Moshe regards Yosef as the head or prince of his brothers and is compared to a wild ox. His blessing focusses on both his role as a warrior and on the bounty of his land.

About Yosef he said: "May the LORD bless his land with the precious dew from heaven above and with the deep waters that lie below; with the best the sun brings forth and the finest the moon can yield; with the choicest gifts of the ancient mountains and the fruitfulness of the everlasting hills; with the best gifts of the earth and its fullness and the favor of him who dwelt in the bush. Let all these rest on the head of Yosef, on the brow of the prince among his brothers. In majesty he is like a firstborn bull; his horns are the horns of a wild ox. With them he will gore the nations, even those at the ends of the earth. Such are the ten thousands of Ephraim; such are the thousands of Manasseh (Deut. 33:13–17).

---

6. Cf. Rashi, Ibn Ezra, and Nachmanides on Deut. 33:12. Cf. also S.R. Driver, *Deuteronomy* (ICC 21; Edinburgh: T & T Clark, 1978), 404; Jack R. Lundbom, *Deuteronomy: A Commentary* (Grand Rapids: Eerdmans, 2013), 929.

Human/*animal-like description*	*land/* **law**
"Let all these rest on the head of Yosef, on the brow of the prince among his brothers...His horns are the horns of a wild ox."[7]	"May the LORD bless his land...the favor of him who dwelt in the bush...he will gore the nations, even those at the ends of the earth. Such are the ten thousands of Ephraim; such are the thousands of Menashe."

ZEVULUN AND YISSACHAR

Zevulun and Yissachar's blessing depicts them going out to battle followed by their safe return.[8] The blessing concludes with them bringing sacrificial offerings of thanksgiving.

> About Zevulun he said: "Rejoice, Zevulun, in your going out, and you, Yissachar, in your tents. They will summon peoples to the mountain and there offer the sacrifices of the righteous; they will feast on the abundance of the seas, on the treasures hidden in the sand (Deut. 33:18–19).

Human/*animal-like description*	*land*/**law**
Zevulun's blessing describes the tribe in a priestly role, in the act of sacrificial offering.	"Rejoice, Zevulun, in your going out, and you, Issachar, in your tents...the treasures hidden in the sand." The reference to tents here is interpreted by the classical commentators as a poetic reference to Torah learning, or alternatively to their tribal land allotment.[9]

---

7.   The identity of the *re'em* is uncertain. Suggestions range from unicorn, wild bull or buffalo, to white antelope. Cf. *HALOT*, "ראם," 1163; Feliks maintains that in ancient times there were two different traditions which identified the re'em in its various spellings as either a wild ox or the Oryx. Cf. Yehuda Feliks, *Nature and Man in* the Bible (London, Jerusalem, New York: Soncino, 1981), 263. The belligerent nature of the animal described here strongly suggests the wild ox.

8.   Ibn Ezra Deut. 33:18. Cf. Num. 27:17.

9.   Cf. Onkelos, Rashi, Ibn Ezra, Rashbam and Nachmanides on Deut. 33:18.

GAD

Gad is compared to a lion. His blessing speaks of both his choice land and his judgements relating to the divine law.

> About Gad he said: "Blessed is He who enlarges Gad's domain! Gad lives there like a lion, tearing at arm or head. He chose the best land for himself; the leader's portion was kept for him. When the heads of the people assembled, he carried out the LORD's righteous will, and his judgments concerning Israel (Deut. 33:20–21).

*Human/***animal**-*like description*	*land*/law
"Gad lives there like a *lion*"	"He chose the best land for him- self…he carried out the LORD's righteous will, and his judgments concerning Israel."

DAN

Dan is also compared to a lion. His land is located in the Bashan region.

> About Dan he said: "Dan is a lion's cub, springing out of Bashan" (Deut. 33:22).

*Human/***animal**-*like description*	*land*/law
"Dan is a lion's cub"	"…springing out of Bashan." Dan's blessing implies a victory in battle over his land allotment.

NAPHTALI

The relevance of Naphtali's blessing to the human/animal theme which is being charted here will be addressed in the evaluation of the blessings as a unit. Naphtali's inheritance is described in abundantly rich terms.

> About Naphtali he said: "Naphtali is abounding with the favor of the LORD and is full of His blessing; he will inherit southward to the lake" (Deut. 33:23).

Human/*animal-like description*	*land*/law
Naphtali abounds with God's blessing, (synonymous with the *priestly blessing*, cf. Num. 6:27). His satisfaction שבע רצון brings to mind the description of the High Priest who wore the golden diadem upon his forehead as an expression of God's רצון. "It will be on Aharon's forehead, and he will bear the guilt involved in the sacred gifts the Israelites consecrate, whatever their gifts may be. It will be on Aharon's forehead continually so that they will be acceptable, לרצון, to the LORD" (Ex. 28:38).	"he will inherit southward to the lake."

ASHER

Asher bathes his feet in oil, dwelling in his land in peace and security.

> About Asher he said: "Most blessed of sons is Asher; let him be favored by his brothers, and let him bathe his feet in oil. The bolts of your gates will be iron and bronze, and your strength will equal your days (Deut. 33:24–25).

Human/*animal-like description*	*land*/law
"let him bathe his *feet* in oil"	"The bolts of your gates will be iron and bronze" Asher is described to be dwelling securely in his land.

Evaluation of the Tribal Blessings

Several observations emerge from this survey. To begin with, when viewed as a complex set, the blessings of Moshe form a composite picture of a human being. The figure that emerges has hands (Yehudah and Levi), legs (Asher), a head (Yosef), and shoulders (Binyamin). In addition to featuring body parts, the figure is adorned with the priestly breast plate (Levi), wears the priestly diadem ציץ (Yosef and Naphtali), and is engaged in the act of offering a sacrifice (Zevulun and Yissachar). The blessings of Moshe appear to conjure an image representative of the priesthood, an institution originally intended to include the entire nation of Israel (Ex. 19:6). Viewing each of the individual tribal blessings as components of a larger tapestry explicates the relevance of Naphtali's blessing to the larger set. Naphtali is described by Moshe as being "full of blessing." Aside from the sacrificial rites conducted within the confines of the Temple, another fundamental priestly ritual function was the conferring of God's blessing upon Israel.

So they will put My name on the Israelites, and I will bless them (Num. 6:27).

A further observation which emerges is the casting of three tribes as animals: an ox (Yosef), and two lions (Gad and Dan). It is noteworthy that the animal designations in Moshe's blessings are different than those found in Yaakov's blessings in Genesis 49, (where Yehudah is associated with a lion, Yosef and Gad aren't compared to animals at all, and Dan is compared to a snake). The differences between the animal descriptions in the two sets of tribal blessings would indicate that Moshe was innovating with his animal characterizations as opposed to confirming Yaakov's earlier designations.

A broad view of Moshe's blessings portrays the tribes of Israel as a compound human/priest/lion/ox. Yechezkel's description of the *kruv* in ch. 28, situated atop God's holy mountain and inlaid with the same rare and precious gems associated with the breastplate worn by the high priest, strongly suggests a close correlation between the *kruvim* and the priesthood.[10] Yechezkel describes the *kruvim* as composite beings that combine the features of a man, a lion, an ox, and an eagle.

Their faces looked like this: Each of the four had the face of a human being, and on the right side each had the face of a lion,

---

10. Ezek. 28:13–14. A relationship between the priesthood and the angelic *kruvim* is also strongly suggested by Mal. 2:7.

and on the left the face of an ox; each also had the face of an eagle (Ezek. 1:10).

Yechezkel, in ch. 41, again describes the *kruvim*, although these *kruvim* combine only the human and leonine features, without the bovine and aquiline features (Ezek. 41:18–19). This description reinforces that it is not imperative for Moshe to have clearly referenced eagles, נשר, in order for it to be possible to discern a hint to the *kruvim* in his blessings. Another physical trait of the *kruvim* described by Yechezkel is their straight, ישר, legs, רגל, made of copper, נחשת (Ezek. 1:7). Fascinatingly, the only other place in the Bible where these three words appear together is in Moshe's blessing to the tribe of Asher:

> About Asher he said: "Most blessed of sons is Asher; let him be favored by his brothers, and let him bathe his feet רַגְלוֹ in oil. The bolts of your gates will be iron and bronze, וּנְחֹשֶׁת and your strength will equal your days. There is no one like the God of Jeshurun, יְשֻׁרוּן who rides across the heavens to help you and on the clouds in His majesty" (Deut. 33:24–26).

While it is not imperative for the eagle to appear in Moshe's Blessings in order to be able to infer references to the *kruvim*, the metaphor comparing God and Israel to eagles in ch. 32 may be viewed as having implications for ch. 33 as well, as these chapters share a close literary relationship (Deut. 32:11). For example, chs. 32 and 33 refer to Israel using the rare terminology Yeshurun, ישורון (Deut. 33:5, 26). This appellation appears only four times in the Bible; twice in our chapter (33: 5, 26), once elsewhere in Deuteronomy, (32:15), and once again in Yeshayahu (44:2). Another strong lexical link connecting chapters 32 and 33 is the word ערף, meaning "to drip," which appears exclusively in these two chapters in the Bible (Deut. 32:2, 33:28). Furthermore, both texts use the word ערף to describe gentle dew which settles upon Israel. Deut. 32:11 compares God to an eagle and Israel to His nestlings. Deut. 33:26 also describes God as being bird-like when it refers to Him as though riding the skies רוכב שמים. Further descriptions of God as eagle-like may be identified in ch. 33, in the word אשדת, upon which I will now elaborate.

Chapter 33 features the hapax אשדת, which was assumed by the classical biblical commentators to be a combination of אש and דת or a

"fiery law."[11] The difficulty with the classical rendering is that the word
דת has been presumed to be a Persian loanword, thus presenting as an
anachronism. This difficulty led many scholars to conclude that the
word is utterly unintelligible.[12] More recently however, Steiner and
Leiman have presented credible evidence for redefining the word and
its etymology.[13] Steiner suggests that the word דת is in fact a contraction
of the word דאת[14] which exhibits an archaic third person feminine
perfect singular form of the verb "to fly or swoop down."[15] He cites
another example of this archaic form in Deut. 31:29, in the word וקראת.[16]
This analysis renders אשדת as "from his right, fire flew to them," which
matches the overall sense of the verse by summing up the four previous
clauses.[17] The only other appearance of the verb דאה in the Pentateuch
may be found just a few chapters earlier in Deut. 28:49, lending further

---

11. Cf. Rashi, Ibn Ezra, and Nachmanides on Deut. 33:2; The Vulgate renders
    אשדת as *ignea lex* ("fiery law") and the Samaritan Targum has "fire of Torah."
    Cf. A. Tal, *The Samaritan Targum of the Pentateuch: A Critical Edition* (Tel
    Aviv: Tel Aviv University, 1981), 2.392, 399. The Targum and Midrashim also
    reference Torah and fire here.

12. Cf. Patrick D. Miller, "Two Critical Notes on Psalm 68 and Deuteronomy 33,"
    HTR 57 (1964), 240–243, esp. 241; D.N. Freedman, "The Poetic Structure of
    the Framework of Deuteronomy 33," pages 25–46 in *The Bible World: Essays
    in Honor of Cyrus H. Gordon* (ed. G. Rendsburg; New York: New York Univ.
    Press, 1980), 30; G. Rendsburg, "Hebrew sdt and Ugaritic isdym," *JNSL* 8
    (1980), 81–82, esp. 81.

13. Richard C. Steiner, "Dāt and ʿēn: Two Verbs Masquerading as Nouns in
    Moses' Blessing (Deuteronomy 33:2, 28)," *JBL* 115.4 (1996), 693–717; Richard
    C. Steiner and Sid Z. Leiman, "The Lost Meaning of Deuteronomy 33:2
    as Preserved in the Palestinian Targum to the Decalogue," pages 157–166
    in *Mishneh Todah: Studies in Deuteronomy and Its Cultural Environment in
    Honor of Jeffrey H. Tigay* (ed. Nih S. Fox, David A. Glatt-Gilad, and Michael
    Williams; Winona Lake, IN: Eisenbrauns, 2009).

14. Steiner points out that this contraction is attested to elsewhere in the Bible;
    Gen 25:24, Deut. 28:57, 1 Sam 1:17, 2 Sam 22:40, Ps 22:22. Steiner explains that
    contractions of this nature are due to "the elision of א between identical or
    similar vowels. Cf. Steiner, "Dāt and ʿēn," 695.

15. HALOT, "דאה," 207.

16. Steiner, "Dāt and ʿēn," p. 695; More examples of this linguistic phenomenon
    are brought by Gesenius in, *Gesenius' Hebrew Grammar*, 74g.

17. Ibid, 695–696.

support to Steiner's thesis.[18] Leiman brings further support for Steiner's hypothesis by demonstrating that "traces of the original interpretation can still be detected in the Palestinian Targum (to Exod. 20:2), especially when it is read in conjunction with the Siphre (to Deut. 33:2)."[19] Biblical evidence in support of the rendering of מימינו אשדת as "fire flew from his right hand" may be observed in Habakkuk's parallel description of God's approach from Teman and Mount Paran in which rays of light are observed emanating from His right hand, reminiscent of the flames which flew forth from God's right hand in Deut. 33:2:

> God came from Teman, the Holy One from Mount Paran. His glory covered the heavens and His praise filled the earth. His splendor was like the sunrise; rays flashed from His hand, where His power was hidden (Hab. 3:3–4).

The verb דאה is found in the bible exclusively alongside either eagles or fiery *kruvim*.[20] Furthermore, the nominal form of the root דאה may be interpreted to be an eagle.[21] Identifying one of the compound roots of the word אשדת as deriving from דאה strongly suggests an allusion in ch. 33 to eagles and to the *kruvim* at one and the same time.

The tension inherent in ch. 33's description of the tribes as simultaneously human/priestly, together with the undercurrent of their angelic qualities, fits the gestalt of the chapter's outer framework, in which Moshe is described as being both mortal and a man of God (Deut. 33:1), and in which God arrives at Sinai accompanied by an entourage at once human and angelic.[22]

---

18. Ibid.

19. Steiner and Leiman, "The Lost Meaning," 159. Lewis adds that Steiner's understanding is fully congruent with what we know about how divinity could be represented in ancient Israel both textually and ichnographically. Cf. Theodore J. Lewis, "Divine Fire in Deuteronomy 33:2," *JBL* 132. 4 (2013), 791–803.

20. Deut. 28:49, Jer. 48:40 and 49:22 feature the verb דאה in relation to eagles, and Ps. 18:11 features דאה in its description of the *kruvim*.

21. *HALOT*, "דאה," 207.

22. The Septuagint strongly attests to the tradition of an angelic presence accompanying God, "with myriads of holy ones, from his right-hand angels with

The Relationship between the Blessings and the Outer Structure

The suggestion of the two halves of the outer framework to be forming a chiasmus was noted above.[23]

> A. (v. 2) God comes to deliver His people.
>> B. (v. 3–4) God protects and provides for His people.
>>> C. (v. 5) God is king over Yeshurun.
>>> C. (v. 26) There is no God like the God of Yeshurun.
>> B. (v. 27–28) Israel is secured in and blessed by God.
> A. (v. 29) Israel is delivered by God.

The suggested equation between Israel's deliverance by God in vs. 29 and the giving of the law in vs. 2 was noted earlier for seeming to be a bit of a stretch. However, when we approach the tribal blessings with a sensitivity to their collective allusion to the tribes' *kruv*-like qualities, then we gain an appreciation for both the meaning of the outer hymnal structure, and of the relevance of the tribal blessings to that outer structure. The *kruvim* were charged with protecting the divine law as they held up God's throne and His footstool/Holy Ark which contained the Decalogue.[24] They also functioned as the guardians of Israel in times of war.[25] The correspondence between vs. 2 and 29 is an apt reflection of that dichotomy; in which Israel's deliverance by God is parallel to the giving of the Decalogue: "Blessed are you, Israel! Who is like you, a people saved by the Lord?" (vs. 29), "The Lord came from Sinai" (vs. 2). Insinuations to the *kruvim* in the outer hymn are further supported by vs. 3 and its *kruv*-like description of Israel at God's feet holding up the Decalogue:[26]

---

him." Cf. Allen, *Deuteronomy and Exhortation in Hebrews,* pp. 105–6; James Kugel, *Traditions of the Bible,* 670; Ibn Ezra on Deut. 33:2 renders the literal meaning of רבבות קדש as angels, and כל קדשיו from vs. 3 as referring to the tribe of Levi. Targum Onkelos renders כל קדשיו from vs. 3 as referring to all of Israel.

23. Christensen, "Two Stanzas," 382–389.
24. The Bible often refers to the Temple as God's place of rest, and to the Holy Ark as his footstool: Isa. 66:1; Ps. 132:1–7.
25. The *kruvim* were traditionally brought out to the battlefield together with the Holy Ark as a means of protection. Cf. Num. 10:35; 1 Sam. 4:4.
26. Cf. Ibn Ezra on Deut. 33:3 who reads this verse as a description of the Levites carrying the Ark of the Law.

Surely it is You who love the people; all the holy ones are in Your hand. At Your feet they all bow down, and from You receive instruction (Deut. 33:3).

In the parallel verse of the chiasmus, Israel is protected beneath God's outstretched arms.[27]

The Temple *kruvim* epitomized awe and reverence before God as well as a yearning for intimacy with the divine. The analogy between Israel and the *kruvim* in the Blessings of Moshe communicates that duality through the description of the tribes as at once prostrate before God's feet, תכו לרגליך,[28] and as ידידי-ה, "God's lover" (Deut. 33:12). The Blessings of Moshe paint a remarkably vivid picture of the tribes of Israel with both *kruv*-like and priestly qualities. The relationship between the *kruvim* and the institution of the priesthood was noted earlier to be inferred from references in Yechezkel and Malachi (Cf. Ezek. 28:13–14, Mal. 2:7). It is also noteworthy that the book of Enoch preserves an ancient tradition of *kruvim* ministering in God's heavenly Temple.[29]

---

27. The phrase גבעת עולם, commonly rendered "everlasting hills," recurs in Moshe's blessing to the tribe of Yosef in Deuteronomy, and again in Habakkuk's theophany (Hab. 3:1). God is referred to by Avraham as א-ל עולם in Genesis, thereby linking God with עולם (Gen. 21:33). Van Den Branden argues that עולם alone may be used as an appellation of the deity, even when not associated with א-ל. Cf. A. Van Den Branden, "Les Dieux des Patriarches," *Bibbia e Oriente* 162 (1990), 27–53, esp. 36. He reads the phrase זרועות עולם not as 'ancient/eternal arms' but rather as the arms of God. The Talmud supports the approach to עולם as a divine epithet. Cf. BT *Hagigah* 12b, where the Sages attribute storms to the hands of God based on ומתחת זרעת עולם.

28. Deut. 33:3; Cf. HALOT, "תכה," 1730. The etymology of the word is unclear and is the subject of debate; Driver suggests the meaning "followed" citing Ibn Ezra and Kimchi, yet states that "The versions and Jewish authorities render no help, in most cases merely conjecturing from the context." Cf. Driver, *Deuteronomy*, 390, 394 nt. 3. Driver however fails to take into account Ibn Ezra's commentary on Prov. 29:13, in which he relates the word תכו from our vs. to תככים, deriving from תוך, meaning "trampled underfoot." Cf. HALOT, "תוך," 1729. Konig suggests that תכו is related to the Arabic *taka'a, ittak'a*, meaning to lie down. Cf. Konig, HALOT, "תכה," 1730.

29. See 1 Enoch 14. While the book of Enoch is not included in the Jewish canon, it may nonetheless have been used as an interpretive tool by the traditional commentators. It is likely that Nachmanides and Ibn Ezra made limited use of Enoch. In his commentary on Lev. 16:8, Nachmanides explains *Azazel*

The Midrash reinforces the priest-*kruv* connection with its description of Solomon's towering *kruvim* as a pair of priests poised in the act of conferring the priestly blessing upon Israel.[30] This is particularly interesting in light of the Akkadian *karabu*, meaning "to bless." The words ברך, "bless," and רכב, "ride," two actions closely associated with the *kruvim*, are believed by many scholars be related to the root כרב through metathesis.[31]

The blessings of Moshe are introduced with a description of God as supreme monarch:

> He was king over Yeshurun when the leaders of the people assembled, along with the tribes of Israel (Deut. 33:5).

Whereas this verse is ambiguous regarding the referent of "he": Moshe or God,[32] as noted in the discussion of the Song of the Sea, Moshe's coronation moments before his imminent death would certainly be anticlimactic. Furthermore, the closing verses of Deuteronomy 33 continues with a description of God's monarchic ascension:

---

from the rite of the sending of the scapegoat as "the prince who rules over wastelands." This statement seems to correlate with the description in 1 Enoch 10:4–6 of *Azazel* having been cast into the wilderness. The term for wilderness found in Enoch, τὴν ἔρημον, matches the same term found in the LXX for the word wilderness in Lev. 16:8. Ibn Ezra also seems to hint that *Azazel* was a kind of a demon. He proposes a riddle; only those who reach thirty-three will understand. Thirty-three verses later, in Lev. 17:7, *seirim*, "demons," are mentioned. Cf. Onkelos, ad. loc., who renders *seirim* to be demons. Also, in his long commentary on Gen. 5:29, Ibn Ezra mentions that Enoch foresaw Noah's survival of the flood, and that he composed books of great wisdom that are still extant.

30. Pesikta Zutreta *(Lekach Tov) Shemot, Terumah,* 25.

31. D.N. Freedman and M.P. O'Connor, "kerub," *Theological Dictionary of the Old Testament* 7:307–320, esp. 308. While Freedman and O'Connor reject the relationship to רכב, the deliberate juxtaposition of these two words in Ps. 18:11, 'וַיִּרְכַּב עַל־כְּרוּב' appears to support the close etymological relationship between these two words. A relationship between the biblical *kruvim* and the Mesopotamian *karibu*, composite guardian creatures whose name means "one who blesses," has also been suggested. Cf. Alice Wood, *Of Wings and Wheels: A Synthetic Study of the Biblical Cherubim* (Berlin: Walter de Gruyter, 2008), 338.

32. Cf. Ibn Ezra, Deut. 33:5, who maintains that Moshe is the king. Nachmanides and Rashi however agree that God is the referent in the verse.

There is no one like the God of Jeshurun, who rides across the heavens to help you and on the clouds in His majesty, ובגאותו שחקים (Deut. 33:26).

Blessed are you, Israel! Who is like you, a people saved by the LORD? He is your shield and helper and your glorious sword, חרב גאותך. Your enemies will cower before you, and you will tread on their heights (Deut. 33:29).

When we reflect further on the totality of the blessings of Moshe's, a broader picture emerges. The blessings (beginning with Yehudah), begin in the Negev, Israel's southernmost boundary, and proceed in a north-easterly direction, traversing the Transjordan territories and reaching their northernmost point in the Bashan region with the blessing of Dan. From there, the blessings change course, moving in a westerly direction, reaching their conclusion with Asher, on the coast of the Mediterranean. Asher's blessing depicts him dwelling in peace and security, "The bolts of your gates will be iron and bronze" (Deut. 33:25). This description reflects not only the safety of Asher's borders, but the security of all the tribes, who are charged with ensuring the security of the Divine presence in their collective midst. When we observe the Blessings of Moshe as a set, it becomes apparent that the order of the presentation reflects their function. The Blessings of Moshe emerge as an exposition on Israel's role as a kingdom of priests and holy nation, ממלכת כהנים וגוי קדוש, tasked with safeguarding the covenant in an eternal expression of their unmitigated acceptance of the yoke of heaven, קבלת עול מלכות שמים.

Review

The Theological Role of Torah Songs and Blessings

קבלת עול מלכות שמים

Acceptance of the Yoke of Heaven

Song of the Sea	The chiasmus which unifies the Song of the Sea equips it with form as well as function. The Song's outer layer celebrates God's coronation and future enthronement, while its inner strata centers on the eradication of evil. The Song's celebration of God's coronation is the theological underpinning of the Israelite monarchic idea.
Song of the Well	The Song of the Sea's exultation of Israel as the beneficiaries of God's lovingkindness offers an alternative yet complementary message to that proposed by the Song of the Sea. Whereas the main thrust of the Song of the Sea is God's military victory over the Egyptians, the Song of the Well emphasizes Israel as the object of God's love and benevolence.

קבלת עול מלכות שמים

Acceptance of the Yoke of Heaven

Song of
Moshe

The Song of Moshe explores God's dominion through-out history, from the dawn of time and into the distant future. Whereas the Songs of the Sea and the Well pay homage to God as king, the Song of Moshe explores the parameters of that allegiance. The Song of Moshe articulates the consequences of the rejection of God's dominion. Israel's willingness to accept the potentially harmful consequences inherent in this relationship is an accurate measure of their unconditional allegiance and dedication. The reciprocal love and devotion expressed in the first two poems of the Torah is finalized by the acceptance of consequences in the third. Understanding the Song of Moshe as a celebra-tion of Israel's acceptance of the yoke of heaven with all of its potential caveats, clarifies its placement at the conclusion of the Torah.

ממלכת כהנים וגוי קדוש

Israel, a Kingdom of Priests and a Holy Nation

Yaakov's
Blessings

Yaakov's blessings establish the dual institutions of Israelite leadership, the monarchy and the priesthood. These establishments are charged with promoting alle-giance to the kingdom of God and dedication to its precepts. Yaakov's prayer for heavenly salvation at the epicenter of the tribal blessings points to the kingdom of God as the fulcrum of the two harmonious realms of Israelite leadership. Yaakov's blessings emerge as an exposition on Israel's fundamental mission as a nation of priests, ממלכת כהנים, charged with supporting the kingdom of God.

ממלכת כהנים וגוי קדוש
Israel, a Kingdom of Priests and a Holy Nation

Bilam's Blessings

Bilam's blessings draw upon imagery from Yaakov's blessings specifically relating to the idea of the Israelite monarchy. Bilam's orations move the idea of Israelite leadership forward by suggesting a synergistic correlation between the Israelite monarchy and the kingdom of God. The absence of any reference to the institution of the Israelite priesthood in Bilam's blessings is ultimately addressed in the blessings of Moshe. The blessings of Bilam, like the Blessings of Yaakov, relate directly to the fundamental theological tenet of both קבלת עול מלכות שמים, acceptance of the yoke of heaven, as well as the idea of Israel as a holy nation, a גוי קדוש.

Blessings of Moshe

The blessings of Moshe paint a vivid composite picture of the tribes of Israel with both *kruv*-like and priestly qualities. The relationship between the *kruvim* and the institution of the priesthood is inferred from references in Yechezkel, Malachi and the Midrash. The blessings are introduced and concluded with a description of God's monarchic ascension. The Blessings of Moshe emerge as an exposition on Israel as a holy nation of priests, ממלכת כהנים וגוי קדוש, accepting the yoke of heaven, קבלת עול מלכות שמים, entrusted with the task of safeguarding the covenant.

Conclusion

When we reflect upon the sum total of the Torah's extended blessing units, they emerge as an integrated exposition on Israel's Sinaitic mission of becoming "a kingdom of priests and a holy nation."

> Now if you obey Me fully and keep My covenant, then out of all nations you will be My treasured possession. Although the whole earth is Mine, you will be for Me a kingdom of priests and a holy nation. These are the words you are to speak to the Israelites (Ex. 19:5–6).

The foundation of Israelite leadership was established by Yaakov in his blessings which laid out the blueprint for the dual institutions of the monarchy and the priesthood. The blessings of Bilam draw upon imagery from Yaakov's blessings and move the idea of Israelite leadership forward, synthesizing the Israelite and Divine monarchy. The multiple intertextual markers that reverberate throughout the blessings of Bilam and Yaakov draw attention to Bilam's curious silence on the priesthood. The Midrash would seem to be alluding to this lacuna with its assertion that a key element is glaringly absent from Bilam's prophecy.[1] Bilam's omission is ultimately rectified by Moshe, whose blessings employ vivid imagery that collectively points to the priestly role of the tribes, who are positioned around God's presence in their midst.

The mandate to become "a kingdom of priests and holy nation" has been interpreted by the commentators in a variety of ways. Rashi,

---

1. Pesikta de Rav Kahana, (ed. Mandelbaum), addendum 1, s.v. *Vezot Haberacha.*

Rashbam, Ibn Ezra, and Nachmanides understand the term "priest" here in its more general sense, stressing the broader notion of service of God, as opposed to the ritual service associated specifically and exclusively with the priesthood.[2] Maimonides adds that Israel's role as a "kingdom of priests" implies "knowledge of Him."[3] This understanding finds support in Yeshayahu's prophecy of national restoration in which Israel's priestly role on a national scale is at the very crux of Yeshayahu's message.

> The Spirit of the Sovereign LORD is on me, because the LORD has anointed me to proclaim good news to the poor. He has sent me to bind up the brokenhearted, to proclaim freedom for the captives and release from darkness for the prisoners, to proclaim the year of the LORD's favor and the day of vengeance of our God, to comfort all who mourn, and provide for those who grieve in Zion – to bestow on them a crown of beauty instead of ashes, the oil of joy instead of mourning, and a garment of praise instead of a spirit of despair. They will be called oaks of righteousness, a planting of the LORD for the display of His splendor. They will rebuild the ancient ruins and restore the places long devastated; they will renew the ruined cities that have been devastated for generations. Strangers will shepherd your flocks; foreigners will work your fields and vineyards. And you will be called priests of the LORD, you will be named ministers of our God. You will feed on the wealth of nations, and in their riches you will boast. Instead of your shame you will receive a double portion, and instead of disgrace you will rejoice in your inheritance. And so you will inherit a double portion in your land, and everlasting joy will be yours (Isa. 61:1–7).

The singular historic experience of revelation at Sinai charged the nation of Israel on a communal level with nothing less than bringing heaven down to earth. The directive to aspire to becoming a "kingdom of priest and a holy nation" challenges the nation of Israel to seek out God's involvement in human affairs. Rav Kook expounds on these ideas

---

2.   Cf. Rashi, Rashbam, Ibn Ezra and Nachmanides, idem.
3.   Maimonides, *Guide to the Perplexed* 3:32.

in his discussion on Israel's imperative to become a kingdom of priests and a holy nation:[1]

> The Torah and the polity in Israel, are interconnected by an unbreakable bond.... Acceptance of the Torah within Israel is in fact a double acceptance; an individual acceptance of the holy ordinances of the nation, on the part of the individual affiliated with the nation, and a group acceptance, as a nation charged with conducting its communal and national life. Indeed, Torah observance on a national level is especially difficult, ... requiring the cooperation of society on all levels in the managing of matters of state. This is far more complicated than the effort of individuals responsible only onto themselves... Our responsibility is not only to be holy as individuals, but rather, and foremost, to be a kingdom of priests and a holy nation; to aspire to the establishment of a holy polity that is worthy of its name.

The experience of revelation at Sinai transformed the people of Israel from an amalgam of individuals to a cohesive nation bound together by a Divine mission. At the very core of Torah theology lies the essence of the Sinaitic mandate, that finite human beings unite and build a society worthy of hosting God the infinite. The three extended blessings of the Torah operate together, reinforcing Israel's fundamental role as witnesses to and conduits for God's continued involvement in history.

Rabbi Joseph B. Soloveitchik, in his discussion on the nature of the relationship between the nation of Israel and God, explains the covenant to be twofold.[2] The first, a covenant of fate, involved God imposing Himself on Israel, "I will take you as My own people, and I will be your God. Then you will know that I am the Lord your God, who brought you out from under the yoke of the Egyptians" (Ex. 6:7). It was only with the second covenant, the covenant of destiny, in which Israel willingly accepted the Torah, that they were charged with becoming a kingdom

---

1. Rabbi Abraham Isaac Kook, "Mamlechet Kohanim," pp. 173–174 in *Mamarei HaRaΛYaH* (Jerusalem, 1988), (Heb.).
2. Joseph B. Soloveitchik, *Fate and Destiny: From Holocaust to the state of Israel* (New York: Ktav, 2000).

of priests and a holy nation. Rav Soloveitchik stresses that this elevation in status brings with it a national, shared responsibility. Israel's ongoing role as keepers of the covenant of destiny is the common thread that binds together the Torah's three blessing units.

The first half of *Torah Song* probed the motivation behind the inclusion of the Torah's extended poetic units. The analysis presented in *Torah Song* showed the Song of the Sea to be a celebration of God's coronation and an articulation of the Israelite monarchic idea. The Song of the Well's exultation of Israel as the beneficiaries of God's lovingkindness was shown to offer an alternative yet complementary perspective on the benevolent nature of the Divine monarchy. Instead of showcasing God's indomitable strength, as in the Song of the Sea, the Song of the Well focuses on Israel as the object of God's love, devotion, and commitment. Finally, the Song of Moshe and its reflection on Israel's irrevocable bond with God, was shown to be an amalgamation of both core ideas. The acceptance of the yoke of heaven, קבלת עול מלכות שמים, on the one hand, and Israel's role as a kingdom of priests and a holy nation, ממלכת כוהנים וגוי קדוש, on the other; two core principles expounded upon in the Torah's extended units of songs and blessings, are the very bedrock of Torah theology.

In the opening discussions of this book, the question was raised: why did the Torah's recounting of God's revelation at Sinai, arguably the most defining moment in Israel's history, not merit its own hymn of praise? Our survey of Torah songs and blessings as self-contained units, and as a loosely connected corpus, offers perspective. The poetry of the Torah forms a coherent, integrated network of musings on Israel's role as keepers of the Divine covenant. The songs and blessings of the Torah emerge as a broad meditation on Israel's enduring role in the establishment and preservation of the covenant of destiny established at Sinai.

Excursus

Lamech's Song (Gen. 4:17–26)

יז וַיֵּדַע קַיִן אֶת־אִשְׁתּוֹ וַתַּהַר וַתֵּלֶד אֶת־חֲנוֹךְ וַיְהִי בֹּנֶה עִיר וַיִּקְרָא שֵׁם הָעִיר
כְּשֵׁם בְּנוֹ חֲנוֹךְ. וַיִּוָּלֵד לַחֲנוֹךְ אֶת־עִירָד וְעִירָד יָלַד אֶת־מְחוּיָאֵל וּמְחִיָּיאֵל יָלַד
אֶת־מְתוּשָׁאֵל וּמְתוּשָׁאֵל יָלַד אֶת־לָמֶךְ. וַיִּקַּח־לוֹ לֶמֶךְ שְׁתֵּי נָשִׁים שֵׁם הָאַחַת
עָדָה וְשֵׁם הַשֵּׁנִית צִלָּה. וַתֵּלֶד עָדָה אֶת־יָבָל הוּא הָיָה אֲבִי יֹשֵׁב אֹהֶל וּמִקְנֶה. וְשֵׁם
אָחִיו יוּבָל הוּא הָיָה אֲבִי כָּל־תֹּפֵשׂ כִּנּוֹר וְעוּגָב. וְצִלָּה גַם־הִוא יָלְדָה אֶת־תּוּבַל
קַיִן לֹטֵשׁ כָּל־חֹרֵשׁ נְחֹשֶׁת וּבַרְזֶל וַאֲחוֹת תּוּבַל־קַיִן נַעֲמָה. וַיֹּאמֶר לֶמֶךְ לְנָשָׁיו
עָדָה וְצִלָּה שְׁמַעַן קוֹלִי נְשֵׁי לֶמֶךְ הַאְזֵנָּה אִמְרָתִי כִּי אִישׁ הָרַגְתִּי לְפִצְעִי וְיֶלֶד
לְחַבֻּרָתִי. כִּי שִׁבְעָתַיִם יֻקַּם־קָיִן וְלֶמֶךְ שִׁבְעִים וְשִׁבְעָה. וַיֵּדַע אָדָם עוֹד אֶת־אִשְׁתּוֹ
וַתֵּלֶד בֵּן וַתִּקְרָא אֶת־שְׁמוֹ שֵׁת כִּי שָׁת־לִי אֱלֹהִים זֶרַע אַחֵר תַּחַת הֶבֶל כִּי הֲרָגוֹ
קָיִן. וּלְשֵׁת גַּם־הוּא יֻלַּד־בֵּן וַיִּקְרָא אֶת־שְׁמוֹ אֱנוֹשׁ אָז הוּחַל לִקְרֹא בְּשֵׁם ה'.

Kayin knew his wife, and she became pregnant and gave birth to
Chanoch. Kayin was then building a city, and he named it after
his son Chanoch. To Chanoch was born Irad, and Irad was the
father of Mehuyael, and Mehuyael was the father of Metushael,
and Metushael was the father of Lamech. Lamech married two
women, one named Adah and the other Tzilah. Adah gave birth
to Yaval; he was the father of those who live in tents and raise
livestock. His brother's name was Yuval; he was the father of all
who play stringed instruments and pipes. Tzilah also had a son,
Tuval-Kayin, who forged all kinds of tools out of bronze and iron.
Tuval-Kayin's sister was Naamah. Lamech said to his wives, "Adah
and Tzilah, listen to me; wives of Lamech, hear my words. I have
killed a man for wounding me, a young man for injuring me. If
Kayin is avenged seven times, then Lamech seventy-seven times."
Adam knew his wife again, and she gave birth to a son and named

him Seth, saying, "God has granted me another child in place of
Abel, since Kayin killed him." Seth also had a son, and he named
him Enosh. At that time people began to call in the name of the
Lord (Gen. 4:17–26).

Introduction

The Kayin genealogy of Gen. 4:17–26 features a cryptic poem, "Lamech's
Song":

> Lamech said to his wives, "Adah and Tzilah, listen to me; wives of
> Lamech, hear my words. I have killed a man for wounding me, a
> young man for injuring me. If Kayin is avenged seven times, then
> Lamech seventy-seven times" (Gen 4:23–24).

The opaque message of Lamech's song and its curious placement
interrupting a terse genealogical table has perplexed the interpreters of
the text. Some scholars have argued that Lamech's song does not move
the text forward in any significant way.[3] Does Lamech's song contain
nothing more than "the rantings of a vicious tribal head," as Speiser
suggested?[4]

This essay explores the meaning of Lamech's song and demonstrates
its relevance within the larger context of the Kayin narrative. The ambiguity of the poem's content is starkly contrasted by its adherence to a
variety of poetic forms and conventions. This essay suggests that the
formal eloquence of the poem is directly related to its core message; that
those men who pose a threat or challenge of any kind will be terrorized,
and those women who Lamech finds pleasing may be forcibly seized.
Anomalies in Gen. 4:23–24 regarding the names and biographical information of Lamech's children prompt analysis which points to their significance as echoes of both Kayin and Hevel. Identifying the references

---

3. Murdoch writes that "Neither of the Lamechs, the Cainite nor the Sethite,
    is really very important. Modern commentaries on Genesis do not have
    very much to say about either of them." Cf. Brian O. Murdoch, *The Medieval
    Popular Bible: Expansion of Genesis in the Middle Ages* (Cambridge: DS Brewer,
    2003), 71.

4. Ephraim A. Speiser, *Genesis* (AB, 1; New York: Doubleday, 1964), 37.

to Kayin and Hevel in Lamech's progeny leads towards an understanding of Lamech's legacy as an attempt to appropriate the combined roles of Adam, Kayin, and Hevel. The unusual textual stress placed on the names of Lamech's wives and his daughter suggests Lamech to be a man who used his power to take women whom he found to be physically appealing. This reading of the Lamech narrative and poem portrays Lamech as representing an even more egocentric and morally corrupted version of Kayin. Understanding the message of Lamech's song as an articulation and adulation of what made Kayin so corrupt leads to an appreciation of the poem's placement in the center of the Kayin-Lamech narrative, and in the opening pages of the book of Genesis.

1. Lamech's Song; Observations

Genesis 4:19–24 contains a cryptic story and poem in the section devoted to the genealogy of Kayin. This narrative bears several anomalies that place it in stark contrast to the rest of the genealogical record of Genesis 5 on a number of accounts:

1. Throughout the genealogies, women are not identified by name, and their very existence is not mentioned. By contrast, Lamech, the sixth generation from Kayin, takes two wives, who are introduced by name; Adah, and Tzilah.

2. Lamech fathers three sons who are all called by a variation of the same root י.ב.ל.; Yaval, Yuval, and Tuval-Kayin. His daughter, Naamah, is also referred to by name.

3. Lamech's sons are credited with pioneering institutions of a cultured and more developed urban society: animal husbandry, the manufacture of musical instruments and the fashioning of copper and iron. By contrast, the Bible does not provide any biographical information on Naamah. This omission is significant as the Bible broke with its own convention in this section by mentioning her at all.

This essay appears in *Scandinavian Journal of the Old Testament* 31.2 (2017), 275–293. I gratefully acknowledge Dr. Joshua Berman's valuable advice and input in the preparation of this essay.

4. The section concludes with an enigmatic song composed by Lamech in which his wives are once again identified by name. The message of the song is unclear and the subject of much debate. It is insinuated that someone has either *been* killed by Lamech or *will be* killed by him:[1] "For I have slain a man to my wounding, and a young man to my hurt" (Gen. 4:23).

5. Lamech concludes with the strange yet terrifying boast that if Kayin's murderer was to be avenged seven-fold, then Lamech's avenger shall surely be punished seventy-seven-fold.

In what way does this digression contribute to the genealogy of Kayin? A close reading of Lamech's song will put all of our above noted observations into context.

2. Poetic Structure

Lamech's song and its surrounding narrative rely heavily on the number seven, a number noted for representing the notion of the ideal in the Bible.[2] In addition to the terms שבעתים, and שבעים ושבעה, the entire poem is based on the number seven. There are fourteen words contained in the first verse of the poem (a multiple of seven), and seven words in the second. It is also interesting that there are seven proper names mentioned in the Lamech narrative.[3] The entire Lamech account contains a total of seven verses (Gen. 4:18–24). In addition, the Kayin genealogy concludes with the children of Lamech, who are the seventh generation from Kayin. Indeed, both Lamechs (from the genealogy of Kayin – Genesis 4, and from the genealogy of Seth – Genesis 5), are

---

1. Modern scholarship is uniform in its understanding of the text as a threat. This is likely due to the fact that there is no murder account recorded in the text. Ibn Ezra (Gen. 4:23) takes a similar approach. Kimchi also understands the song as Lamech's threat to kill his own wives. Onkelos and Bechor *Shor* read the song as a rhetorical question. The Sages and most of the classical exegetes, including Rashi, interpret the phrase as referring to a murder that took place. Cf. *Midrash Tanchuma*, ed. Warsaw, Gen. 11.

2. Umberto Cassuto, *A Commentary on the Book of Genesis: From Adam to Noah*, vol. *I* (Jerusalem: Magnes, 1944), 12–13.

3. Lamech, Adah, Tzila, Yaval, Yuval, Tuval-Kayin and Naamah.

sevenths. Lamech, the descendant of Kayin, is the seventh generation from Adam, and Lamech, the descendant of Seth, is the seventh generation from Enosh, whose name meaning "man" suggests his being a "new Adam."[4] This may be interpreted to suggest the opportunity for renewal, and rectification. Notwithstanding Adam still being alive at the time, the period of Enosh is noted by the text as having been a watershed, ushering a new era in which 'calling out in the name of God' became commonplace (Gen. 4:26).

The observations noted above regarding the careful adherence to form in both the poem itself and the surrounding narrative serve to underscore the poem's ambiguous message, implying that the poem must convey a message of significance which contributes in a meaningful way to the development of the greater literary context. Nachman Levine nonetheless concluded that "There is nothing there but the virtuosity of his [Lamech's] eloquent incoherence, its form its only substance."[5] Levine's assertion that Lamech's song is all form and no substance serves to intensify our initial question concerning the poem; why would a poem whose apparent sole contribution to the text is its formal elegance, interrupt the genealogy of Kayin?

Benno Jacob comments that while the message of the poem is obscure, it is the first example of Hebrew poetry. "Lamech might be called the inventor of poetry. The intention may be to establish this."[6] Jacob suggests that the inclusion of the poem in the genealogy is essentially in order to establish Lamech as the first biblical poet.[7] This is interesting in light of the fact that the text went out of its way to point

---

4. Richard S. Hess, "Lamech in the Genealogies of Genesis," *Bulletin for Biblical Research* 1 (1991), 21–25.

5. Nachman Levine, "Lamech's Song: Narrative Context and the Poetry of Violence," *Milin Havivn* 2 (2006), 128–143; Cf. M. Weinfeld, "שירת למך," *Olam Hatanach*, Gen (Heb.), 47, for a discussion of the meticulous format of Lamech's poem.

6. Benno Jacob, *The First Book of the Bible: Genesis, Augmented Edition* (ed. and trans. Ernest I. Jacob and Walter Jacob; Jersey City, NJ: Ktav, 2007), 38.

7. Robert North also comments that Lamech's song is "uniformly singled out by critics as the earliest example of Israelite rhapsody." Cf. Robert North, "The Cain Music," *SBL* 83.4 (1964), 373–389.

out that Lamech's children were also "firsts" in their respective cultural fields. This approach, however, does not solve the problem of relating the substance of the song to the surrounding narrative.

Cassuto attributes the song's inclusion to its glorification of violence. The song demonstrates that "material progress did not go hand in hand with moral advancement."[8] Others attribute its inclusion to the fact that it commemorates the invention of weapons, signaling the degeneration in culture.[9] These approaches understand Lamech's song as playing an integral role in the Kayin narrative, as they connect the violence of Lamech to Kayin's legacy of murder.

The culture of violence endorsed in Lamech's poem taken together with its careful adherence to poetic form and structure suggest that Lamech's viciousness was a carefully thought-out, pre-meditated affair. This becomes even more apparent when we observe the poem's exacting adherence to a wide variety of poetic conventions.

3. Poetic Conventions

Lamech's poem increases in its intensity from the first half of each verse to the second:

נשי למך **האזנה** אמרתי   עדה וצלה **שמען** קולי

וילד לחברתי: כי **איש** הרגתי לפצעי

ולמך **שבעים ושבעה**:   כי **שבעתים** יקם קין

In the first line, the word שמען, or hear, conveys an essentially passive activity. האזנה, or lending one's ear, requires a more active focusing of one's attention.[10] This is observed in Psalms, where the Psalmist entreats God to hear his words of prayer, לשמע, but to pay closer attention, להאזין, to its substance, to his crying out:

Hear my prayer, LORD, listen to my cry for help... (Ps. 39:13).
LORD, hear my prayer, listen to my cry for mercy... (Ps. 143:1).

---

8.   Cassuto, *From Adam to Noah*, 244.

9.   John Skinner, *Genesis* (*ICC* 1; *Edinburgh*: T. & T. Clark, 1969), 115, 120.

10. Cf. "אזן," BDB, 24; Cf. also Rabbi Meir Leibush ben Yechiel Michel, (Russia 19th cent. also known as 'Malbim'), Deut. 32,1.

The second line of the poem opens with the killing of a man, and concludes with the killing of a child, a far more chilling act of cruelty.[11] In the final line there is a clear increase from seven-fold to seventy-seven-fold.

Lamech's song is written in poetic verse.[12] Alter observes that biblical poetry is characterized "by an intensifying or narrative development within the line...the poetry of the Bible is concerned above all with the dynamic process moving toward some culmination...."[13] We noted how Lamech's song increases in its intensity as it progresses. Lamech's song also conforms to a wide variety of poetic conventions. It is written in deliberate balance, constructed of three parallel lines, which include rhyme – a rare phenomenon in biblical poetry:[14]

עדה וצלה שמען קולי נשי למך האזנה אמרתי
כי איש הרגתי לפצעי וילד לחברתי:

While the first line of the poem contains a one-to-one ratio of parallel words, the ensuing lines contain fewer parallel words in the second half of each verse. "There ensues a rapid and continued disintegration of

---

11. Hamilton notes that the words איש and ילד don't form a word pair anywhere else in the Bible, further highlighting the questions regarding this unusual word pair. Cf. Victor P. Hamilton, *The Book of Genesis* (vol. 1 of *The New International Commentary on the Old Testament* ed. Robert L. Hubbard Jr.; Grand Rapids: Wm. B. Eerdmans Publ., 1990), 239.

12. Lamech's song is considered poetry, even though it is surrounded by prose. J.P. Fokkelman describes the abrupt transition from prose to poetry: "In the case of Lamech's song of revenge and Jacob's blessings, the transition is achieved by a formal beginning, an adjuration to be attentive...." Cf. J.P. Fokkelman, "Genesis," in *The Literary Guide to the Bible*, (ed. R. Alter and F. Kermode; Cambridge: Harvard University Press, 1987), 38; Cf. Rabbi Chaim Paltiel, (a Tosafist from Germany, 14th cent.) on Gen. 4:23. Paltiel notes that Lamech quotes his name in the beginning of the poem, which further indicates the text's status as poetry.

13. Robert Alter, "The Characteristics of Ancient Hebrew Poetry," pp. 611–624 in *The Literary Guide to the Bible* (ed. Robert Alter and F. Kermode; Cambridge: Harvard University Press, 1987), 620.

14. James L. Kugel, *The Idea of Biblical Poetry: Parallelism and its History* (Baltimore: Johns Hopkins University Press, 1998), 233–250.

the (biblical) tradition of fixed pairs...."[15] While in the first and final verses of the poem, each half line contains either three or four words, the center line contains only two words in its second half. By reducing its length in contrast to the rest of the poem, the center line attracts the attention of the listener. This has the effect of highlighting its message and intensifying its ambiguities. What event is being described? Why should an ambiguous event be highlighted by the poem?

4. The Message

Scholars approach our text as a threat to violence.[16] They assume it to have been composed in honor of the creation of weapons by Tubal-Kayin, and refer to it as the "sword song."[17] Perhaps whether or not the song recounts an actual murder is not the crux of the matter: "The

---

15. S. Gevirtz, "Lamech's Song to His Wives," in *I Studied Inscriptions from Before the Flood: Ancient Near Eastern Linguistic Approaches to Genesis 1–11* (ed. Richard S. Hess and David Toshio Tsumura; Winona Lake: Eisenbrauns, 1994), 405–406.

16. Ibn Ezra also reads the verse as a threat, wherein the perfect tense verb, הרגתי, describes an act not yet actualized. Cf. Ibn Ezra Gen. 4:23. The Sages interpreted Lamech's song as referring to a murder which had taken place. Cf. *Midrash Tanchuma*, ed. Warsaw, Gen. 11; *Midrash Aggadah*, ed. Buber, Gen. 4:3; Cuthbert A. Simpson agrees with this approach. Cf. Simpson, "The Book of Genesis: Exegesis," pp. 465–832 in George A. Buttrick (ed.), *The Interpreter's Bible: General Articles on the Bible. Genesis. Exodus* (vol. 1 Nashville: Abingdon Press, 1951). The LXX, Vulgate, and Peshitta reflect this tradition in their rendering of the text. Cf. Albert Pietersma and Benjamin G. Wright, *The New English Translation of the Septuagint*, (Oxford: OUP, 2007), 8; R. Coyne, *The Holy Bible Translated from the Latin Vulgate*, (Dublin, 1847), 5; George Mamishisho Lamsa, *The Holy Bible from the ancient Eastern text: George M. Lamsa's translations from the Aramaic of the Peshitta*, (online ed.), Gen. 4:23; Onkelos and Pseudo-Jonathan read the text as a rhetorical question.

17. Cf. Skinner, *Genesis*, 120; Speiser, *Genesis*, 37; Herman Gunkel, *Genesis*, (Georgia: Mercer University Press, 1997), 52; Murdoch, *Expansion of Genesis in the Middle Ages*, p. 81; J.G. Vos, *Genesis*, (Pittsburgh: Crown & amp; Covenant Pub., 2006), 105; S.R. Driver, *The Book of Genesis*, (London: Kessinger pub., 1926), 70.

terrifying moral standards his words reflect are unambiguous."[18] The
fact that the text remains ambiguous indicates that it is not critical to
know whether or not there actually was a murder. The point of the
text is to convey Lamech's conviction that on principle, he could kill
with impunity. Fretheim sums up the point of the song well: "The song
shows how violence has been intensified through the generations. This
is an important point, because it shows how the sword song is part
of the build-up to the moral decay that is the proximate cause of the
flood. Sin progresses as civilization progresses."[19] The intensification of
violence can be seen in the shift in the second verse from the first half
to the second: "For I have slain a man to my wounding (לפצעי) and
a young man to my hurt (לחבורתי)" (Gen. 4:23). The words פצע and
חבורה, a frequent word pair in the Bible, have different nuances.[20] פצע
can function as both a noun and a verb. It connotes both a wound and
the act of infliction.[21] The word חבורה however, functions exclusively
as a noun. It lacks the force inherent in the verb potential of the word
פצע. Bauer and Leander relate the word חבורה to the word חברברות, the
skin spots of the tiger.[22] The connection is also made to the Akkadian
ibaru, meaning "birthmark," and to the Aramaic חברברתא which refers
to a variety of spotted-snake. The word חבורה connotes the topical
mark left by the blow, or its appearance on the skin, as opposed to פצע
which implies a blow with greater life-threatening potential.[23] Kimchi

---

18. Shamai Gelander, *The Good Creator: Literature and Theology in Genesis 1–11*
    (Atlanta: Scholars Press, 1997), 58.

19. Terence E. Fretheim, *The New Interpreters Bible* (vol. 1; Nashville; Abingdon
    Press, 1994), 375.

20. The sequence that the Bible uses here is deliberate and significant, as there
    is an instance where the opposite order is employed; Prov. 20:30: חברות פצע
    תמריק ברע ומכות חדרי בטן. In this verse it is the topical wound, and
    its medicinal treatment that is being described. The lack of severity of the
    wound is indicated by the primacy of the word חבורה relative to פצע. In this
    verse the subject is the physical discomfort of the wound. In all other cases
    of the word pair פצע and חבורה, the word פצע appears first, indicating a more
    serious wound.

21. *HALOT*, "פצע," CD-ROM ed., 954.

22. *HALOT*, "חבורה," and "חברברות," *HALOT*, 285, 288.

23. In 1 Kings 20,37, an unnamed prophet disguises himself before King Ahav by

comments on our verse that a פצע, in contrast to a חבורה, is a wound that is accompanied by the flowing of blood.[24] At first glance it would appear that the פצע־חבורה word pair in our verse moves the verse from a higher intensity to a lower intensity, where a life-threatening blow is followed by a topical wound. This seems to go against the forward movement of the other components of the poem, and against the flow of intensification indicative of biblical poetry.

Lamech boasts that he may murder a man in response to serious bodily injury, or a פצע. Alter comments that this act is followed by the taking of the life of an innocent child for merely hurting him.[25] Kimchi uses the discussion on the פצע וחבורה as an opportunity to address the question of why a child is mentioned in the second half of the verse, and suggests that a child would be more susceptible to die from a חבורה than an adult.[26] This interpretation of the verse understands all of the components of the song to work together in increasing the intensity of the poem. The חבורה־פצע word-pair is thereby harmonized with the surrounding couplets, which as noted earlier, moves from a lower intensity to a higher intensity. This reading of the poem also offers further insight into the depraved nature of the song.

Lamech threatens violent retaliation against any man who would dare to cause him harm, or even against a child who might bruise him. Weinfeld notes that Lamech's song has parallels in ancient Arabic "sword songs" which also describe vengeance as vital for the maintenance of honor. There are songs from this genre which depict vengeance upon tens of people in retribution for the death of one. According to one way in which vengeance was practiced, it was permissible to kill the child of the murderer to avenge a homicide.[27]

It remains unclear however how Lamech's terrifying song relates

---

having a wound inflicted upon himself – פצע, in order to appear as having returned from the battlefield. The context strongly suggests that the פצע is an open wound accompanied by a flow of blood.

24. Qimhi Gen 4,23.

25. Robert Alter, *Genesis: Translation and Commentary*, (New York: W.W. Norton, 1997), 20.

26. Qimhi, Gen 4,23.

27. Weinfeld, "שירת למך", 47.

to the surrounding narrative. A return to the Kayin narrative, which is directly referenced by Lamech in his song in Gen. 4:24, will reveal how Lamech set himself up to be an even more ruthless and corrupted version of Kayin.

5. Adam, Kayin, and Lamech

Gen. 4 opens with the story of Kayin and moves quickly within the space of a single verse, to the Kayin genealogy (Gen. 24:18), and from there into the Lamech material. The close proximity of the two accounts strengthens the argument that the Lamech genealogy and song may be properly understood only when viewed against the backdrop of the Kayin narrative.

The motivation for the murder of Hevel was jealousy, Kayin's most essential and key characteristic. Note the similarity between the root of the name Kayin, קנה, and the root קנא, meaning "jealousy."[28] This relationship is implied by the verse in Ezekiel where the two roots appear in consecutive words:[29]

וישלח תבנית יד ויקחני בציצת ראשי ותשא אתי רוח בין הארץ ובין השמים
ותבא אתי ירושלמה במראות אלהים אל פתח שער הפנימית הפונה צפונה
אשר שם מושב סמל **הקנאה המקנה**: (Ezek. 8:3)

Sawyer observes that "the gratuitous mention of Kayin's wife in 4:17 has the effect of, among other things, highlighting the comparison with Adam and Eve, (Gen. 4:1), and raising Kayin to the same level of importance as Adam."[30] Kayin's initial act following the murder, the establishment of a new family, presents Kayin as Adam's replacement and heir apparent. Lamech, following in his forebears' footsteps, attempts to replace both Kayin and Hevel. One of the final verses of the chapter,

---

28. Rabbi Yaakov Tzvi Mecklenberg, (1789–1865) *Ha-Ketav Ve-Hakabbalah*, (Jerusalem: Am Olam), 1969. (Heb.), Gen. 4:1; John F.A. Sawyer, "Cain and Haphaestus: Possible Relics of Metalworking Traditions in Genesis 4," *Abr-Nahrain* 24 (1986), 155–166, esp. 159. Sawyer also suggests an etymological relationship to the root נקם.

29. Levine, "Lamech," 139.

30. Sawyer, "Cain," 158.

which recounts the birth of Seth, confirms that the replacement of earlier
players is at the heart of the Kayin-Lamech narrative:

> Adam *knew* his wife again, and she gave birth to a son and named
> him Seth, saying, "God has granted me another child *in place of*
> Abel, since Kayin killed him" (Gen. 4:25).

While it is unclear from Lamech's song if he has actually committed
a murder, or if he is threatening murder, it is clear that Lamech, like
his forebear Kayin, has become obsessed with homicide. In the case of
Kayin, God vows:

$$\text{וַיֹּאמֶר לוֹ ה' לָכֵן כָּל הֹרֵג קַיִן שִׁבְעָתַיִם יֻקָּם ...(Gen. 4:15)}$$

What is meant by the word שבעתים? *HALOT* and *BDB* define it as
seven-fold.[31] Kimchi defines שבעתים in the context of our verse as many
vengeances, which will be meted out upon he who dares to kill Kayin.[32]
Lamech's statement following his self-incrimination is similar to God's
vow regarding Kayin:

$$\text{וַיֹּאמֶר לוֹ ה' לָכֵן כָּל הֹרֵג קַיִן שִׁבְעָתַיִם יֻקָּם. (4:15)}$$

$$\text{כִּי שִׁבְעָתַיִם יֻקַּם קָיִן וְלֶמֶךְ שִׁבְעִים וְשִׁבְעָה. (4:24)}$$

Lamech boasts that he, like Kayin, will surely evade Divine justice.
If Kayin's avenger is to be punished seven times more harshly than
Kayin himself, then it is highly unlikely that anyone would ever dare to
exact punishment for his crime. Lamech predicates his assertion that
he will surely evade justice on the lessons learned from Kayin's legacy.
The man who will attempt to bring Lamech to justice for his crimes will

---

31. Westermann, "שבע," *HALOT*, 1399; BDB, "שבעתים," 988; Onkelos, who usually
    renders texts according to the plain sense, applies the rabbinic definition for
    שבעתים, rendering it as a referring to the seventh generation. This deviation
    from the plain sense of the text is likely due to Onkelos' practice of follow-
    ing the rabbinic approach in poetic units. Cf. Yehuda Komlush, *Hamikra
    Beor Hatargum*, (Tel Aviv: Devir, 1973), 11, (Heb), for a discussion of this
    phenomenon in Onkelos.
32. Kimchi, "שבע," *Sefer Hashorashim* (Heb.).

be punished seventy-seven-fold![33] The implication is abundantly clear. With a threat of retribution so severe, Lamech is free to commit murder with guaranteed impunity.

Whereas in the Kayin text, it is God who promises to mete out punishment, in the Lamech text, Lamech boasts that he will be the one to mete out the punishment. While the word for "revenge" is passive in both texts, יֻקַּם, it is understood from the context of Lamech's boast that he is personally threatening retribution.[34] This is why scholars adopted the name "sword song" for Lamech's poem. Skinner writes that "It is almost universally assumed that it [the song] commemorates the invention of weapons by Tubal-Kayin, and is accordingly spoken of as Lamech's 'sword song.'"[35] The surrounding text may be understood as suggesting that Lamech was brandishing a freshly sharpened sword developed by his son Tuval-Kayin, as a prop, during his declamation. Mathews draws attention to the relationship between Lamech and Kayin: "Lamech's gloating over a reputation more ruthless than infamous Kayin's shows the disparagement of human life among Kayin's seed that was fostered by his murder of Abel."[36] Simpson describes the transition from Kayin to Lamech well: "Kayin was a murderer, but at least he had remorse; Lamech, his descendant, not only could kill but could celebrate that killing in the fierce triumph of his taunting song."[37]

Lamech outdoes his ancestor Kayin. Kayin established the first city (4:17). Lamech is credited with parenting אבות or "inventors," who developed fundamental institutions of civilization. Lamech not only adopts the role of Kayin, he takes it even further. Whereas Kayin killed his brother in a fit of jealousy, Lamech's threat lays the foundation for pre-meditated murder.

---

33. This interpretation is supported by Cassuto who points out that the use of double digits in Ugaritic was a common form of hyperbole. (Note the double digits in the phrase שבעים ושבעה). Cf. Cassuto, *From Adam to Noah*, 243.
34. Skinner, *Genesis*, 122. Skinner writes that "The vengeance of Lamech knows no limits."
35. Ibid, 120.
36. K.Λ. Mathews, *Genesis 1–11*, (vol. 1 *The New American Commentary*; Nashville: B&H Publishing Group, 1996), 289.
37. Simpson, "The Book of Genesis-Exegesis," 522.

Kayin's murderous act is attributed to his inability to control his intense jealousy:

> But on Kayin and his offering He did not look with favor. So Kayin was very angry, and his face was downcast. Then the LORD said to Kayin, "Why are you angry? Why is your face downcast? If you do what is right, will you not be accepted? But if you do not do what is right, sin is crouching at your door; it desires to have you, but you must rule over it" (Gen. 4:5–7).

Kayin's "fallen face" betrays his inner turmoil. God warns Kayin and exhorts him to control his temper, lest it take control of him. Lamech, on the other hand, suffers from no such pangs of conscience.

Sawyer sees in the text a hint to the occasion that inspired Lamech's song. Lamech's son Tuval-Kayin is described as לטש כל חרש נחשת וברזל, a sharpener of weapons. He explains that the verb לטש describes a very specific technical process in the manufacture of weapons, specifically – the affixing of the fine edge. Sawyer's insight into the inspiration for the song calls further attention to the viciousness of Lamech's boast.

Lamech's arrogant song highlights his attempt to finish the job begun by Kayin. Lamech's sons' names, and their correspondence to both Kayin and Hevel, underscores Lamech's attempt to assume both the role of Kayin and Hevel. Kayin is described in Gen. 4:1–2 as עבד אדמה, an agricultural worker, while Hevel is a רעה צאן, a shepherd. Lamech's family took over both of those roles. Yaval was a rancher, אֲבִי יֹשֵׁב אֹהֶל וּמִקְנֶה, and Tuval-Kayin was a forger of metal instruments, לֹטֵשׁ כָּל חֹרֵשׁ נְחֹשֶׁת וּבַרְזֶל, suggesting that he manufactured farming implements in addition to weapons.[38] Kugel suggests a further connection between Lamech and Kayin through the use of the word איש by both:[39]

---

38. The Bible contains many examples of verses which express a tension between farming implements and weapons. Cf. Isa. 2:4 וְכִתְּתוּ חַרְבוֹתָם לְאִתִּים וַחֲנִיתֹתֵיהֶם לְמַזְמֵרוֹת; Mic. 4:3; Joel 4:10.

39. James Kugel, "Why Was Lamech Blind?" *Hebrew Annual Review* 12 (1990), 91–103.

וְהָאָדָם יָדַע אֶת חַוָּה אִשְׁתּוֹ וַתַּהַר וַתֵּלֶד אֶת קַיִן וַתֹּאמֶר קָנִיתִי אִישׁ אֶת ה':
וַיֹּאמֶר לֶמֶךְ לְנָשָׁיו עָדָה וְצִלָּה שְׁמַעַן קוֹלִי נְשֵׁי לֶמֶךְ הַאְזֵנָּה אִמְרָתִי כִּי אִישׁ
הָרַגְתִּי לְפִצְעִי וְיֶלֶד לְחַבֻּרָתִי: (Gen. 4:1,23)

To review, Lamech, Kayin's descendant, follows in Kayin's footsteps, and presents himself as Kayin's physical and ideological heir. If Kayin will be avenged sevenfold, then Lamech will be avenged seventy-sevenfold! Lamech deliberately gave his children names that suggest the usurping of both the legacy of Kayin and Hevel, which I will now present in detail. In so doing, Lamech subtly asserts his triumph in taking over the combined heritage of both Kayin and Hevel.

6. The Names

The names of the characters in the Genesis genealogical table take on a literary and almost poetic significance. Hess writes that "the personal names play a role in the literary environment of Gen. 1–11 which corresponds to the role exerted by the name bearers in their history.... The key to understand Gen. 1–11 lies in appreciating the role of the name as well as the name bearer."[40] He continues, "The etymology and wordplay of the personal names serve to carry the narrative forward and to provide important clues as to its theme and direction."[41]

Avishur understands Kayin's name to derive from the Ugaritic divinity qayn.[42] Cassuto relates it to the Akkadian, qyn, meaning "smith" or "metal-worker."[43] He further notes the relationship to the Arabic qayun, and the Aramaic qenaya, also meaning smith. This interpretation is especially interesting in light of Tuval-Kayin's role as an inventor of ironwork.

Lamech's sons' names suggest the names of both Kayin and Hevel, furthering the presumption of a connection between the Lamech material and its larger literary framework within the Kayin genealogy. Cassuto

---

40. Richard Hess, *Studies in the Personal Names of Genesis 1–11*, (Winona Lake: Eisenbrauns, 1993), 162.

41. Ibid, 161.

42. Y. Avishur, "קין," *Encylopedia Mikrait*, 2,40. (Heb.)

43. Cassuto, *From Adam to Noah*, 197.

relates all of the names of Lamech's sons to Kayin.[44] He interprets Yaval as deriving from the word יבול or "produce," relating back to Kayin's agricultural vocation.[45] Cassuto connects the name Yuval, who is associated with the production of musical instruments, to קינה or lamentation, which sounds like the name קין. Cassuto bases this observation on what he believes to be the musical quality inherent in both names.

We have seen that Lamech's song may either be characterized as a lamentation of a murder which already took place, or alternatively as a lamentation over a future murder.[46] Tuval-Kayin, the metal-worker, bears both the name of Kayin, as well as a hint to his relationship with his ancestor Kayin, through his metal forging occupation, which includes the making of weapons designed for killing. Tuval-Kayin is described by the text as being לטֵשׁ כָּל חֹרֵשׁ נְחֹשֶׁת וּבַרְזֶל.[47] While the word לטש, or "to sharpen," can be associated with farm implements, as in 1 Sam. 13:20, its earliest connotation seems to be associated with weapon making. Gordon relates the word לטש to the Ugaritic word *lts*, which means "to brandish a sword."[48] Sawyer adds that the verb לטש refers to a technical process in the manufacture of weapons.[49] Levine observes that Tuval in Sumerian also means an "iron smith." The name Tuval-Kayin may be a Hebraized combination of these two words which share a common definition.[50] The word קין is also used in the Bible to refer to weaponry:

וישבי בנב אשר בילידי הרפה ומשקל קינו שלש מאות משקל נחשת והוא
חגור חדשה ויאמר להכות את דוד (2 Sam. 21:16)

---

44. Cassuto, *From Adam to Noah*, p. 233.

45. Hess also notes the possibility of interpreting all three brothers' names as deriving from the root *yvl*, but in the sense of bringing forth, common to the meaning behind the word produce, יבול, and the act of giving birth. Cf. Hess, *Personal Names*, p. 128.

46. The prophets are replete with prophecies that lament future events that have not yet transpired. For example Jer. 30:7 laments the future day of doom; Cf. Midrash Yelamdenu Yalkut Talmud Torah, Gen. 22.

47. Gen. 4:22.

48. Gordon, "לטש," *HALOT*, 528.

49. Sawyer, "Cain and Haphaestus," 155–166.

50. Levine, "Lamech," 137.

The names Tuval, Yaval, and Yuval may also be seen as echoes of Hevel who was a shepherd, similar to Yaval who was a rancher.[51] The three names derive from the word *yovel*, a ram's horn which is a wind instrument.[52] Shepherding, Hevel's vocation, was associated in the ancient world with music, and in particular with the flute, a wind instrument.[53] Evidence of the close relationship in the ancient Near East between the flute and shepherding is found in a variety of sources. A relief from Nippur from the second millennium BCE depicts a crouching/dancing shepherd (and a swineherd) playing the lute.[54] In the Babylonian Gilgamesh Epic, Gilgamesh prays to the gods of the netherworld and names the gifts that he is burying with Enkidu for his journey in the afterlife:

> He displayed to the sun god a *flute* of carnelian.
> For Dumuzi, the *shepherd* beloved of Ishtar.
> *May* Dumuzi, the *shepherd* beloved of Ishtar accept this.
> May he welcome my friend and walk by his side.[55]

Gilgamesh is observed offering a flute to the shepherd god Dumuzi. Dumuzi appears again with a flute in "The Death of Dumuzi," a Sumerian

---

51. Benno Jacob has been credited with being the first to suggest that the names of Lamech's children represent echoes of Hevel. Cf. Gordon J. Wenham, *Genesis 1–15*, (WBC 1; Texas: Word, 1987), 112; Rabbi Avraham Yaakov Sabba, (15th century, Verona, Italy, also known as *Tzror Hamor*) in his commentary on Gen. 4:19–22 comments on the relationship between the names of the sons of Lamech to both Kayin and Hevel.

52. Exod. 19:13, Josh. 6:4–5.

53. Note David's role as shepherd and musician, 2 Sam. 1:16–19; Cf. Raymond Monelle, *The Musical Topic: Hunt, Military and Pastoral* (Bloomington, IN: Indiana University Press, 2006), 208. Monelle draws attention to the repeated use of the syrinx or Pan flute by shepherds throughout Homer, considered a quintessentially pastoral instrument.

54. Harvey Turnbull, "The Origin of the Long-necked Lute," *The Galpin Society Journal* 25 (1972), 58–66. This piece of the text appears in book VIII of the epic, lines 144–149.

55. Andrew R. George, *The Babylonian Gilgamesh Epic-Introduction, Critical Edition and Cuneiform Texts vol. 1* (Oxford: Oxford University Press, 2003), 67–68.

myth. Dumuzi, the shepherd of Erech has a premonition that death is imminent and laments:

> The *shepherd* – his heart was filled with tears,
> He went forth to the plain,
> He fastened his *flute* about his neck,
> Gave utterance to a lament.[56]

At the time of Dumuzi's descent into the netherworld the demons are heard saying:

> The *shepherds* play not the *flute* and the *pipe* before him.[57]

By bridging the opinions relating the etymologies of the sons of Lamech to concomitantly relate to both Kayin and Hevel, the names emerge as a combination of the key elements from both of their lives.[58] Each of Lamech's sons' names represents a composite of the larger amalgam, hinting to both characters.[59] Lamech's sons names may be understood to represent their father's perceived success in arrogating the combined legacy of Kayin and Hevel.

Lamech's wives, who we will now examine, also contribute to the degenerate family culture, playing into Lamech's power-hungry worldview, where appropriating others and their legacies is considered a virtue.

7. The Wives

The Bible draws the reader's attention to Lamech's wives by mentioning their names three times.[60] The Bible employs an unusual phrase here for

---

56. Samuel Noah Kramer, *The Sumerians: Their History, Culture and Character* (Chicago: University of Chicago Press, 1963), 156.
57. Samuel Noah Kramer, "Inanna's Descent to the Netherworld Continued," *Proceedings, American Philosophical Society* 94.4 (1950), 361–363.
58. Hess adds the possibility that the name הבל may derive from the Sumerian word for heir, *ibila*, or from the Arabic word for bereaving a mother of her son, *habala*. Cf. Hess "Lamech," 27.
59. Hess writes "the similarity of the roots of the names, Jabal, Juval, Tubal-Cain, and Abel further associate Cain and Abel with this latter generation." Cf. Hess, *Personal Names*, 126.
60. Harper suggests that the attention paid to Lamech's wives is part of the overall

taking a wife. Whereas the term usually found for marriage in the Bible is ויקח את, here we read ויקח לו, "and he took for himself." Interestingly, we find this unusual term for marriage once again in another Genesis text (Gen. 6:2), following the account of a different Lamech, who was a descendant of Seth and the father of Noah. It is also noteworthy that in both of these texts it is implied that the taking of wives involved the abuse of power.

The second Lamech is recorded as having died at the conspicuous age of seven hundred and seventy-seven! The Sages attribute to Lamech's son Noah the sharpening of a metal instrument as well, but this one was an agricultural plow.[61] The second Lamech also authors a short song, but his song announces the promise of comfort as opposed to revenge:[62]

זה ינחמנו ממעשנו ומעצבון ידינו מן האדמה אשר אררה ה' (Gen. 5:29)

Like the first Lamech's song, the second Lamech's poem is also carefully constructed.[63] It is composed of ten words, (another significant number in Genesis – Noah is the tenth generation from Adam), with each line containing exactly five words.[64] This poem however emphasizes the community, as opposed to the individual in the first Lamech's song:

---

thrust of chronicling the development of sin and corruption. He attributes this to fact that this is the first recorded instance of polygamy. Cf. Harper, "The Fratricide: The Cainite Civilization. Genesis IV," *Quarterly calendar* 3.4 (1894), 264–274; Jacob notes that while the Bible doesn't prohibit polygamy, the practice of polygamy is in direct contradiction to God's directive to man, that he cleave to his wife and become one flesh. Cf. Jacob, *Genesis*, p. 38; Vos asserts that Lamech's polygamy is highlighted here to suggest a direct correlation between Lamech's character and the development of evil in the line of Kayin. Cf. Vos, *Genesis*, p. 98; Kimchi and Bechor Shor on Gen. 4:23–24 also view the polygamy of Lamech negatively.

61. Levine, "Lamech," 143; Cf. Rashi, Gen. 5:29.

62. Levine, "Lamech", 141.

63. Scholars who subscribe to the Documentary Hypothesis agree that Gen. 5:29 and Gen. 4 are part of the same J source. Cf. Gordon J. Wenham, *Genesis 1–15* (WBC 1; Waco: Word, 1987).

64. Gen. 5.

זה ינחמנו ממעשנו ומעצבון ידינו עדה וצלה שמען קולי נשי למך האזנה
אמרתי כי איש הרגתי לפצעי וילד לחברתי:

Whereas the first Lamech's poem highlights himself ולמך שבעים
ושבעה, the second Lamech's poem mentions only God by name. There
is a clear distinction between the two Lamechs suggested by the text.
Both men shared the same name, but their character could not be more
different. Whereas Lamech I may be characterized as an egocentric
megalomaniac, Lamech II is prayerful and relates optimistically to
mankind's physical and spiritual future.

The names in the genealogies of Kayin and Seth in chapters four and
five are strikingly similar:

קין	שת
חנוך	אנוש
עירד	קינן
מחויאל	מהללאל
מתושאל	ירד
למך	חנוך
יבל, יובל, תובל קין	מתושלח
–	למך
–	נח

These two lists are similar enough to draw our attention, but different
enough to stress their dissimilarities. This lends further support for
the contention that Adam in Gen. 4:25 was attempting to turn the tide
away from the Kayin-Lamech line by replacing Hevel with Seth. Aaron
Lichtenstein observes this phenomenon and suggests that what is being
hinted at by the text here is "an effort at redemption of the accursed
family by re-naming and re-living."[65]

Immediately following the story of the second Lamech and the birth
of Noah we read a laconic account of marriages which took place in
the days of the second Lamech, which contributed to God's decision

---

65. Aaron Lichtenstein, "Redeeming Cain: A Comparative Literary Reading of
Genesis," *Dor Le Dor* 13 (1985), 199–200.

to destroy that civilization.[66] Both of the marriage accounts associated with the two Lamech texts are introduced by a similar phrase:

ויקח לו למך שתי נשים שם האחת עדה ושם השנית צלה: (4:19)

ויראו בני האלהים את בנות האדם כי טבת הנה **ויקחו להם** נשים מכל אשר בחרו: (6:2)

This unusual phrase for marriage, ויקח לו־להם, "and he took for himself (Lamech)/themselves (בני האלהים)" as opposed to simply taking, in both of the Lamech accounts, lends further support to the position that there is an inherent relationship between these two texts.

The conspicuous role of the women in the first Lamech text demands our attention. We observed earlier the critical importance that names play in the Genesis genealogies.[67] Lamech's wives' names, עדה and צלה appear in parallel positions in the poem, which led scholars to look for analogous definitions in deciphering the meaning behind the names. Some relate their names to light and dark; deriving צלה from צל, meaning "shade," and עדה from the Babylonian Goddess of light (Hera or Juno).[68] Others related the name עדה to the word for dawn in Assyrian-Arabic.[69]

Garsiel relates the name צלה to צליל or "cymbals."[70] Hess notes that *sll* in Ugaritic is a cymbalist.[71] Most scholars agree that עדה derives from the word עדי or "ornament."[72] Cassuto notes that these two names reflect the two main characteristics of feminine beauty: appearance and song. Cassuto sees this reflected in the verse from Canticles:[73]

---

66. Gen. 6:1–8.

67. Cassuto, *From Adam to Noah*, 233.

68. W.H. Bennett, *Genesis: Introduction; Revised Version with Notes*, (*The New Century Bible*, 1; Edinburgh: T.C. & E.C. Jack, 1904), 21.

69. Driver, *Genesis*, 69.

70. Moshe Garsiel, *Biblical Names: A Literary Study of Midrashic Derivations and Puns* (Ramat Gan: Bar-Ilan Press, 1991), 95.

71. Hess, *Personal Names*, 48–49.

72. Wenham, *Genesis 1–15*, 112; Cf. Hess, *Personal Names*, 47, Harper, *the Biblical World*, 271; Sawyer, "Cain and Haphaestus," 159.

73. Cassuto, *From Adam to Noah*, 233.

"My dove in the clefts of the rock, in the hiding places on the mountainside, show me your face, let me hear your voice; for your voice is sweet, and your face is lovely" (Cant. 2:14).

עדה, which means "ornament," is a name which relates to the feminine practice of adorning the appearance with jewelry, which are, in effect, beautiful ornaments. צלה, meaning cymbals, or the sound produced by cymbals, is a reflection of the beauty of the female voice.

Cassuto also notes the similarity between the name נעמה and *n'm*, the musician who sings before the Baal in Ugaritic poems.[74] We find that the root נ.ע.מ. appears in the Bible, as well, in the context of song.[75] Taken together, according to Cassuto, all three of the female names in the Lamech narrative reflect idealized feminine beauty.

Hess comments that if we understand the name צלה to mean "cymbal," as Cassuto suggests, then an implicit word play with עדה may be suggested. He explains both names as referring to the arts. Hess concludes that either option is possible (light/dark, or culture related).[76]

Mathews attributes Naamah's inclusion in the genealogy to the text's desire for balance; two children for each of Lamech's wives.[77] That balance is also borne out in the language of the verses: אחיו\אחות:

וְשֵׁם אָחִיו יוּבָל הוּא הָיָה אֲבִי כָּל־תֹּפֵשׂ כִּנּוֹר וְעוּגָב: וְצִלָּה גַם־הִוא יָלְדָה אֶת־תּוּבַל קַיִן לֹטֵשׁ כָּל־חֹרֵשׁ נְחֹשֶׁת וּבַרְזֶל **וַאֲחוֹת** תּוּבַל־קַיִן נַעֲמָה: (Gen. 4:21–11)

While symmetry is certainly a priority in the text, of equal value is the meaning and significance of the names within the context of the genealogy. The interpretation of the feminine names in the narrative as relating to idealized feminine beauty may shed light on the problem of the text's silence regarding Naamah; her name alone attests to her contribution to the family culture of objectification. The premium that the poem places on feminine beauty is especially interesting in light of the poem's emphasis on structural perfection.

---

74. Cassuto, *From Adam to Noah*, 233.

75. 2 Sam. 23:1: "וְאֵלֶּה דִּבְרֵי דָוִד הָאַחֲרֹנִים נְאֻם דָּוִד בֶּן יִשַׁי וּנְאֻם הַגֶּבֶר הֻקַם עָל מְשִׁיחַ אֱלֹהֵי
יַעֲקֹב וּנְעִים זְמִרוֹת יִשְׂרָאֵל"

76. Hess, *Personal Names*, 49.

77. Mathews, *Genesis*, 286.

Lamech's wives and daughter share the dubious distinction of being highlighted by the text for a combination of distinctly feminine traits: physical beauty, and the proclivity to please. When taken together with Lamech's penchant for arrogating the legacies of those who preceded him and threatening those who might harm him, his objectification of women is but another indicator of his egocentric and corrupted nature.

8. Reasons for the Song's Inclusion

We have considered a variety of approaches to the problem of the inclusion of the song of Lamech in the Genesis genealogy. Opinions ranged from those which did not view Lamech's poem as an integral part of the Kayin-Lamech narrative, to those which understood the poem to be part of the general message of the surrounding text. Taking the latter approach, we may ask: in what way has the text been transformed by the inclusion of Lamech's song? Gelander suggests "The terrifying moral standards his [Lamech's] words reflect are unambiguous.... It is implied that he intended that this should be his wives' teaching to his descendants."[78] The implied message of the text's unusual attention to the wives is that Lamech intended for them to play a key role in the transmission of his corrupt legacy.

Lamech followed in the footsteps of Kayin, the builder of the first city, in both deed and spirit. He fathered the inventors of fundamental societal institutions and predicated the development of that society on a culture of violence. The *a fortiori* construct of the concluding verse of his song affirms that if Kayin was essentially able to get away with murder, then Lamech can do the same, and even better (Gen. 4:24). His poem reflects his goals and aspirations for the future development of mankind: "might makes right." Lamech's philosophy venerating the supremacy of power is seen as well in the names of his sons, which reflect back on the lives of Kayin and Hevel, and the names of his wives and daughter, whose contribution to the family lies in their ability to please. The poetic symmetry and careful structure of his song are an integral

---

78. Gelander, *The Good Creator*, 58.

part of its core message. Lamech's song unveils his worldview, where visceral force, physical perfection, and corporeal beauty embody the ideal. This hedonistic worldview left little room for the development of a moral civilization.

Conclusion

Lamech's song and the prominent role that it plays in the Genesis genealogy have puzzled traditional exegetes and contemporary scholars alike. Through an examination of the structure and substance of the text, and a careful examination of the meaning and connotations of the names highlighted in the narrative, we arrive at an understanding of why the song was placed in the center of the Kayin genealogy. Lamech's song exposes his egocentric attempt to appropriate and replace the legacies of Kayin and Hevel. The etymologies of Lamech's sons' names harken back to both Kayin and Hevel, suggesting that Lamech intended for them to combine all the essential characteristics of their predecessors. The conspicuous role of the women in the Lamech narrative, and the etymologies of their names, points to their literary significance as the objects of Lamech's pleasure and desire. Lamech was a man who perceived men as the recipients of either his vengeance or terror and women as nothing more than objects for his pleasure and amusement.

What emerges is the realization that Lamech's brief, yet vicious, song is hardly insignificant. Lamech's "sword song" has ramifications far beyond the chapters of the Genesis genealogies. Through its neat and concise format Lamech articulates his hedonistic and brutal worldview: "might makes right." Lamech's song presents a moral challenge which relates directly to both the chronicle of the development of sin and evil opening the first chapters of Genesis, and to its subsequent chapters which continue to track the moral decline of mankind leading up to the flood.

www.ingramcontent.com/pod-product-compliance
Lightning Source LLC
Chambersburg PA
CBHW031246090426
42742CB00007B/334